2004

Adolescent Assessment

◆

Adolescent Assessment

♦

Jann Gumbiner

WILEY

John Wiley & Sons, Inc.

Copyright © 2003 by John Wiley & Sons, Inc., Hoboken, New Jersey. All rights reserved.

Published simultaneously in Canada.

Library of Congress Cataloging-in-Publication Data:
Gumbiner, Jann.
    Adolescent assessment / Jann Gumbiner.
        p.   cm.
    Includes bibliographical references and index.
    ISBN 0-471-41981-8 (alk. paper)
    1. Behavioral assessment of teenagers.   2. Teenagers—Psychological testing.   I. Title.

BF724.25.G86 2003
155.5′18′0287—dc21   2003000581

Printed in the United States of America
10 9 8 7 6 5 4 3 2 1

To the men in my life: Charles Gumbiner, my father; Bruce Gumbiner, my brother; Albert Ezroj, my husband; and Aaron, Daniel, and David, my sons, for guidance, advice, encouragement, and meals.

◆ Contents

Preface

Adolescent Assessment was written to help adolescents and mental health professionals. By providing a methodical approach to assessment, *Adolescent Assessment* aims to help adolescents receive more thorough assessments, more accurate diagnoses, and more effective interventions. It includes practical information on adolescent development, adolescent mental health, special populations, basic psychometrics, testing, ethics, and general assessment principles. Resting on a solid foundation of theory, scientific research, and ethics, this book is clearly and succinctly written. Guidelines for sound assessments are presented in an accessible format. Most of all, *Adolescent Assessment* aims to be useful.

Adolescent Assessment is written for experienced practitioners and for graduate students. For experienced practitioners, *Adolescent Assessment* offers a handy professional reference guide. It contains key information necessary for written reports and courtroom testimony. Test summaries, reliability, and validity coefficients are provided. For graduate students and clinical interns, it contains introductory material and test reviews.

Adolescent Assessment begins with an overview of the assessment and testing process. Assessment as science, purposes of assessment, steps in the assessment process, advantages of psychological tests, test selection, and ethics are all covered in chapter 1. Adolescent development, the study and history of adolescence, biological development, cognitive development, intelligence, psychological development, and social development are covered in chapter 2. The *DSM-IV-TR* categories; special diagnostic issues of adolescents; gender, age, and ethnic concerns; anxiety disorders, conduct disorders and delinquency, depression, oppositional defiant disorder, sexual abuse, substance-related disorders, and suicide risk are covered in chapter 3. Chapter 4 covers assessment of diverse populations. Topics include culture, test fairness, language, acculturation, gender, age, learning disabilities, and physical disabilities.

The second half of *Adolescent Assessment* focuses on testing issues and test reviews. Chapter 5 presents an overview of psychometric principles. It reviews correlation coefficients, standardization, norms, the normal probability curve, standard deviations, percentiles, reliability, standard errors of measurement, validity, and short forms. Chapter 6 contains reviews of psychological tests most widely used with adolescents. Each test was carefully selected for sound theoretical and psychometric principles. A wide range of methods, including observational techniques, self-report inventories, and standardized intelligence tests are included to encourage a multimethod test battery. Test facts including purpose, theory, administration, scoring, reliability, and validity are presented in an accessible format for quick reference.

Adolescent Assessment contains a review of the following tests: the Achenbach System of Empirically Based Assessment, the Beck Depression Inventory–Second Edition, the Goodenough-Harris Drawing Test, the MacAndrew Alcoholism Scale–Revised (MAC-R), Millon Adolescent Clinical Inventory (MACI), the Minnesota Multiphasic Personality Inventory–Adolescent (MMPI-A), the Rotter Incomplete Sentences Blank, the Strong Interest Inventory–II, the Wechsler Intelligence Scale for Children–Third Edition, The Wide Range Achievement Test–3, the Woodcock-Johnson III Tests of Cognitive Abilities, and the Woodcock-Johnson III Tests of Achievement.

Several special features of *Adolescent Assessment* are included in the appendixes. The appendixes aim to help the reader apply knowledge and principles covered in previous chapters. Appendix A is a list of adolescent psychological tests organized by use. Commonly used tests are listed and referenced by their best uses, allowing the test examiner to select a test for a specific purpose, such as measuring depression. Appendix B presents a table for conducting problem-focused assessment. Appendix C consists of case studies organized by presenting problems. They allow the reader to think through presenting problems, case examples, diagnostic hypotheses, testing rationales, and suggested test batteries. A unique feature of this book is the combination of case studies, *DSM*-related diagnostic hypotheses, and test batteries for adolescents. Appendix D consists of a copy of the 2002 APA Ethics Code section on assessment. It includes ethical bases for assessments, uses of assessments, informed consent, interpretation, test security, and other pertinent ethical information. Appendix E is a list of publishers, addresses, phone numbers, and web sites enabling readers to purchase tests.

Adolescent Assessment is a useable and compact reference on assessment, ethics, adolescent development, adolescent mental health, diverse populations, psychometric principles, and test use. Rapid reference tables help the reader select appropriate tests and provide important data on reliability and validity. If *Adolescent Assessment* helps one teenager receive a more thorough assessment or if it helps one clinician have a less stressful day, then it would have been worth the large investment of my time.

No single book is perfect, and every book is an innately human effort. To be as current and accurate as possible, many resources and colleagues were consulted. Test manuals, ethical codes, test reviews, and psychometric texts were pored over. Even though our scientific knowledge is constantly growing and quickly outdated, some basic principles are timeless. Sound assessments will always be client centered, based on multiple methods, justified by a sound rationale, and conducted by competent clinicians.

Adolescent Assessment represents the culmination of more than two decades of education, training, clinical experience, and teaching. During those years, the author learned a lot from teachers, clients, and students. However, some mentors stand out with a special warmth and brilliance. The author would like to thank Dr. Carol Whalen at the University of California, Irvine, who first taught her about reliability and validity; Dr. Blake Keasey, her clinical supervisor at Loma Linda Medical University; and Dr. Robin DiMatteo, Dr. Howard Friedman, and Dr. Robert Singer at the University of California, Riverside, for graduate school funding and intellectual rigor. In the clinical arena, Dr. Curtis Booraem and Dr. John Flowers deserve thanks for supervision and mentoring.

Many colleagues read drafts of *Adolescent Assessment* during its preparation. University professors with special expertise in testing, measurement, ethnic differences, and specific tests reviewed the manuscript. In particular, the author would like to thank June Havlena at California State University, Fullerton; Dr. Ronald Scott at Chapman University; and Dr. Roberto Velasquez at San Diego State University for their invaluable feedback. Graduate student Erika Woolf Frady and practicing psychologist Dr. Jule Marini Biesiada also provided insightful comments. Dr. Jack Lipton, provided consultation on ethical and legal dilemmas. Technical support came from the editors at Wiley and from typist Jackie Franza. A special thanks goes to editor Tracey Belmont at Wiley for her continued interest, positive feedback, suggestions, and patient reading of numerous drafts. Susan Dodson, at Graphic Composition, applied a keen eye and rigorous review to the copy editing. The author would also like to thank the many behind-the-scenes folks at John Wiley & Sons who helped a proposal become a book.

Writing a book takes a concentrated and focused effort over years. This effort could never have been sustained without many friends. Friends were a constant source of informal feedback, advice, encouragement, and humor. Among them the author would like to thank Harriet and Homer Brown, Tara Brown, Kim and Peter Gerrard, Susan Martincek, Margie Medrano, Jamoa Moberly, Valeri Okun, Dana Tatom, Bill Wakefield, Lou Ann Wieand, and Renie Wong.

Jann Gumbiner
Irvine, California

One

— ◆ —

The Assessment and Testing Process

— ◆ —

ASSESSMENT AS SCIENCE

Adolescent Assessment applies scientific thinking to the assessment process. Psychology is part science, part religion, and the practice of it is an art. Yet, assessment, diagnosis, and treatment should be as scientific as possible for several reasons. First, the science of psychology is supported by the Educational Directorate of the American Psychological Association (APA). APA is the oldest and largest national organization of psychologists. The Educational Directorate consists of many of the profession's most highly regarded university professors. These university professors, who represent thousands of psychologists, view scientific thinking as an important objective of psychological training. By planning university curricula, they are planning the future of psychology. The future of psychology is science.

Second, science aims to be objective, empirical, and self-correcting. When scientific thinking is applied to the assessment process, assessments become more systematic. They are more thorough and less likely to miss potentially important information. The objectivity of a well-constructed psychological test provides a second professional opinion and is less apt to be biased than a single interview. A major conclusion of the APA Psychology Assessment Work Group (PAWG), which studied the validity of psychological assessment, was that clinicians relying exclusively on interviews are prone to incomplete understanding (Meyer et al., 2001). Next, clinical hypotheses can be formulated and data can be collected to test

1

Rapid Reference 1.1
Purposes of Assessment

- To describe functioning
- To form clinical impressions
- To make diagnoses
- To plan treatments
- To evaluate treatments
- To limit legal risk to the clinician
- To provide empathic feedback

these hypotheses. Most important is that when assessments are incorrect, empirical checks provide a feedback mechanism for revising the original assessment. Thus, science is self-correcting.

Scientific thinking (as compared to a haphazard or strictly intuitive approach) is systematic, objective, and testable. Nowhere is this feature more important than in the field of psychological assessment. Assessment is the foundation of diagnosis and treatment. Without thorough and accurate assessments, adolescents are less likely to be correctly diagnosed and effectively treated. The scientific method may not always result in the correct answer, but to quote Sir Francis Bacon, "truth is more likely to arise from error than confusion."

PURPOSES OF ASSESSMENT

The main purpose of psychological assessment is to gather information and aid in decision making. In 1996, The American Psychological Association (APA) formed a Psychological Assessment Work Group (PAWG) and charged it with reviewing scientific evidence on the efficacy of psychological assessment (Meyer et al., 2001). One hundred and twenty-five meta-analyses and 800 samples were examined. The committee reviewed assessments conducted in many settings, including health care, forensic, school, and clinical settings. According to the PAWG, the purposes of psychological assessment in the health care setting are to describe current functioning; to confirm or refute clinical impressions; to aid differential diagnoses; to identify treatment needs, help select appropriate treatment, and predict likely outcomes; to monitor treatment over time; to limit legal risk to the clinician; and to provide skilled, empathic, assessment feedback as a therapeutic intervention in its own right.

More specifically to adolescents, psychological assessment can provide empathic feedback, counsel and guide parents and teens, and help them understand what is "normal." Psychological assessment can facilitate decision making regarding placement in educational programs, career goals, treatment, intervention, rehabilitation, and forensic decisions. Finally, developmentally appropriate assessments can monitor changes due to intervention and growth.

GUIDELINES FOR SOUND ASSESSMENTS

Guidelines for sound assessments have been proposed by the APA, the American Educational Research Association (AERA), the National Council on Measurement in Education (NCME), and many psychometrists and psychologists (APA, 1999, 2002). Anastasi and Urbina (1997), Kaufman (1990), and Sattler (2001, 2002) each offer direction and insight. Furthermore, APA's test interpretation and diversity is an excellent resource for culturally sensitive assessments (Sandoval, Frisby, Geisinger, Scheunemean, & Grenier, 1998). The goal of a quality assessment is to obtain optimal test performance of the individual; this may involve special accommodations or testing in a native language. Sound assessment is based on valid and reliable tests and on multimethod techniques. In the end, the test examiner is ultimately responsible for selecting, administering, and interpreting appropriate psychological tests. The following list presents some guidelines for sound assessments:

1. Read the test manual and become thoroughly familiar with the test. Be aware of the groups on which the test was normed and profile patterns of diverse groups.
2. Practice within your area of competence. Refer to an expert if necessary.
3. Have a sound rationale for the selection of each test.
4. Select tests that are appropriate for the individual and the referral question.
5. Select tests that are normed on a standardization group representative of characteristics of the individual being tested (when possible).
6. Establish rapport with the examinee.
7. Make sure the examinee understands and follows the directions.
8. Be cautious in your interpretation; make sure cultural and socioeco-

nomic contexts are reported in the written report. Become knowledgeable about the specific culture of the individual. Consider using an acculturation measure.

9. Consider the impact of the decision based on the testing. Some decisions, such as educational placement carry high stakes. Be especially cautious with high-stakes interpretations.

10. Remember any single test score is just one sample of behavior on any given day.

11. Multiple test scores provide convergent sources of data and strengthen the accuracy of results and interpretation. No decision should be based on a single test score. Multiple measures of the same construct are much stronger, and an assessment battery always consists of more than one test.

STEPS IN THE ASSESSMENT PROCESS

A good assessment is thorough, ethical, scientifically sound, and guided by a defensible rationale. Although the terms *tests* and *assessments* are frequently used interchangeably, they do not mean the same thing. An assessment is more comprehensive than a test and involves many steps. The assessment process begins with a referral, and it involves collecting background information on an adolescent; formulating testable hypotheses about diagnosis and treatment; designing a test battery with a sound rationale; administering, scoring, and interpreting tests; refining hypotheses; developing intervention strategies; and communicating the results of the assessment to the teen, parents, and important community members. A strong rapport with the teen and parents is essential, and a well-conducted assessment takes considerable clinical skill. Poor assessments can have disastrous consequences—hasty assessments of a sad, 19-year-old college student resulted in diagnoses as disparate as adjustment disorder and bipolar disorder. Furthermore, using tests with questionable reliability and validity puts the clinician at legal risk.

A comprehensive assessment should be based on multiple methods. An assessment includes subjective information (e.g., an interview with the teen and parents), objective information (e.g., psychological testing), and clinical impressions. Basing clinical decisions on multiple sources of data is a way of increasing validity, providing checks and balances, and getting a second opinion. In addition, relying on multiple measures in a test battery is a practice that provides the examiner more than one method of operationally defining a construct. For example, depression as measured by the Minnesota Multiphasic Personality Inventory–Adolescent (MMPI-A) is slightly different from depression as measured by the Beck Depression Inventory–Second Edition (BDI-II). Administering both instruments will yield more information for the clinician and often more accurate diagnoses, treatment, and evaluation of therapy. Objective tests also provide hard evidence for clinical decision making and are usually well accepted in a court of law. The assessment report by the PAWG for APA provided considerable empirical evidence that a single method of measurement is less likely to be valid (Meyer et al., 2001). Clinicians who rely on a single method of measurement (e.g., self-report interview) are more likely to provide a biased diagnosis, to compromise the validity of the assessment, and ultimately to put themselves at greater legal risk. Finally, multiple measures provide objective checks on clinical impressions or biases in normal judgment and maximize the validity of clinical judgment. No important decision should ever be made on the basis of a single test. A decision should be made only after a thorough assessment using multiple methods has been conducted.

RAPPORT

A strong client-therapist rapport eases the assessment process and aids intervention. Building rapport can be especially challenging with adolescents. Frequently, adolescents are in therapy against their will—perhaps forced by their parents, their school, or the judicial system. If therapists can relate to the phenomenal reality of the adolescent, they may be able to develop rapport. Understanding adolescent development, employing good listening skills, empathizing with the teen, and taking an interest in his or her music or dress may assist rapport. Nonverbal communication is especially important to teens, who usually feel that they are constantly being watched and judged.

Moreover, the clinician will need to establish a strong rapport with both teens and parents. Often, the teen is fighting with the parents, and the clinician's interacting with parents may be perceived as a betrayal. Because teens are minors, certain ethical considerations apply. For example, Section 9 of the APA Principles of Psychologists and Code of Conduct apply to assessment and confidentiality (APA, 2002). Every attempt should be made to protect the confidence of the minor; at the same time, however, the minor and legal representatives must be informed of the uses of testing and the limits of confidentiality.

REFERRAL

All assessments start with a referral. The clinician should know who referred the teen and the reasons for the referral. Referrals provide insightful clues. For example, the source of the referral may suggest the severity of the problem. When the referral is from the school, the problem is probably less serious than it is when the referral is from the courts. It is highly recommended that the referral source be contacted. A school counselor, for example, can tell the clinician important information about the teen's academic and social behavior.

COLLECT BACKGROUND INFORMATION AND DATA

Important information about the adolescent's background can be collected from reports and interviews. Medical records documenting physical development should be consulted when they are available. Written reports from agencies provide an outside description of problem behaviors. Clinical interviews with the adolescent and parents can provide valuable insight. When possible, extended family, teachers, friends, school counselors, and community members should be interviewed to give the clinician additional perspective. All of these sources provide an important multimethod approach to formulating and verifying clinical hypotheses.

When collecting data from reports and interviews, the clinician should examine the physical, developmental, educational, and social history of the adolescent. Previous diagnoses by medical doctors, psychologists, and social workers should be reviewed. The clinician may discover, for example, that the adolescent has been diagnosed and treated for ADHD by a medical doctor since middle childhood. Educational information may indicate the teenager had speech problems at age 5 that led to excessive shyness and trouble making friends. Commonly, report cards and school records can document a history of learning disabilities and disruptive classroom behavior. A thorough assessment should include a physical history (including medications), a developmental history, a social history, and educational history.

FORMULATE TESTABLE HYPOTHESES

Almost immediately and automatically during the assessment process, clinicians start to form hypotheses. For example, when a 16-year-old male client is called a perpetrator in court transcripts, it is tempting to make certain assumptions. Unfortunately, these assumptions are not always very scientific. However, keeping an open mind and using an unbiased approach with adolescents are imperative. Adolescents are young; they are not fully grown and they are very easily influenced. Unquestioned assumptions and premature diagnoses can lead to misdiagnoses, labeling, social expectations, and even self-fulfilling prophecies (Rosenthal & Jacobson, 1992). Furthermore, a young, vulnerable, and confused adolescent may accept the opinion of a doctor and become further depressed or anxious.

Early in the assessment process, clinical hypotheses can be formulated. A hypothesis is a conjectural statement that can be tested (Kerlinger, 1975). Clinical hypotheses that are behaviorally specific are more scientific; are easier to verify, reject, or revise; and communicate more information. As much as possible, clinical hypotheses should be stated in clear, specific, and measurable terms. For example, it would be better to say that the 14-year-old girl was involved in sex crimes and sold pornography than to simply label her as incorrigible. This hypothesis can then be verified or revised with more information from outside sources, client report, clinical observation, and testing. Clinical hypotheses should also be based on the referral question and background information.

RATIONALE

Every assessment should have a sound rationale (Meyer et al., 2001). The rationale for any test at any time should be determined by what is in the best interest of the client (APA, 2002). In their APA report, Meyer et al. (2001) stated that assessors should provide a sound rationale for their work and be expected to justify the cost-benefit ratio. For example, giving a full-scale IQ test to an adolescent with high grades who is referred due to parental divorce is probably too time costly to justify the benefit. A more common mistake is administering a test that is too brief. Using a 10-min brief IQ test with unknown reliabilities and validities to make a school placement for a potentially gifted child is probably not in the client's best interests.

Meyer et al. (2001) encouraged questioning bureaucratic rules for appropriate testing. According to Meyer et al. (2001), there is no routine, standard battery appropriate for all clients. The appropriate use of tests should flow from the presenting problem and be customized for each client. Testing is highly individualized and should be determined by each unique client and each unique circumstance. Decisions based on background information, testable hypotheses, adolescent development, and scientifically solid tests should guide testing selection. Assessors can be held responsible for providing an assessment rationale that is in their client's best interests. Examples of test batteries guided by presenting problems, rationales, and case studies can be found in the appendix.

CONDUCT TESTING

Guidelines for administering, scoring, and interpreting tests can be found in three valuable sources. They are (a) *Ethical Principles of Psychologists and Code of Conduct* published by the APA (2002) and commonly referred to as the APA ethical code; (b) *The Standards for Psychological and Educational Testing,* published by AERA; and (c) the individual test manual for each psychological test. It is assumed that the reader of this book has had a basic undergraduate course in psychological testing and that this book is a review. Many excellent texts have been written on the topic. Two of them are *Psychological Testing* by Anastasi and Urbina (1997) and *Assessment of Children* by Sattler (2001, 2002).

According to Anastasi and Urbina (1997), "a psychological test is essentially an objective and standardized measure of a sample of behavior" (p. 5). A larger sample of behavior—meaning more test items—is a more reliable sample of behavior. From this sample of behavior, other related behaviors can be extrapolated. The sampled behaviors are not always identical to the predicted ones. What is important is that there is a strong empirical relationship between the test and the predicted behaviors. A diagnosis, in this terminology, is a form of prediction. *Adolescent Assessment,* like Anastasi and Urbina (1997), refers to testing as a sample of behavior.

A norm-referenced test, or standardized test, can be thought of as a yardstick. Because uniform items are administered under standardized conditions, individuals can be ranked and compared to each other. The goal is not to pigeonhole or label teens; rather, it is to view them in the context of their peers. A single test may have been administered to thousands of teens. The aim is a fair comparison to other similar adolescents who have taken the test in the past. A teenage boy whose parents are complaining that he is too much of a thrill seeker may not seem so when the boy is compared to other teens on an MMPI-A. Similarly, by comparing test performance to that of other teens, a test may be used to document a learning disability and obtain special educational services. No single test is error free. However, a psychometrically sound test includes a measurement of its own error in the form of reliability, validity, and confidence intervals; this allows the practitioner to gauge the degree of certainty of the test results. These statistical concepts are discussed in more detailed in chapter 5.

The test examiner should be very familiar with the test manual for the test being used. Test manuals provide information on administration, scoring, and interpretation of tests. They also provide important psychometric information such as validity and reliability. Psychometric data should be reviewed by the clinician who is selecting a test, and these data should be presented in written reports. Validity and reliability may be requested in a court of law. The test manual should be reviewed prior to administering the test, may be used during administration, and should be referred to afterward for test interpretation. It is absolutely essential for the test examiner to thoroughly read the test manual.

Failure to be familiar with the test manual can result in poor decision making and even legal risk. For example, a school counselor administered a brief intelligence test to a fifth grader to screen for admission to a gifted program. Basing his decision on the results of the 10-min test, the counselor told the mother that the boy had an average IQ and did not qualify for the gifted program. The counselor justified the placement decision by saying that the test correlated with the Wechsler Intelligence Scale for Children–Third Edition (WISC-III). When he was asked the size of the correlation, the counselor rolled his eyes, said he did not know, and handed the manual to the parent. The manual was still wrapped in plastic, unopened, and it clearly had never been read. When the mother opened it and looked for the correlation with the WISC-III, it didn't exist. This school counselor had based an important educational decision on a quick test with unknown reliabilities and validities. Furthermore, he hadn't even reviewed the test manual. Not only did the counselor cheat the fifth-grade boy, but he also placed the school at legal risk.

Standardized administration procedures should be followed very closely. If they are not, test validity may be compromised. Each test manual provides directions on how to administer the test. Some tests, such as the WISC-III, have clear rules about phrasing questions and time limits.

Accurate test interpretation depends on strict adherence to the administration procedures. Likewise, tests are normed on specific populations, and test interpretation is most valid when similar populations are tested. For example, if a test is normed on 14- to 18-year-olds, it is not valid for 13- or 19-year-olds. Occasionally, it is necessary to use a test on a population different from the norm group; in these cases, the test examiner should explain the circumstances in the written report (see chapter 4 on diversity).

Test scoring may be done by hand or computer. Computer *scoring* is a great aid to busy clinicians. Computers are fast and accurate. They can process data rapidly and save the clinician a lot of time. Computerized *test interpretations,* on the other hand, vary in quality. Some interpretations are quite good and others are very general. All focus on clinical deficits. Very few say anything positive about the adolescent. APA ethics mandate that the clinician is responsible for the validity of the computerized interpretation. Computerized test interpretations are not always as valid as traditionally scored test interpretations reported in test manuals. The software interpretations may be based on archival data or on clinical opinion. It is up to the clinician to be responsible for this information. A competent test examiner should know the theory, data bank, statistics, and software used to design the computerized test interpretation.

The selection of tests and the creation of a test battery are just as important as administering, scoring, and interpreting the results. Selection of tests should be guided by a sound rationale and the client's best interests. Knowing what is in the client's best interest requires knowledge of adolescent development, adolescent mental health problems, psychometric properties of tests, and ethics. *Adolescent Assessment* aims to help clinicians select and use developmentally appropriate and scientifically sound testing instruments. It contains a review of adolescent development, mental health problems, common diagnoses, ethics, statistics, widely used tests, and case study examples. This information should help adolescents receive competent assessments and help clinicians conduct them.

SYNTHESIS, REVISION, AND FEEDBACK

The final step in the assessment process consists of synthesis, revision, and feedback. Interviews have been conducted and tests scored. At this point, the practitioner reviews all of the data and synthesizes it. He or she rejects, revises, or reformulates hypotheses. For example, a teenage girl was re-

Rapid Reference 1.2
Steps in the Assessment Process

- Develop rapport.
- Follow up on the referral.
- Collect background information and data.
- Formulate testable hypotheses.
- Establish a rationale.
- Conduct testing.
- Synthesize all sources of data, revise hypotheses, draft a written report, and provide feedback.

ferred for depression. It was hypothesized that she was depressed, lonely, and having school problems. However, after interviews with family members and a review of her test battery, it was discovered that she had an eating disorder. The original hypotheses were reviewed, and the major focus of diagnosis and intervention became the eating disorder.

Next, the clinician prepares feedback. Generally, the feedback is in written and oral form. Excellent guidelines for report writing can be found in *Assessment of Children* by Sattler (2002). A written report typically includes the following: identifying information of the adolescent and test examiner; the reason for the referral; background information; behavioral observations; a description of the tests administered, along with reliability, validity, and confidence intervals; test results; clinical impressions and syntheses; and recommendations.

Finally, the results of the assessment are often presented to parents and adolescents. Feedback should be clear and simple. The APA Ethics Code states that reasonable steps be taken to give explanations of results to the individual or designated representative (APA, 2002). A description of the tests, their uses, and their limitations is important. The purpose of the assessment and conclusions should be indicated. The clinician should try to identify strengths as well as weaknesses. When making recommendations, he or she should use clear, specific behavioral recommendations rather than broad, global diagnoses. Providing feedback requires clinical sensitivity; the clinician needs to be familiar with confidentiality guidelines but must also anticipate emotional responses. Anastasi and Urbina (1997) emphasized the importance of understanding the examinee's educational level and emotions. Certainly, the limits of testing should be explained.

For example, a low score on an IQ test may be due to a bad day. In the case of disappointing or confusing feedback, Anastasi and Urbina (1997) encourage the availability of counseling to cope with assessment results.

In sum, psychological assessment is essentially a problem-solving process. The clinician is presented with a problem and asked to form an opinion and make recommendations. To accomplish these tasks, the clinician gathers information. This problem-solving process proceeds more methodically when scientific thinking is applied to the steps in the assessment process. The steps in the assessment process include developing rapport, following up the referral, collecting background information, formulating testable hypotheses, developing a sound rationale, conducting testing, and synthesizing information with feedback. Finally, parents and teens should be encouraged to ask questions and share insights; this step is especially important because assessment is so frequently misinterpreted.

The deductive-inductive loop of science can be applied to these steps (Babbie, 1997). Based on the referral and data collection process, the practitioner formulates clinical hypotheses; this is deductive reasoning. These hypotheses, such as diagnoses, are then tested. Testing takes the form of objective and subjective observations; this includes formal psychological testing instruments, trained clinical impressions, clinical interviews, and observations by others. For example, consider again the case of the teenage girl referred for depression. After conducting a test battery, reviewing written reports, and interviewing the family, the clinician discovers an eating disorder. From the observations, new generalizations are induced. The diagnosis may be revised and a treatment plan is formulated. Thus, both deductive and inductive reasoning are applied to the assessment process. The use of a loop diagram represents the self-correcting nature of science (see Figure 1.1). Psychology is part science, part religion, and the practice of it is an art. For the purposes of this book, however, I have applied the rigor of scientific thinking as often as possible.

ADVANTAGES OF PSYCHOLOGICAL TESTS

Psychological tests offer many advantages over unstructured interviews. Tests provide uniformity, measure a broad range of characteristics, provide empirically quantifiable information, permit comparisons with relevant peers, provide measurable estimates of their own error, and provide cross-checks. The many advantages to using psychological tests as part of an assessment package were outlined by the APA's PAWG in the *American*

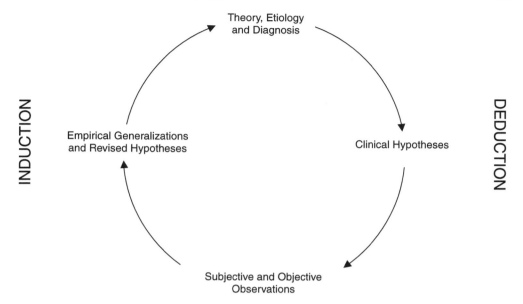

Figure 1.1. Assessment as science.

Psychologist (Meyer et al., 2001). A test is a structured interview. It may consist of 500 self-report items, or it may consist of 20 items rated by a teacher. Each time the test is administered the test items are the same. This allows for consistency and reproducibility. As stated previously, the uniform nature of tests, standardized administration, and norms provide a yardstick for comparison. Norms allow the teen to be compared to a relevant group of peers. The clinician can see the teen in context with adequate base rates. For example, a depressed adolescent in Orange County, California, can be compared to thousands of depressed adolescents across the country. Tests measure a broad range of personality, cognitive, and neuropsychological characteristics simultaneously. They contain items that may be overlooked by even the most experienced clinician.

Tests provide empirically quantifiable information. For example, the BDI-II takes an emotion like depression and applies numbers to the emotion. The numbers can be used to assess the severity of the depression. By comparing a client's score to those of other individuals, the clinician can determine whether the depression is mild or severe. Tests provide objectivity, and because they are objective, they function like a second opinion. This feature reduces legal and ethical problems and protects clinicians from allowing unintentional personal biases to enter their assessment.

Another form of quantification includes measuring bias. Tests are unique in that they can estimate their own error. By using reliability and validity coefficients along with confidence intervals, a skilled clinician can explain the strengths and weaknesses of various scores. Another form of measurable bias enters assessment in the form of test-taking attitudes. Some psychological tests contain scales that measure lying, inconsistency, malingering, apathy, and other biased presentation styles. So, an adolescent who is lying on the MMPI-A can be identified with scales measuring test-taking attitude.

By using multiple methods, a test battery provides cross-checks. Multiple methods provide converging lines of evidence. Whereas a BDI-II may offer quick screening for severity of depression, an MMPI-A adds detailed data describing somatic and other symptoms. Each test adds new information to the battery and provides a verification of other tests.

Tests have many advantages, but they will never replace an experienced clinician. They cannot empathize. They cannot provide support or encouragement. Only a skilled clinician can synthesize diverse sources of information in an assessment and pull them together to form a clinical opinion. Remember that the assessment process is essentially a problem-solving process, and tests are only one component of the process.

SELECTION OF TESTS FOR THIS BOOK

Each test included in this book was very carefully selected. Several criteria were applied. Not all criteria apply to each test, but the reader is advised when they do not. The main criteria were that the test is (a) widely used with adolescents, (b) developmentally appropriate, and (c) psychometrically sound. Tests were selected that sample different domains of adolescent abilities and use different methods. The goal was to offer a range of good-quality tests that would allow the practitioner to construct a multitrait, multimethod test battery. Tests are included that sample academic achievement, behavior, career interests, learning disabilities, mental health, personality, and more. Several different types of tests were also selected so that a test battery would consist of multiple methods. For example, self-administered personality inventories, professionally administered intelligence tests, and parent-teacher observation rating scales were included. Both objective tests and projective tests are included. Using multiple methods, as compared to one test, increases information and validity. Practical matters, such as ease of administration; availability of the test; time to administer, score, and interpret; and economics were also considered.

According to a survey conducted by Archer, Maruish, Imhof, and Piotrowski (1991), the psychological tests most commonly used with adolescents are the Wechsler Intelligence Scales, Rorschach Inkblot Test, Bender-Gestalt Visual Motor Test, Thematic Apperception Test (TAT), Sentence Completion Tests, MMPI-A, Human Figure Drawings, House-Tree-Person test, Wide Range Achievement Test (WRAT3), Kinetic Family Drawing, BDI-II, Millon Adolescent Personality Inventory (MAPI), MacAndrew Alcoholism Scale, Child Behavior Checklist (CBCL), Woodcock-Johnson Comprehensive Battery (WJ III), and Peabody Picture Vocabulary Test. Based on this list, tests were selected that sample a range of abilities and use different techniques. This book includes tests for eating disorders, substance abuse, ADHD, academic problems, and the many clinical and ordinary needs of adolescents. Appendix A lists tests by usage to enable the clinician to easily find a test for a specific problem.

Some tests are conspicuously absent from this book. The TAT, the Rorschach Inkblot Test, and the Halstead-Reitan Neuropsychological Battery, for example, were not overviewed. Two of these tests, the Rorschach and Reitan, are too lengthy for a book of this nature. They require specialized training beyond the scope of this book to administer and interpret. Finally, in an age of managed health care, lengthy projective tests, such as the TAT and Rorschach, are being used less frequently than in the past.

ETHICS AND TEST USER QUALIFICATIONS

Guidelines for the ethical behavior of psychologists can be found in the APA's (2002) Ethics Code. Specific guidelines as they pertain to assessment can be found in Appendix D. Additional standards for the practice of assessment come from *Standards for Educational and Psychological Testing,* published jointly by the AERA, APA, and NCME (1999). Every mental health professional should read these codes. Those conducting and using assessments should be very familiar with the guidelines specific to assessment. The most pertinent points are reviewed here.

Test user qualifications are discussed in detail in the APA article entitled, "APA's Guidelines for Test User Qualifications" (Turner, DeMers, Fox, & Reed, 2001). In this article, the APA task force expresses a growing "concern over the misuse of tests" (p. 1100). Most commonly the problem is due to a lack of competence by individual test users. To remediate this problem the task force offers guidelines for knowledge and skills of competent test users. "The test user's key function is to make valid interpretations of test scores and data often collected from multiple sources, using proper test selection, administration, and scoring procedures" (p. 1104). To do this, test users must be able to integrate psychometric and methodological principles, know the theory and empirical literature behind the tested construct, and understand the specific individual and context of testing. More specifically, core knowledge for the appropriate selection of tests includes but is not limited to knowledge of scaling, item format, difficulty level, reliability, validity, test bias, standardization norms, administration procedures, test-taker variables, and special requirements or limitations of the test. Beyond these academic requirements, competent test users should be knowledgeable about legal rights of test takers, safeguards for protecting tests and protocols, and test use with diverse groups. For more information on the specific guidelines for test user qualifications, the reader is directed to Turner et al. (2001).

The preamble to the Ethics Code (APA, 2002) begins with the statement that "psychologists are committed to increasing scientific and professional knowledge" and to use this knowledge to help others (p. 3). In other words, the leading national organization of psychologists believes that the purpose of the profession is humanistic work based on scientific evidence. When this belief is applied to assessment, it means that the examiner is responsible for selecting tools that are valid, reliable, and based on scientific research. After emphasizing the importance of a science-based discipline, the preamble states that the goal of the profession is the "welfare and protection of the individuals and groups with whom psychologists work" (p. 3). It is expected that scientific knowledge is used to improve the conditions of individuals, groups, and society.

The preamble of the code is followed by general principles. These principles include beneficence-nonmaleficence, fidelity-responsibility, integrity, justice, and respect. Psychologists strive to benefit others and do no harm. They establish relationships based on trust. Responsibility refers to conducting oneself in a professional and ethical manner and consulting with a colleague when necessary. On occasion, a psychologist meets an ambiguous assessment or ethical issue. For example, at what age is a child or adolescent included in the presentation of testing results? Or perhaps a therapist's personal life is interfering with the ability to work. In these instances, it is important to consult with a colleague or professional organization. Integrity means being accurate, honest, and truthful; this means avoiding misleading statements. For example, the teen and parents should be advised in advance about the purposes of testing, the limits, and the expenses involved.

Whereas the code's preamble and principles are aspirational goals, the standards are enforceable rules of conduct. Violations of standards put the practitioner at risk for legal and licensure consequences. Standard 2, competence, is especially important. To be competent means to know the boundaries of one's expertise and to provide only those services for which one is qualified by education, training, supervised experience, consultation, study, or professional experience. Although many parts of the code pertain to assessment, one standard in particular—Standard 9—focuses exclusively on assessment. This standard reviews the rules regarding bases for assessments, use of assessments, informed consent, release of test data, test construction, interpretation of assessment results, assessment by unqualified persons, obsolete tests and outdated test results, explaining assessment results and maintaining test security (see Appendix D).

According to Standards 9 and 2.04, psychologists should base their recommendations, reports, and diagnostic or evaluative statements on established scientific knowledge. Findings in reports should be substantiated, and one of the most effective ways to do this is with multiple methods and tests that are reliable and valid. Furthermore, it is expected that psychologists use assessment techniques appropriately and in light of research evidence. Assessment tools are to be used whose reliability and validity have been established for use with members of the tested populations; when this is not possible, it is expected that psychologists describe the limitations of test results and interpretation.

Although the 2002 Ethics Code is similar to previous versions, some important changes were made. Among these changes was an increased emphasis on informed consent for assessment (see Appendix D). Psychologists should obtain informed consent in language that is reasonably understandable to the client. There are a few exceptions to this guideline (e.g., when assessment is mandated by law), which are detailed in Standard 9. A careful reading of this section of the Ethics Code is strongly advised.

The standards require that when psychologists provide test interpretations, they should accurately describe the purpose, norms, validity, reliability, and applications of the procedures. When scoring and interpretation services are used, including computer-automated scoring, these services are selected on the basis of evidence of the validity of the program. Finally, psychologists are expected to maintain the security of test materials such as manuals, instruments, protocols, and test questions. For further detail on specifics of ethical assessment procedures, the reader is directed to the Ethics Office of the APA, the Ethics Code (APA, 2002), and Appendix D.

Two
— ♦ —

Adolescent Development
— ♦ —

Adolescence is a time of rapid change. Between 12 and 20 years of age, very rapid biological, psychological, and social changes take place. The word *adolescence* comes from the Latin root *adolescere,* which means *still growing.* Adolescence is defined as the state or process of growing up. It is the stage of life between puberty and maturity that terminates legally at the age of majority. Adolescence is a transitional period. It is a bridge connecting childhood and adulthood. Teenagers are neither children nor adults.

HISTORY

Although the scientific study of adolescence is a young discipline, theorists have noticed and commented on these changes since the time of the ancient Greeks. Over 2,000 years ago, Plato and Aristotle noticed that adolescents are impulsive, are prone to excess, and enjoy arguing for its own sake. For example, Plato (4th century B.C./1968 translation) believed that boys should not drink until the age of 18 because they were excitable and "fire must not be poured on fire." According to Aristotle (4th century B.C./1941 translation), young people entered adolescence as unstable, and by the end of the period, they developed a sense of self-control. To Aristotle, the most important characteristic of adolescence was the ability to choose. The world is determined for children by adults, but adolescents start to make their own choices.

18

Rapid Reference 2.1
What Is Adolescence?

- Adolescence means *still growing.*
- Adolescence is a time of rapid change.
- Adolescence is a transition between childhood and adulthood that lasts from puberty until independence.
- Plato believed that adolescents were impulsive, were prone to excess, and enjoyed arguing.
- Aristotle saw adolescents as unstable and learning self-control.
- Aristotle thought adolescents needed to make their own choices.
- Stanley Hall saw adolescence as a time of storm and stress.
- The media has perpetuated stereotypes of adolescents as substance abusers and prone to violence.
- Most adolescents make the transition to adulthood smoothly and are hard-working and healthy.

It has been argued that the existence of adolescence as a period of development is an invention of society (Fasick, 1994). The developmental stage of adolescence as we know it today was the result of several societal trends occurring around the beginning of the 20th century. At this time, the industrial revolution caused massive changes in the economy and the way people lived. Prior to the industrial revolution, the United States had been primarily an agrarian society. The farm and home were the center of family life. All skills and services originated from the home. Children were apprenticed to their parents and learned about life and survival from their parents. For example, a father would teach his son how to milk the cows and run the farm. In adulthood, the farm would become the son's inheritance. Some boys were apprenticed to blacksmiths and printers. Girls learned to cook and sew from their mothers. Food, education, and health care were all provided on the family farm. Elderly persons were cared for by family and died at home. If young people were educated, the Bible was their primary reference. Schools were rare. When children did go to school, they often attended one-room schoolhouses where the students ranged in age from 10 to 28 years.

The industrial revolution caused large-scale migration to the cities from rural communities. Society changed drastically, both in work and home life. Work that had previously been centered at home now took place outside the home. Children were employed in factories. They worked 10–12 hours a day at highly mechanized tasks, such as assembling automobiles or clothing. Working conditions were deplorable, and children and women worked long hours for low wages. Eventually, child labor laws were passed to protect children, and school attendance increased.

The migration from rural areas to the cities also altered family life. Caregiving, previously provided by the family, became institutionalized. Education, medicine, and religion now took place in schools, hospitals, and churches. Children were taught by professional teachers rather than by parents, and doctors healed sick persons in sanatoriums. The Bible was supplemented by educational textbooks, and experts on child rearing, mental hygiene, and medical cures flourished.

Wealthy families began to realize that education helped their children maintain higher social status. More specialized jobs required a higher level of education. At the beginning of the 20th century, there was a rapid increase in the number of schools, academies, and colleges. Education exploded. Congregated in cities and freed of farm labor, children and teenagers were able to attend school. At first, high school education was reserved for the wealthy, but with time, middle classes began to see the importance of education beyond the sixth grade. Laws were passed that made education compulsory. School attendance soared. When families could afford it, parents encouraged their children to stay in school longer. From 1890 to 1900, the rate of high school graduates increased by 116%, and from 1910 to 1920 they increased by 112%. The entire period of 1910 to 1930 saw high school graduates increase by 600% (Santrock, 2000). These social trends—compulsory education, age segregation in schools, specialized divisions of labor, separation of work and home, and the appearance of youth groups such as the YMCA and Boy Scouts all contributed to the emergence of adolescence as a unique period of development.

Observing these changes in society and the new expectations of young people, Stanley Hall published his classic two-volume work, *Adolescence,* in 1904. His book and ideas initiated the scientific study of adolescent development as a special stage (Hall, 1904). Hall's work emphasized the biological, psychological, and social nature of adolescence. Chapters in his book describe adolescent growth in terms of height and weight, growth of body organs, diseases, and sexuality. Several chapters focused on education and religion. One of the concepts Hall is best remembered for is his notion of *adolescent storm and stress.* He believed that the years between 12 and 23 were turbulent years characterized by mood swings. They were years of rapid oscillation between conceit and humility, goodness and temptation, and happiness and sadness.

Rapid Reference 2.2
Societal Changes Leading to Adolescence

Around the turn of the century, the industrial revolution led to many changes resulting in adolescence as a unique stage of development. Among these social trends were

- Changes from an agrarian society to an industrial one.
- Massive migration from farms to cities.
- Shift from a home-centered life and education to institutions (e.g., schools, hospitals, etc.).
- Loss of apprenticeship method of job training (e.g., farmers, printers, etc.).
- Increase in mechanized, assembly line jobs.
- Rapid increase in number of schools, academies, and colleges.
- Compulsory education.
- Age segregation in schools.
- Youth groups (e.g., YMCA).

Although adolescence is a period of rapid change and emotional fluctuation, images of angry, violent teenagers are not consistent with contemporary scientific opinion of normal adolescents. Adolescents are frequently portrayed as rebellious, impulsive, undisciplined, violent, angry, and depressed. These dramatic images are perpetuated by film and newspapers. Each decade has at least one Hollywood hit that glamorizes teen rebellion such as *Rebel Without a Cause, Easy Rider, Colors,* and *Boys N the Hood.* In a similar fashion, the media publicize incidents of adolescent suicide and homicide. Although these problems do exist, the image of rebellion as normal is largely a stereotype of adolescents based on a small number of highly visible teens. Most teenagers are not alcoholics or juvenile delinquents. Most contemporary adolescents are hardworking, well informed, and healthy. Adolescents today attend school, participate in extracurricular activities, hold down part-time jobs, and maintain relationships with friends and family.

THE STUDY OF ADOLESCENCE

As teenagers grow, they develop internally and externally. Their minds and bodies grow internally, but they grow in the context of their environment,

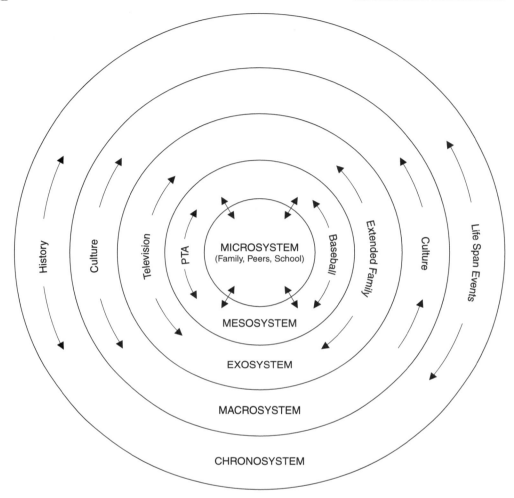

Figure 2.1. Bronfenbrenner's ecological model.

family, peer group, and community. Without light, an infant's visual system doesn't develop properly. Without love, a baby doesn't thrive. A useful framework for understanding the relationship of adolescents to their
environment is provided by Urie Bronfenbrenner.

Bronfenbrenner's ecological model (1986, 1995) consists of five environmental systems: the microsystem, mesosystem, exosystem, macrosystem, and chronosystem. These systems can be thought of as concentric
circles beginning with the individual and working themselves outward
(see Figure 2.1). The *microsystem,* or smallest system, is the individual's
primary setting or where he or she lives; it includes family, peers, school,
and teachers. The *mesosystem,* or middle system, connects other systems

and consists of relations between other systems, such as the parents participating in coaching the baseball team or the overlap of school and a part-time job. The *exosystem* is the outside or system external to the teen that influences the teen's life. An example of the exosystem's influence is the mass media's portrayal of thin models and how it affects dieting patterns in teenage girls. The macrosystem consists of the individual's culture. An adolescent girl in some cultures is expected to study and prepare for college. Other cultures prohibit her from attending school and expect her to cook, clean, and help the family. Finally, the *chronosystem* pertains to the personal and historical chronology of life events. A dramatic example is the adolescence of Anne Frank. Anne Frank recorded the unfolding of her adolescence in a diary while hiding from the Nazis in a small, confined attic. Obviously, Anne's relationship to her mother, her beginning of menstruation, and her infatuation with the adolescent boy, Peter, were all influenced by the war and her captivity.

The human being is an organic whole. Biological development influences psychological development. The onset of puberty and hormones affects body image, dating patterns, and self-esteem. Biology influences intelligence, and intelligence affects the types of environments in which individuals place themselves. Biology, psychology, and cognition are interdependent. This phenomenon is what Bandura (1997) calls *reciprocal determinism*. Behavior, cognition, and environment interact and are reciprocal rather than unidirectional (see Figure 2.2).

The act of observing, categorizing, and describing human development is an academic exercise. According to Carl Jung (1965) all of art, science, and philosophy is a projection of the human psyche. As such, dividing the human being into biological, cognitive, and psychological development is

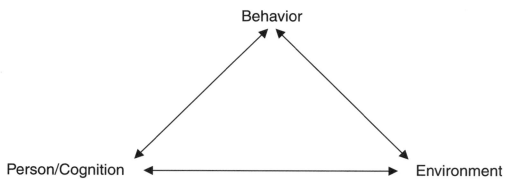

Figure 2.2.   Bandura's reciprocal determinism.

somewhat arbitrary but still necessary. The amount of knowledge is so voluminous, it is impossible to study ourselves otherwise. To be consistent with previous research, the material presented in the following section is organized according to these familiar categories; however, when assessing adolescents, the psychologist faces unique living, breathing teenagers. In other words, the whole is greater than the sum of the parts.

BIOLOGICAL DEVELOPMENT

The beginning of adolescence is not clearly defined, but a universal biological marker can be found in the onset of puberty. Triggered by hormonal events in the brain, the first visible external events are growth spurts and sexual maturation (Berger, 2000; Santrock, 2000).

GROWTH SPURT

One of the first noticeable physical developments of puberty is a sudden growth spurt (see Rapid Reference 2.3). Girls mature earlier than boys. At about age 10.5, girls begin a period of rapid growth that lasts about 2 years. It is natural for girls to gain weight first. The weight gain is then followed by a spurt in height. The height gain continues with an average increase of about 3.5 inches per year. Weight gain may be a focus of concern to the girl or her mother in today's fashion-conscious society. Mothers and daughters should be assured that a weight gain prior to puberty is natural and followed by a spurt in height. As long as good nutrition and exercise are practiced, this weight gain should not be the focus of undue anxiety.

In general, boys begin their growth spurt at about 12.5 years (see Rapid Reference 2.3). Like that of the girls, this growth spurt also lasts about 2 years. Each boy differs in his rate of growth, but on average boys may grow about 4 inches per year. In our culture, height is highly esteemed in men, and short boys are often teased by their peers.

Growth charts in doctor's offices are based on statistical averages of large cohorts of data. Few children ever represent the average. Some children will be taller and some shorter; some will mature earlier and some later. More than one boy has passed through the high school years as the smallest boy in his class, only to begin his growth spurt after high school and ultimately become more than 6 feet tall. There is a wide range of *normal* development, and normal should not be confused with *average*.

Rapid Reference 2.3
Biological Changes of Puberty

Sex	Average Age Range[a]
Girls	
Height spurt	10.5–15
Breast growth	11–15
Pubic hair	11–14
Menarche	13
Boys	
Height spurt	12–16
Testicular development	11–15
Penile growth	12–15
Pubic hair	12–15.5

[a]These are approximate average age ranges, and a wide range of normalcy exists.

SEXUAL MATURATION

Following the growth spurt, the next visible change in biological development is sexual maturation. Puberty begins in the brain with the pituitary gland. The pituitary gland and hypothalamus trigger hormones, called *gonadotropins,* to stimulate the testes in boys and the ovaries in girls. Through a sophisticated feedback loop originating in the human brain, the endocrine system and several hormones stimulate sexual maturation. In boys, *testosterone* is the primary hormone stimulating sexual maturation. In girls, it is *estrogen.*

Sexual maturation follows a common sequence of events. In girls, puberty begins with an increased production of estrogen and progesterone in the ovaries at about age 9. Next, the uterus and vagina begin to grow larger. These changes are followed by the beginning of breast development. Growth of pubic hair, widening of hips, and menstruation all begin around age 13. First ovulation usually begins about a year after the beginning of menstruation, and final development of secondary sex characteristics is generally completed by the end of high school. Bear in mind that these ages are averages and a wide range of normal development exists. Menarche, or the first period, is considered normal if it begins anytime between the ages of 9 and 15. If a parent or counselor is concerned, a medical doctor should be consulted.

In boys, the pattern of pubertal events is as follows: Testes increase pro-

duction of testosterone, penis and testicle size increase, pubic hair appears, the voice changes, first ejaculation occurs (usually through masturbation or a wet dream), onset of maximum growth occurs, hair begins to grow in armpits, more detectable voice changes occur, and facial hair begins to grow. Like girls, boys can show a wide range of normal age development. In general, the age range for the beginning of puberty is 11 and the end is 16–17 years. During this stage, boys develop a noticeable increase in upper body strength and muscles; as a result, they may be fascinated by flexing their muscles, wrestling, and competing in displays of strength and height.

EARLY AND LATE MATURERS

Each human's biology unfolds at its own rate. However, to study the relationship between physical and psychological development, researchers categorize boys and girls into early and late maturers. Girls who develop earlier are more likely to date at a younger age and seek independence from their parents. They may also be at risk for smoking, drinking, depression, eating disorders, and sexual advances from older men (Santrock, 2000). Boys who develop at a younger age—especially if they are tall and muscular—are likely to be more confident than other boys.

BODY IMAGE

An important developmental task of adolescence is adjustment to a changing body. Adolescents are fascinated by the changes in their own bodies, and they think that everyone else is, too. This excessive preoccupation with oneself during adolescence was termed *imaginary audience* by David Elkind (Elkind, 1976). Adolescents think that everyone is looking at them and that everyone notices each pimple on their faces. The media and fashion industries capitalize on these adolescent fantasies. Consider that the people of the island of Fiji had almost no eating disorders until they received cable TV. With the advent of cable TV and the flood of images of thin women, teenage island girls began to diet and develop anorexia. Body dissatisfaction is especially strong in early adolescence, but self-acceptance generally increases with maturity. Boys, especially, become more self-accepting. Girls, however, become more dissatisfied and more focused on thinness. The most extreme cases of a distorted body image in girls and special pressure to be thin can result in serious illnesses like anorexia nervosa and bulimia.

Many studies have attempted to study the relationship between physical and psychological development. Puberty affects each adolescent differently. Depression, violence, and teen pregnancy have all been blamed on raging hormones. However, when puberty is carefully studied, its effects seem to be exaggerated. Some adolescents do struggle with the adjustment. The role of parents, teachers, and friends can influence this adjustment. Nevertheless, most adolescents pass through puberty and adjust to their changing bodies uneventfully.

COGNITIVE AND MORAL DEVELOPMENT

COGNITIVE DEVELOPMENT

Thinking changes both *quantitatively* and *qualitatively* during adolescence. Adolescents can think faster and more efficiently than children. Mathematical operations are conducted more rapidly. The way adolescents think about themselves and their world is also qualitatively different from the way children think. Reality is no longer black and white, right or wrong, but shades of gray. Life is full of complexities and what-ifs. Situations that were previously concrete are now hypothetical. Mom and Dad, who used to know everything, now have faults. Some of these changes in thinking are captured by the theories of Piaget, Elkind, and Kohlberg (Elkind, 1976; Kohlberg, 1958, 1976, 1986; Piaget, 1952).

Jean Piaget was trained as a zoologist, and he brought these skills to the observation of his own children. Trained as a scientist, he was fascinated by the development of logic and *scientific thinking* in children. He watched the growth and evolution of thinking in his own three children and devised theories and experiments. Piaget believed that thinking was an active process and that children were born intelligent. He even called the inquisitive toddler, forever curious and exploring his world, a little scientist (Piaget, 1952).

Piaget used the term *schema* to describe intellectual frameworks. Children have mental frameworks, or schemata, for observing and interpreting their experience. Through the process of *assimilation,* experience is fitted into existing schemata. Conversely, the process of *accommodation* adjusts the schema to the world. For example, a toddler who saw a deer for the first time called it a "big woof-woof." The child's *schema* for four-legged animals was a dog, and a deer was simply a large dog. This is an example of assimilation.

Piaget differed from previous theorists by seeing children, even infants, as intelligent beings actively organizing their world. Prior to Piaget, John Locke called a child a tabula rasa or blank slate. The behaviorist, John Watson, believed that any infant could be shaped into a beggarman, thief, doctor, or lawyer. To Piaget, on the other hand, the infant was born not blank but rather intelligent, active, and ready to learn. His ideas were labeled *cognitive* (in contrast to behaviorist), meaning that children are innately intelligent. Intellectual development unfolds at its own pace and is a function of an interaction between biological maturation and the environment. It can't be rushed.

According to Piaget, even infants are organizing their world intellectually. A baby, from approximately birth to 2 years, is in what Piaget termed the *sensorimotor stage* of development. The baby is coming to know his or her world through the senses, such as taste and touch, and through motor functions, such as crawling and walking. When children were around 2 years of age, Piaget noticed that thinking changed. Piaget called this stage *preoperational thinking*. During this stage of cognitive development, children begin to represent the world with images and symbols; this is the beginning of symbolic logic, which allows language development. However, preschoolers rely on intuition rather than logical reasoning for problem solving.

The two most important stages of cognitive development to the study of adolescence are *concrete operations* and *formal operations*. *Concrete operations* is characterized by logical reasoning about concrete objects. Children in this stage are also able to classify objects in hierarchies more systematically than they were previously able to do. This stage marks the beginning of children's understanding of addition, subtraction, and scientific taxonomies. Early elementary-aged children can understand set theory as long as hands-on manipulatives, such as popsicle sticks or crayons, are used to organize groups by size or color. This stage involves doing mental operations that were previously done physically. Children can logically infer relationships between objects and reverse them mentally. Piaget believed that this stage lasted approximately from 7 to 11 years. This change in thinking is best demonstrated by Piaget's classic experiment on conservation.

The conservation experiment is conducted by presenting two beakers of water to a child. Both of them contain the same amount of water. One beaker is tall and thin, and the other is fat and wide. The child is asked to pour the water from the smaller and wider beaker into the taller one. The child is asked which beaker has more water. The preoperational child will answer that the wider beaker has more water but won't be able to explain why; this demonstrates intuitive thinking. The concrete operational child will answer that the water is the same in both beakers and can provide an explanation. This simple experiment has been replicated thousands or millions of times and demonstrates a basic difference between the thinking of younger versus older children. This experiment demonstrates conservation and reversibility. Through the principle of reversibility, children come to understand that because the water is the same in both containers, the operation is reversible. This same reversibility allows children to put themselves in others' shoes. This stage of concrete operations sees the beginning of empathy and understanding toward others.

According to Piaget, the stage of *concrete operations* is followed by *formal operations. Formal operational thinking* is the final stage of cognitive development and represents a fully mature, adult way of viewing the world. Adolescents in this stage perform logical operations and hypothetical-deductive reasoning. They form hypotheses and then deduce answers. The hypotheses may be about algebraic functions, real-world dating situations, or even dreams of perfect parents. Whereas elementary-aged children live in a world of concrete reality, adolescents dream and fantasize. They dream about perfect parents and ideal worlds. They argue and philosophize about hypothetical situations. They have brilliant futures. It is abstract, formal thinking that allows adolescents to use satire and metaphor. Writing, mathematical operations, and analytic thinking all improve.

Piaget's theories have tremendous implications for working with adolescents. First, understanding the *qualitative* changes in the way adolescents think about their world helps adults communicate with them. For example, you can argue relentlessly with a preoperational child about conservation and never persuade him or her that the amount of water in the two beakers is the same. Therapists, teachers, and counselors need to try to identify with young people and understand how they see the world to help them change.

Understanding cognitive development helps parents understand their teenagers. It helps them understand the rejection that comes with increased independence. Only a few years earlier, their children worshiped them. Now their sons and daughters are constantly comparing them to their friends' parents and finding faults in them. As adolescents mature and become more self-reliant, they push away from their parents. At the same time, they see their parents' faults. It is the leap in adolescent cognitive development that allows them to imagine perfect parents; this is nor-

Rapid Reference 2.4
Piaget's Theory of Cognitive Development

Concepts

- *Schema:* mental framework for observing and interpreting experience
- *Assimilation:* fitting experience into an existing schema
- *Accommodation:* stretching the schema to fit new experience

Stages of Cognitive Development

- *Sensorimotor:* coordination of sensory and motor movements, 0–2 years
- *Preoperational:* symbolic thinking, using images and words to portray the world, beginning language, 2–7 years
- *Concrete operations:* logical reasoning about concrete objects, classification skills, conservation, 7–11 years
- *Formal operations:* logical reasoning, hypothetical-deductive reasoning, abstract thinking, 11–15 years

mal cognitive and emotional development for the adolescent, but it feels like rejection to most parents.

Finally, Piaget's theory has implications for education and curriculum design. The California state curriculum, for example, mandates that algebra be taught in 8th or 9th grade. However, tests of Piaget's theories indicate that only 17–67% of college students are thinking in formal operational ways (Elkind, 1961; Tomlinson-Keasey, 1972). Many adolescents and adults never reach Piaget's stage of formal operations. They view the world in concrete and tangible realities; this means that a lot of students and teachers are being frustrated by unrealistic expectations and that the curriculum should probably be adjusted to the abilities of the students.

SOCIAL COGNITION

While adolescent thinking about logical, scientific processes changes, so does their thinking about social situations. Some ideas from Piaget and Elkind are also very helpful in understanding social cognition. David Elkind (1985) was a student of Piaget and believed that formal operational

Rapid Reference 2.5
Social Cognition

Formal operational thinking allows adolescents to view their social world differently than they did as children. Some of Elkind's (1985) and Piaget's (1952) ideas help understand adolescent thinking. They are

- *Egocentricism:* a heightened sense of self-consciousness and a tendency to believe the world revolves around oneself
- *Imaginary audience:* the feeling of being on stage all of the time, that others are always watching
- *Personal fable:* a sense of grandiosity and uniqueness, alone and the center of their own story
- *Invincibility principle:* a sense of immortality, the idea that nothing can hurt or kill them

thinking explains adolescent *egocentricism, imaginary audience,* the *personal fable,* and the *invincibility principle.* Adolescents are *egocentric* in nature. They believe that the whole world revolves around them. They have a heightened sense of self-consciousness and believe that everyone else is as focused on them as they are on themselves.

Imaginary audience is a term used by Elkind to explain the concept that adolescents think that everyone is watching them all of the time. They feel that they are on stage and that every pimple is a public announcement. Boys and girls spend long hours staring in the mirror and may be obsessed with their appearance. The *personal fable* refers to the adolescent's sense of uniqueness and grandiosity. Adolescents feel they are unique, alone, and the center of their own story. A teenage girl can't imagine that her own mother ever experienced the pain of a breakup with a boyfriend. Adolescents often think they are capable of saving the whole world, of reconciling religion and science, or of becoming powerful world leaders. Finally, the *invincibility principle* pertains to an adolescent's sense of immortality; most adolescents believe they are immortal. They believe that they can drive too fast and nothing will happen to them. They believe that other girls get pregnant, but that they will not. A common problem among college students is that they overextend themselves. They think they can study, work, exercise, and socialize—all on little or no sleep. These ideas, egocentricism, imaginary audience, personal fable, and the invincibility principle help adults understand the way adolescents think about social situations.

MORAL DEVELOPMENT

In addition to coping *with* the many other changes that are taking place in them, adolescents are reevaluating their morals. Teenagers are evaluating their parents' morals and forming their own personal ethics; this pertains to standards in appearance, academic behavior, and sexual morals. Adolescents are questioning their parents' values and the rules of society. They are forming ideologies that will guide their decisions and behavior. One way to understand moral development during adolescence is through the theories of Lawrence Kohlberg and Carol Gilligan. Kohlberg (1958) designed a theory to study moral reasoning. His theory consists of several stages of moral development. In the lower-level stages, moral reasoning is based on externalization of values; in other words, morals are determined by others, like parents, teachers, and police. At the higher levels of moral development, morals are internalized and based on an internal code of morals. As children grow and evolve, so do their morals. Younger children are more controlled externally, and older ones are more controlled internally. It is important to note that moral reasoning and moral behavior are not the same thing. An adolescent may know the right thing to do and still behave immorally.

Kohlberg's theory consists of three levels with two stages within each level. In the lowest level, *Level 1: Preconventional reasoning,* moral reasoning is controlled by external rewards and punishments. In Stage 1, *Punishment and obedience orientation,* moral thinking is determined by fear of punishment. For example, children and adolescents behave because they are afraid of being punished by their parents or teachers. Students maintain good grades and control themselves in class out of fear of detention. In Stage 2, *Individualism and purpose,* moral reasoning is based on rewards and self-interest. In other words, a teenager will work hard to obtain good grades to be accepted to a prestigious university.

Kohlberg's *Level 2: Conventional reasoning* is the second or intermediate stage of moral reasoning. Internalization of morals is intermediate; some are governed by internal standards and some by external standards. In Stage 3, *Interpersonal norms,* moral reasoning is guided by a concern for trust, caring, and loyalty to others. This stage explains a lot of adolescent group behavior. An adolescent may break the law to protect a friend. Loyalty to friends is very important to teenagers. Stage 4, *Social systems morality,* is the fourth stage of Kohlberg's theory of moral development. In this stage, moral decision making is based on social order, law, justice, and duty. Adolescents begin to understand that laws serve a purpose of protecting the community.

Level 3: Postconventional reasoning is Kohlberg's highest level of moral reasoning. Moral development at this level is completely internalized. Adolescents are aware of alternatives and select the best moral decision based on an internal moral code. In Stage 5, *Community rights versus individual rights,* morals are seen as relative. It is acknowledged that laws are important, but it is also realized that laws are man-made and can be changed. Some morals, such as justice, even surpass the law. The final stage in Kohlberg's theory is Stage 6, *Universal ethical principles.* At this stage, an individual has a moral standard based on universal human rights. At this level, individuals follow their consciences before the laws of society.

Kohlberg believed that levels and stages were hierarchical and followed an age-related sequence. Moral development was a by-product of cognitive development, and as children mature, their thinking about moral situations matures. Prior to age 9, children reason in a preconventional way. By adolescence, they reason in conventional ways. Most adolescents are in Stage 3, but some are in Stage 2 or 4. Less than 10% of people ever reach Stage 5, but those who do achieve it about age 20 to 22.

Kohlberg tested his theory with a series of stories of moral dilemmas. In other words, he designed examples of conflicts in moral reasoning and asked interviewees a series of 10 questions about the moral dilemma. The most common moral dilemma has to do with a man whose wife is dying and needs an important drug. The drug is available from a druggist at a highly increased price. Interviewees' level of moral development is assessed by the way they respond to this moral dilemma.

Kohlberg has been criticized for emphasizing a Western, male perspective of morals (Gilligan, 1982, 1992). His system of moral development is based on moral reasoning with a strong emphasis on justice. The justice perspective emphasizes the rights of the individual, and individuals make independent moral decisions. In contrast, in her book *In a Different Voice* Carol Gilligan (1982, 1992) emphasized the *care perspective.* The care perspective focuses on the interconnectedness of people, communication, relationships, and concern for others. Women, especially, often make moral decisions on the basis of caring for others. Gilligan and her colleagues interviewed girls from 6 to 18 years of age and found that girls often make decisions by listening to and watching others. They tend to interpret moral dilemmas in terms of human relationships. Further investigation of gen-

Rapid Reference 2.6
Kohlberg's Theory of Moral Development

Level 1: Preconventional reasoning

Stage 1: Punishment and obedience: characterized by fear of punishment (e.g., fear of detention or juvenile hall)
Stage 2: Individualism and purpose: motivation by rewards (e.g., working for praise and good grades)

Level 2: Conventional reasoning

Stage 3: Interpersonal norms: moral reasoning by loyalty, trust, and concern for others (e.g., protecting friends)
Stage 4: Social systems morality: moral decision making based on social order, law, justice, and duty (e.g., laws protect the community)

Level 3: Postconventional reasoning

Stage 5: Community versus individual rights: moral reasoning relative and based on an internal code (e.g., a teenager develops a personal moral code)
Stage 6: Universal ethical principles: moral standards based on universal human rights (e.g., a conscientious objector avoids going to war to prevent killing others)

der differences in moral reasoning does not appear to support gender differences (Santrock, 2000). These studies demonstrated that both men and women can express care and justice perspectives.

Kohlberg has also been criticized for being ethnocentric. American society emphasizes individualism and justice. But many other societies emphasize groups and collectivism. For example, many Asian and Latin cultures are known to be more collectivist than American society. In another example, one study of adolescent Buddhist monks in Nepal found that they were more concerned with the prevention of suffering and the importance of compassion rather than justice. Although Kohlberg's theory of moral development has been criticized for being gender- and culture-biased, it still provides a useful paradigm for understanding the development of moral reasoning in adolescents.

INTELLIGENCE

Intelligence is a multifaceted and dynamic characteristic. There are many differing definitions, theories, and ways of measuring intelligence. Although intelligence has a strong genetic basis and is generally stable over the life span, intelligence test scores are influenced by motivation, culture, and even family problems such as divorce. Any individual who administers intelligence tests and related achievement tests should be familiar with basic terminology, theories of intelligence, testing methods, and how they apply to adolescents.

Anastasi and Urbina (1997) refered to intelligence as abilities necessary for survival and advancement in a specific culture. Because different cultures value different abilities, intelligence varies cross-culturally. Not only does intelligence vary across cultures, but it also varies across the life span. For example, intellectual abilities necessary for elementary-aged children are different from those required of college students or adults. Many intelligence tests were developed for school-aged children and are closely related to school curricula. They test verbal abilities and numerical abilities; these are the skills deemed necessary for survival and advancement in Western, technologically driven cultures.

IQ

IQ, or intelligence quotient, is a term used to summarize test performance on a specific test. It represents behavior on a specific test, at a specific point in time, relative to other individuals at the same time (Anastasi & Urbina, 1997). Among adolescents, IQ may be measured to help with educational and career planning. It is often used in schools to identify gifted or disadvantaged students who qualify for special services. Another use of intelligence tests is the assessment of neurological damage after accidents.

The term *IQ* evolved from Alfred Binet's concept of *mental age*. Commissioned by the French government during the late 19th century to assess the abilities of so-called dull children, Binet reasoned that the intelligence of a "dull" 10-year-old should resemble the abilities of a younger, normal child. Prior to Binet, intelligence had been measured in terms of sensory abilities. In England during the 1860s, Sir Francis Galton, believed that because the world is experienced through our senses, individuals with better senses should be more intelligent. Galton not only precisely measured sensory discrimination and motor abilities, but he was also responsible for developing statistical techniques, such as the correlation coefficient, to measure them. Galton also believed that intelligence was inherited.

In contrast to Galton, Binet and his colleague, Simon, thought that intelligence encompassed more than sensory abilities and that it included judgment, practical sense, initiative, and adaptability. Commissioned by the Paris public schools, Binet and Simon designed a series of items to assess retardation in children. They reasoned that intelligence was age related, and they ranked the items by difficulty. Many of the items, such as naming pictures, perceiving similarities, and vocabulary are similar to items on contemporary intelligence tests. The Binet-Simon Scale was published in 1905 and became the model for future intelligence tests.

Terman imported the Binet-Simon to the United States and revised it. He developed extensive norms and standardized administration procedures and the intelligence quotient. The resulting test became known as the 1916 version of the Stanford-Binet Intelligence Scale, named for Stanford University where Terman was working. Combining concepts of mental age from Binet and mental quotient from Stern (1914), Terman devised the intelligence quotient (IQ). IQ is a ratio of mental age (MA) to chronological age (CA) and is symbolized as $IQ = (MA/CA) \times 100$. So, a bright child would have a mental age greater than chronological age, resulting in an IQ above 100. A retarded child would have mental age lower than chronological age, resulting in an IQ below 100, and an average child would have an IQ equal to 100. To this day IQ is used to summarize intelligence test scores. Although statistical methods for deriving IQ have become more complex and tests differ in their computations, in general 100 still represents an average IQ.

GENERAL *g* OR MULTIPLE INTELLIGENCES?

Intelligence is often thought of as a single ability. Spearman (1927) believed that all intellectual abilities shared a common factor he called *general* g, or simply *g*. To Spearman, general *g* correlated with all important, specific abilities and was the best predictor of a person's intelligence. Therefore, only one test of intelligence is necessary, one that measures general *g*. Raven's Progressive Matrices is a good example of this type of test. It measures reasoning and logic.

In contrast, the Weschler Scales of Intelligence (i.e., the Wechsler Adult Intelligence Scales–Third Edition [WAIS-III] and WISC-III), measure several intellectual abilities. They measure verbal as well nonverbal intelligence and include subtests of vocabulary, arithmetic, sequencing, picture arrangement, similarities, and various visual-spatial tests. During World War I, David Weschler was employed by the military as a test examiner. At the time, the army used two group-administered tests to help with the rapid classification of large numbers of troops. They used the Army Alpha, similar to the Stanford-Binet, and the Army Beta, a nonverbal test for non–English-speaking immigrants. Due to his familiarity with the Army Alpha, Army Beta, and the Stanford-Binet, Weschler incorporated both verbal and nonverbal tests into the development of his Weschler Intelligence scales. As a result, the Weschler tests measure both verbal and nonverbal intelligence. Because the WISC-III provides both overall IQ scores and measures of specific abilities, it has been useful in the diagnosis of learning disabilities.

Recently, Sternberg's (1986) theory of intelligence has been receiving considerable attention. Sternberg proposed a triarchic theory, or a theory with three components. These three components are *componential intelligence, experiential intelligence,* and *contextual intelligence.* The basic unit of intelligence in Sternberg's model is the component. It is the basic unit of information processing that acquires, stores, and retrieves information; it is an internal process. Experiential intelligence to Sternberg is a form of intelligence that connects internal and external worlds. According to Sternberg's theory, novel intellectual tasks become automatic with experience. Finally, the contextual dimension of intelligence deals with the external environment; this is a form of practical or tacit knowledge, such as changing a car tire.

Howard Gardner's (1983) model of intelligence is popular in educational circles. Gardner believes in multiple intelligences. *Linguistic intelligence,* for example, is intelligence that uses language for communication. *Musical intelligence* (e.g., rhythm and pitch), *logical-mathematical intelligence* (i.e., reasoning and mathematics), *spatial intelligence* (i.e., perceiving the world and objects in space, such as Legos, architecture, or three-dimensional graphics), *bodily-kinesthetic intelligence* (e.g., dancing, acting, and athletics), and *personal intelligence* (e.g., sensitivity to moods in oneself and others) are other types of intelligence. These multiple intelligences can provide a useful means for understanding different young adults and their differing abilities.

Standard measures of intelligence have limitations. Because intelligence tests tend to measure verbal and numerical abilities, many types of intelligence are overlooked. Mechanical, musical, and artistic abilities are not

Rapid Reference 2.7
Concepts of Intelligence

- Anastasi and Urbina (1997) define intelligence as abilities necessary for survival and advancement in a specific culture.
- Galton believed intelligence was inherited and measured through sensory and motor tasks.
- Binet and Simon thought intelligence included judgment, practical sense, initiative, and adaptability. With growth, older children have a higher mental age than do younger ones.
- Terman's intelligence quotient (IQ) was a ratio of mental age (MA) to chronological age (CA), or $IQ = (MA/CA) \times 100$.
- To Spearman, intelligence was one global ability, called general g, rather than specific abilities.
- Weschler scales of intelligence, the WAIS-III and WISC-III, measure multiple verbal and nonverbal abilities, including vocabulary, similarities, information, arithmetic, block design, and picture arrangement.
- Sternberg's (1986) triarchic theory consists of componential intelligence, experiential intelligence, and conceptual intelligence.
- Gardner's (1983) multiple intelligences include linguistic, musical, logical-mathematical, spatial, bodily-kinesthetic, and personal intelligences.

measured by standard intelligence tests. Intelligence tests cannot measure creativity, social abilities, or persistence. Some forms of intelligence and factors related to academic achievement go unmeasured by traditional tests of intelligence. For this reason, it is very important that clinicians rely on no single test to make an important decision. Decisions regarding educational and career planning, for example, should be based on multiple sources of information, including work portfolios, grades, students' interest, parents' opinions, test batteries, and counselors' input.

INTELLIGENCE AND AGE

Longitudinal studies of intelligence indicate that intelligence is stable (Anastasi & Urbina, 1997) over time. An early test of third-grade boys in Sweden demonstrated a correlation of .72 with test scores 10 years later (Husen, 1951). A later study, conducted by Harnqvist (1968) showed a correlation of .78 between tests given at 13 and 18 years of age on 4,500 boys.

Follow-up studies on the Stanford Binet indicate retest correlations of .65 at 10-year retest and .59 with 25-year retest (Anastasi & Urbina, 1997).

Even though intelligence does seem to be stable over the life span, individual scores may fluctuate widely at given points in time. Large upward and downward shifts may be affected by changes in an adolescent's life—for example, a parent's divorce, a move, or lack of motivation. In one study of intelligence scores over the period of 6–18 years, approximately 60% of the students' scores changed by 15 points (Honzik, Macfarlane, & Allen, 1948). Many variables can influence a teen's test performance. Birth order, culture, language, socioeconomic status, and parenting have all been studied. Over and over again, the single most important variable related to IQ test scores and academic achievement is parenting (Anastasi & Urbina, 1997). Parenting includes everything from reading books to preschoolers, participating in their children's activities at the school, and providing encouragement for studying to valuing and emphasizing the importance of education. Parents who encourage and reward academic success and structure the home environment to enable success—including making children do their homework—are more likely to have children who succeed in school and on intelligence tests.

MENTAL RETARDATION AND GIFTEDNESS

Schools use intelligence tests to help young people gain access to special services. Intelligence tests are used to assess both mental retardation and giftedness. Mental retardation is defined by the *Diagnostic and Statistical Manual of Mental Disorders–Fourth Edition–Text Revision* (*DSM-IV-TR*) as "significantly subaverage intellectual functioning with onset before age 18 years and concurrent deficits or impairment in adaptive functioning" (APA, 2000, p. 41). Impairments in adaptive functioning refer to problems in self-care, home living, social-interpersonal skills, work, leisure, health, and safety. A standardized, individually administered intelligence test such as a WISC-III or Stanford-Binet is administered to assess intelligence. An IQ score of approximately 2 standard deviations below the mean, or 70 IQ points, is the cutoff. It is recommended that additional information on adaptive functioning be gathered from reliable and independent sources such as teachers, an educational evaluation, or a medical history.

The definition of giftedness varies from school district to school district. Just as mental retardation is defined as 2 standard deviations below the mean, giftedness is often defined as 2 standard deviations above the mean

Rapid Reference 2.8
Intelligence and Age, Retardation, and Giftedness

- In general, intelligence is very stable over the life span.
- Many factors can influence intelligence test scores, including language, family problems, low motivation, fatigue, and culture.
- Mental retardation is defined as "significantly subaverage intellectual functioning with onset before age 18 and concurrent deficits or impairments in adaptive functioning" (APA, 2000, p. 41).
- Mental retardation is often determined by an IQ that is two standard deviations below the mean (i.e., an IQ of about 70 on a WISC-III or Stanford-Binet) *and* an assessment of adaptive functioning in self-care, home living, interpersonal skills, and so forth.
- The definition of giftedness varies from school district to school district but is often defined as two standard deviations above the mean, or an IQ of about 130 on a WISC-III or Stanford-Binet.

(i.e., an IQ of 130 to 132 on a Stanford-Binet Intelligence Scale–Fourth Edition or WISC-III). Sound assessment practices always rely on multiple measures, including student work samples, grades, parent and teacher report, behavior observation, and testing. Useful guidelines and observation tools for identifying giftedness can be found in Sattler (2001, 2002).

Many school districts have special programs for gifted and talented students, and identification of gifted adolescents depends on the goals of the program, availability of funds, and personnel. Some districts have special magnet schools in the arts or sciences. Others have pullout enrichment programs. In California, special funds are allocated for gifted students. Adolescents who excel in art, dance, music, or other creative acts not measured by standard IQ tests are often eligible for these enrichment programs.

A common misconception is that gifted individuals have more psychological and social problems. For example, extremely smart boys may be thought of as nerds who have social problems. Terman's (1925) longitudinal study of highly gifted individuals provides no scientific support for this assumption. In fact, the gifted individuals participating in Terman's study became highly productive and well-assimilated members of society (H. S. Freidman et al., 1995).

Intelligence is a multifaceted and dynamic characteristic; like personality, it cannot be measured as a separate characteristic because the two interact. To classify tests as measures of intelligence or personality is a somewhat arbitrary distinction. For example, a more motivated adolescent may perform better on an intelligence test, yet motivation is a personality characteristic. Many environmental variables influence intelligence test scores as well, such as educational opportunity, previous learning, family problems, low motivation, frustration, and self-concept. For the present, it is important to keep in mind that intelligence is a function of both genetics and environment. Although intelligence is generally stable over the life span, it is also sensitive to environmental factors and may even vary within the same individual.

PSYCHOLOGICAL DEVELOPMENT

TEMPERAMENT

All individuals are predisposed at birth toward a certain temperament, which stays fairly constant over the life span (Berger, 2000). Temperament is similar to what is commonly thought of as personality. Groundbreaking research by Thomas, Chess, and Birch (1963) in the New York Longitudinal Study observed that very young babies differ from each other in nine characteristics of temperament: activity level, rhythmicity, approach-withdrawal, adaptability, intensity of reaction, threshold of responsiveness, quality of mood, distractibility, and attention span. Some babies are happy, adaptable, and sleep well from the first days of life. Other babies kick a lot from the time they are in utero, cry intensely at birth, and rarely sleep. These differences are observed to be consistent over months and years.

Follow-up studies by other investigators have demonstrated evidence for the stability of three temperamental variables in particular: *activity level* (Goldsmith & Gottesman, 1981), *sociability or shyness* (Daniels & Plomin, 1985; Kagan, Reznick, & Snidman, 1987) and *emotionality* (Berger & Thompson, 1991). The active, happy, relaxed infant tends to become a positive child. The negative, intense, avoidant infant tends to become a shy and negative child. Although temperament remains fairly constant over time, temperamental characteristics can be influenced by environment and puberty. For example, parents can encourage a shy child to become more outgoing. Hormones in puberty will make a difference, too. Boys tend to become more aggressive and extroverted, whereas girls may become more withdrawn and eager to please.

Rapid Reference 2.9
Psychological Development

- *Temperament* is a consistent and inherent disposition.
- Activity level, sociability or shyness, and emotionality are very consistent across the life span.
- Shyness, similar to introversion, can be measured and may be an important indication of social interaction and mental health.
- Defenses can be thought of as *coping styles* and include regression, denial, displacement, withdrawal, rationalization, asceticism, and sublimation.
- Coping styles are not necessarily maladaptive. Their clinical significance can be assessed by frequency, intensity, duration, and the extent to which they interfere with normal social and occupational functioning.

The consistency in temperament persists into adulthood. McCrae and Costa (1987) identified five relatively stable temperaments in adulthood: openness to new experience, neuroticism (fearfulness and anxiety), extroversion, agreeableness, and conscientiousness. It is no accident that some of the personality tests reviewed in this book pick up on these consistent differences in temperament. For example, the most stable scale on the MMPI is scale 0, or Social Introversion (*Si*), which measures shyness and extroversion. Shy children tend to be shy adults. Sufficient scientific research exists to support the assumption that temperament—especially activity level, sociability, and emotionality—has a biological basis and is relatively stable into adolescence and adulthood.

COPING STYLES

When they are threatened, people tend to respond differently. Some people run and hide, others lash out, and still others may make friends to protect themselves. It seems likely that persons with different temperaments have different coping styles. For example, young children respond in characteristic and predictable ways while they are still too young to have been instructed by parents. A shy person is more likely to withdraw when he or she is threatened, whereas an intense person may attack someone. Anna Freud (1958) believed that people defended themselves from anxiety with defense mechanisms. In more contemporary terminology, Freud's defenses might be thought of as coping styles. These coping styles could be the natural evolution of different temperaments. The concept of coping styles, or Freud's defenses, is a very useful tool for understanding adolescents.

Some of Freud's defenses were regression, denial, displacement, withdrawal, rationalization, asceticism, and sublimation. *Regression* is a common behavior in children and teens. A preschooler who loses a nanny may return to wetting his bed. A young adult struggling for independence may return to live with parents several times before becoming fully self-reliant. *Denial* means pretending something doesn't exist. Adolescents deny their very mortality. They think car accidents can't happen to them (and even if they did, they wouldn't be fatal anyway). Another example of denial in teenagers is thinking that sex without contraception is okay because they won't get pregnant or contract a sexually transmitted disease (STD). *Displacement* is a way of blaming others for one's feelings. Anger is often displaced on others, and disappointed and angry teenagers may blame their parents for their own poor grades. *Withdrawal* and *avoidance* also are common ways teens deal with anxiety. It is easier for some adolescent boys to bury themselves in books and debate team activities than it is to face girls, for example. *Rationalization* is a way of justifying or explaining away things. A common excuse for not turning in homework used to be that the family dog ate it. These days, computers seem to be eating a lot of homework. College students excel at *asceticism.* Asceticism refers to monk-like behavior that denies bodily needs. Examples include staying up for days on end without sleeping to study for exams or not eating but expecting to perform well on finals. Finally, *sublimation* means channeling emotion into socially appropriate channels. Anger can be directed in exercise. Sadness can be expressed through music.

These defenses are not necessarily maladaptive. Everyone feels threatened from time to time. Everyone withdraws or rationalizes his or her experiences occasionally. Some coping styles are actually healthy. Playing a vigorous game of basketball when one is angry with a teacher is very constructive. These coping styles become maladaptive when they interfere with normal social or occupational functioning. The minimum expectation of normal social and occupational functioning for teens is going to school and spending time with friends. Some teens are able to do this and work, go out with persons of the opposite sex, and pursue extracurricular activities. However, if an adolescent girl is spending excessive time alone in her room, her good grades have fallen, she is not attending school, and she is avoiding her friends, then the withdrawal is maladaptive. The clinical significance of defenses can be assessed by their frequency, intensity, and duration and by the extent to which they interfere with normal social and occupational functioning.

DEVELOPMENTAL TASKS

According to Freud, defense mechanisms protect us from the overwhelming anxiety inherent in living. What then are the anxieties that teens face? Adolescents feel anxious about loss of control, sexuality, dependence-independence, the need to be rational, acceptance by peers, competence, and body image; these are age-appropriate anxieties and are related to the social expectations of that age group. One way to think of these social expectations is as *developmental tasks* (Conger, 1977).

Developmental tasks vary from culture to culture and from time to time, but some are universal expectations to master to become adults. *Developmental* refers to the age span of adolescence. *Tasks* refer to jobs, responsibilities, and social expectations; they include achieving independence from parents, adjusting to sexual maturation, maintaining cooperative relationships with peers, selecting and preparing for a vocation, and developing a sense of identity. It is no wonder that adolescents feel anxious; such tasks are difficult to accomplish, and trying to accomplish them simultaneously and on one's own can be overwhelming.

Achieving independence from parents can take years. In early adolescence this sense of autonomy is often characterized by pushing away from parents. Teenagers may not know what they do want but they do know what they don't want. They don't want to be like their parents. This self-expression takes the form of creative clothes, music, and perhaps even rebellion by choosing friends their parents don't like and staying out too late. Conflict with parents and other authorities (e.g., teachers) is common in adolescence, and most personality tests assess the extent of this conflict. This form of autonomy usually quiets down by late adolescence as teens mature. Becoming fully independent of parents, however, takes a long time in our highly developed civilization. Most adolescents need to attend college or begin a vocation before they are able to fully support themselves.

Adjusting to a changing body is a difficult task for adolescents, especially in early adolescence or middle school. Girls expect themselves to be thin and may even starve themselves. Boys expect themselves to be tall and muscular. Along with learning self-acceptance comes adjusting to a body that is changing sexually, having sexual feelings, and developing sexual

Rapid Reference 2.10
Developmental Tasks

Developmental tasks are age-appropriate, social expectations required to make the transition from childhood to adulthood.
Developmental tasks include

- Achieving independence from parents
- Adjusting to sexual maturation
- Maintaining cooperative relationships with peers
- Selecting and preparing for a vocation
- Developing a sense of identity

morals and a sexual identity. Many adolescents don't even have access to accurate information about sexuality. If their parents are too busy or unable to talk frankly with them, adolescents may be miseducated by their peers and unable to access appropriate health care.

Peer relationships also can be a focus of considerable anxiety. More than any other time in their lives, teens want badly to be accepted by and popular with peers. Because teenagers are becoming less dependent on parents and are trying to be independent, their peer group becomes the focus of self-worth. Some teens regress and make bad choices in order to belong—some examples include drinking, smoking, and driving too fast. These activities may be things that they frowned on at 12 but that now seem exciting to a 15-year-old. Blos (1989) called adolescence a "detour of regression." Teens, especially boys, regress to childlike tendencies such as swearing, telling dirty jokes, and being messy. Teenagers who don't feel accepted may experience loneliness and a sense of alienation. Most scales of adolescent behavior measure alienation and peer relations.

On top of all of these social expectations, adolescents are expected to perform well in school and find their way to careers and economic self-reliance. Unfortunately, teachers and counselors are often overworked and not available to provide the necessary information to help adolescents along. The adolescent who is studious and self-motivated probably has the easiest transition from high school, to college, to work. As society has become highly technological and the apprenticeship model of earlier eras has died out, the transition to adulthood has become more difficult for many teens. These teens would be well served by an increase of vocational training in high schools, mentor programs, and apprenticeship programs.

IDENTITY

Erik Erikson (1963, 1968) thought the major psychological task of adolescence was forming an identity. In *Childhood and Society* and *Identity: Youth and Crisis* he explains his stages of development. Human growth, according to Erikson, is a series of inner conflicts successfully weathered by the vital personality. The central conflict of adolescence is identity versus identity confusion. In this stage, the adolescent develops a personal identity by experimenting with various roles through music, clothes, and so forth. Role experimentation allows young people to find their niche in society, and the way adolescents pass through this stage will have a profound impact on their later life.

The danger at this stage in Erikson's theory is role confusion; this may include confusion about sexual identity or reluctance to commit to a profession. Erikson refers to the adolescent mind as the mind of a "moratorium." This psychosocial moratorium is a delay of adult commitments, or a time-out, between childhood and adulthood. It is "a psychosocial stage between childhood and adulthood and between the morality learned by the child and the ethics to be developed by the adult" (p. 263). Erikson likewise views college life as a moratorium and describes even a year abroad or (in many cases) juvenile delinquency in the same way. Even psychotherapy can be a form of psychosocial moratorium, when it is a self-exploration for young people who would otherwise be "crushed by the standardization and mechanization" of society (Erikson, 1968, p. 157).

Identity confusion explains the vulnerability of young people to cults, superheros, and revolutions. Young people are searching for identity, belonging, and adults to idolize. Roles, rituals, and regalia define experience by providing status and order. For this reason, countries in poverty and chaos, like 1930s Germany, are susceptible to charismatic leaders like Hitler. Hitler appealed to the idealism and identity confusion of adolescents. Hitler was aware of the vulnerability of youth and exploited this weakness to form his own army of youth, called the Hitler Youth. According to a member of the Hitler youth, he even told their parents, "I don't need you. I have your children" (Heck, 1988).

Adolescence is a confusing time, not only because teenagers are changing very rapidly, but also because society sends them ambiguous expectations. One minute they are told that they are too young to do something, and the next minute they are told to grow up. They are told to get a job, but no one will hire them without experience and they can't get experience without a job. With so many changes and so much expected of them, it is

> ***Rapid Reference 2.11***
> **Identity Formation**
>
> - Erik Erikson believed that human growth is a series of conflicts weathered by the vital personality.
> - The central conflict of adolescence is *identity* versus *identity confusion.*
> - Adolescence is a psychological moratorium, or time-out, from adult responsibilities such as earning a living and parenting.
> - Adolescence is a time of role experimentation (e.g., clothes, music, jobs), which helps adolescents find their identities.
> - Identity confusion causes a teenager to be vulnerable to peer pressure, drugs, and even cults.
> - Kurt Lewin called the adolescent a marginal man because he or she has no real status in society and is neither child nor adult.

no wonder they feel confused, lonely, and out of control. Kurt Lewin (1936) called an adolescent a "marginal man" because adolescents have no real status in our society. They have renounced childhood and they are not fully adults. They are partly accepted and partly rejected by the privileged class, adults. One young client called adolescence "no man's land."

SOCIAL DEVELOPMENT

Adolescent growth takes place in a social context. Like Bronfenbrenner's ecological model presented earlier in this chapter, development begins with the individual, but in most cases, the individual grows in a family. To small children, parents, siblings, grandparents, and caregivers are their whole world. As they mature, their sphere expands to include a neighborhood, school, and peers. Although it doesn't always seem so, family is very important to teenagers.

Brothers and sisters have a significant impact on teenagers. Older brothers and sisters are role models and caregivers. When the older brother is a good student, the younger one may compete and become a good student. The older one can help younger siblings by providing a studious atmosphere and doing homework problems with them, quizzing them on test material, and so on. Girls frequently take on a nurturant role, feeding, clothing, and holding younger siblings; they may help younger siblings to cross the street or take them to school. Just as the younger sibling needs the older one, the older one needs the younger one not only to gain companionship, support, and play, but also to have someone to love, someone who needs them, and someone for whom to be responsible. The older one gains confidence and meaning from caring for a younger brother or sister. The relationship between siblings and the way parents utilize it is an area that has largely been ignored by the psychological literature.

PARENTS

Effective parenting of adolescents is different from the parenting of younger children but builds on the same foundation. In a classic study of parenting, Diana Baumrind (1967) studied the parents of competent preschoolers. She defined competent young children as ones who were independent, self-reliant, and confident. After interviewing the parents of these children, Baumrind identified four important characteristics of good parenting: nurturance, setting limits, communication, and maturity demands. Good parents are warm and nurture their children. They also set age-appropriate limits. A 1-year-old is not allowed to decide whether to go into the street. A 4-year-old is expected to pick up his or her own toys. Effective parents communicate with their children by listening, talking, and explaining. They are likely to give reasons for setting limits (e.g., the child's safety). Finally, good parents have age-appropriate maturity demands (e.g., a 3-year-old is expected to be toilet-trained, and a 5-year-old can help make his or her own lunch).

Baumrind (1967) grouped the parents into three parenting patterns. She called the most effective parents *authoritative.* Authoritative parents set limits and enforce rules but are also very warm and listen to their children. Less effective parents were either authoritarian or permissive. *Authoritarian* parents saw their word as law (not to be questioned) and were overly punitive. Maturity demands were high and communication low. This militaristic style of parenting tends to encourage rebellion. *Permissive* parents are very nurturant, communicate with children, are accepting, make few rules, and have few maturity expectations. Permissive parenting may result in children who are controlling, are demanding, are unable to do things for themselves, and have a high sense of entitlement.

Parenting an adolescent is similar to parenting a younger child but is more *democratic.* As mentioned earlier, Aristotle thought that adolescence was about making choices. Adolescents can and should be considered when their parents are making decisions that apply to them. In a very

Rapid Reference 2.12
Family

- Brothers, sisters, and parents are very important to teenagers.
- A good parent to a teenager is *democratic* and guides him or her into making their own well-informed, cautious decisions.
- Teenagers want parents who listen to them.
- Good listening means being available when the teen wants to talk, reading nonverbal communication, paraphrasing, and giving support.

short time, they will be making all of their own decisions. For example, a 16-year-old boy may be asked what time he thinks is a good time to come in on school nights and weekends, and parents can negotiate a reasonable curfew. Parents and adolescents can also discuss household rules, appropriate hangouts, and safety. At times, they will disagree, and this is normal. Some conflict is inevitable; as long as that adolescent is a minor, however, the parent is legally responsible. A useful rule of thumb for adolescent children living at home is that they have the right to be heard but that parents make the rules. Even though parents still hold the authority, the ultimate goal is for the adolescents to become independent and self-reliant. Successful parents and teachers make themselves obsolete. We know we have succeeded when our children don't need us anymore.

Although adolescents should be allowed more decision-making authority, they still need and often want limits. A 15-year-old-girl whose single mother lets her go wherever she wants and stay out as late as she likes may feel unloved. A boy might want his parents to tell him to be in by midnight so that he doesn't have to go drinking with friends. Adolescent lives can be saved by asking, *who, where, and when.* One afternoon when I was calling home from work to check on my 13-year-old son, one of my college students overheard me asking, "Who are you going with?" and "Where are you going and when will you be back?" She turned to me and said, "If my parents had just asked me those questions when I was younger, I would have gotten in much less trouble." Parents set and enforce limits because they love and care about their children.

By the time a child reaches adolescence, a parent needs to have developed a strong rapport with that child. The rapport will be necessary for the times the adolescent feels scared, alone, and confused and when he or she needs an adult to whom to turn. This rapport is the result of years of showing an interest in the child and listening. The previous U.S. Surgeon

General, C. Everett Koop, traveled across the country and interviewed hundreds of teenagers. He interviewed high-achieving adolescents in Catholic schools and interviewed homeless adolescents living on the streets. He asked hundreds of teens, "If there was just one thing you wished your parents would do, what is it?" The universal response was "Listen."

Perhaps the most important role of a being a parent is being available. Adolescents need support and encouragement. They need to know that someone in the adult world cares about them and recognizes the unique persons that they are and can become. Popular psychology abounds with advice for parents, but more important than being so-called professional parents is just being available, taking an interest in their children's lives, and showing that they care. There is no substitute for good old-fashioned love.

FRIENDS

The role of friends to a preteen and teen cannot be overemphasized. Adolescence is a very formative period, and friends made at this stage in life take on a special significance. Years later, well into middle age, friends from childhood and adolescence are remembered with special affection. Few friends made in adulthood ever share that intense bond. A lucky few are able to maintain their adolescent friends throughout their lifetimes.

To a teenager, friends represent a source of belonging, self-worth, companionship, and identity. When friendships don't go well, they cause intense pain. Being accepted at this age is very important, and being popular is enormously important.

Adolescents are very concerned with fitting in socially in middle school, high school, and even early adulthood. One way to make the social transition from middle school to high school is through an extracurricular activity. Adolescents who have interests such as music, sports, or some area in which they can become involved as part of a group have more opportunities to develop competencies and make friends. Many adolescents feel lonely and isolated, and this problem can be exacerbated if they have few or no social outlets. They may view high school as a bad experience to get behind them so that they can get on with their lives.

High school students tend to cluster in cliques, such as the athletes, the studious types, students of the same ethnic group, and those out on the field smoking. The names of the cliques vary with specific schools and generations, but adolescents almost always identify themselves and others

Rapid Reference 2.13
Friends

- Friends represent a source of belonging, self-worth, companionship, and identity.
- When peer relations are strained, adolescents suffer deeply.
- Extracurricular activities like music and sports provide a source of competency, self-esteem, and companionship.
- Adolescents frequently identify with cliques.
- Adolescents are fiercely loyal to friends.
- Isolation from peers can result in loneliness, delinquency, and mental health problems.
- Romantic relationships are a source of joy and pain for teens.
- A thorough psychological assessment needs to include an assessment of friendships and romantic relationships.

by these cliques. Self-concepts formed at this age may persist into adulthood. The nerdy kids who become successful doctors or computer wizards may still perceive themselves as misfits years later.

Good peer relations have an impact on adjustment. When monkeys who have been raised together are separated, they become depressed and regress socially (Suomi & Harlow, 1976). Anna Freud's studies of children who lost their parents during World War II (WWII) demonstrated that these youths formed their own peer-families. They protected and helped each other, and even without parental care, they grew up without becoming delinquents or psychotic. Furthermore, studies of teenage mothers who were abused as children but were exposed to healthy peer mothers showed that these teenagers become good mothers themselves (Berger, 2000). Just as healthy peer relations can improve adjustment, loneliness and isolation have been observed to be related to dropping out of school, delinquency, and mental health problems (Santrock, 2000). Some psychological tests designed for adolescents, like the Millon Adolescent Clinical Inventory (MACI), assess alienation.

Adolescents are fiercely loyal to their friends and may even risk their lives for them. Young adolescents are just beginning to separate from their nuclear families but haven't yet started their own families. For many adolescents, their friends serve as their family when the mother or father or both are emotionally unavailable to them; this explains why gangs are so important and why some adolescents risk their lives for their friends.

Romantic relationships and interest in the opposite sex grow during middle school and high school. During middle school, boys and girls tend to socialize in groups. With time, the groups become smaller and individuals pair off. Romantic relationships can be a source of both satisfaction and pain to adolescents, and they may be terribly confusing. Adolescents may not be able to tell whether somebody likes them. Maybe the timing is off, and he liked her last year and now she likes him. Most adolescents don't understand themselves very well, don't know how to express themselves, and are only beginning to understand others. Rejection and fear of rejection can be devastating. Because of all of the other changes going on in their lives, some teens find it easier to avoid romantic relationships altogether. Romantic relationships are an area of adolescent development that is not well understood, but they are so important that they warrant more study. Perhaps the importance of adolescent romantic relationships is that they provide experience in adult roles. Erik Erikson believed that the most important psychological issue of young adulthood was intimacy versus isolation—that is, to become a vital young adult, one needed to form a close and intimate relationship with another. If adolescents can learn to trust each other and talk openly, they may be developing important relationship skills.

Although the importance of friendships is recognized by adolescents themselves, their parents, popular writing, and adolescent textbooks, it has been generally neglected in psychological assessments. Two very valuable sources of support or conflict are frequently overlooked—siblings and friends. Most personality tests focus on the individual. They ask about somatic symptoms and mood, but they rarely ask about friends. Most tools were originally designed for adults and ask about spouses or family, but they rarely address friendship circles. Tests designed for adolescents do assess conflict with authority (e.g., parents, teachers, and police) but rarely assess quality of peer relationships. Adult therapists who lack experience working with adolescents may accidentally overlook the importance of friends to the mental health of an adolescent.

CONCLUSION

In summary, adolescence is a time of rapid change. It is a period of biological, cognitive, psychological, and social change. Puberty brings a rush of hormones, the development of secondary sexual characteristics, and sexual maturation. Cognitively, the adolescent begins to view the world differently. Cognition changes both qualitatively and quantitatively. Even though they can reason better and faster than ever, adolescents often see themselves as invincible and their parents as at fault for everything.

At birth, each child comes into the world with a unique temperament. The way children cope with experiences is a function of their temperaments. Some children gobble up new experiences, whereas others hide from life. These temperaments interact with parenting styles and life experiences to contribute to the uniqueness of each teenager. In addition to the changes taking place in their bodies, teenagers are expected to become more independent of parents, adjust to sexual maturation, develop cooperative relationships with peers, prepare for a vocation, and develop an identity. Adolescence represents a time-out from adult responsibilities, and this time-out gives them time to accomplish these developmental tasks.

Family and friends are very important to teenagers. Siblings provide role models and companionship. Some parents help their adolescents become independent, and others make it more difficult. Democratic parents assist their teens in making their own decisions. Authoritative or permissive parents may encourage rebelliousness or controlling behaviors in adolescents. Friends can provide support, belonging, and identity. Adolescence is a time of exploring new identities, and much of this exploration comes from peer group association. Stanley Hall, considered the father of the scientific study of adolescence, called this stage a period of storm and stress. He believed that turbulence was a normal part of growing up. Even so, most adolescents make this difficult transition quietly, uneventfully, and successfully.

Three

— ♦ —

Adolescent Mental Health Problems and Diagnoses

——— ♦ ———

Mental health problems of adolescents include anxiety, conduct disorders and delinquency, eating disorders, family and peer problems, sexuality, school problems, substance abuse, and suicidal ideation and suicide. Assessing psychological problems in an adolescent is difficult because adolescents may not recognize their own symptoms. Moreover, they may lack the vocabulary to describe their symptoms, and they may resist treatment. It is also difficult for the clinician to tease out what is normal adolescent development and what may represent personality, situational, or mental disorders. Many problems of adolescence are the result of the transition from childhood to adulthood and are due to accomplishing developmental tasks, such as identity development, separation from parents, and formation of intimate relationships (see chapter 2). Frequently, adolescent problems that are the focus of treatment and that may be causing considerable distress are *not* diagnosable mental disorders. For example, two major developmental tasks of adolescence are peer acceptance and adjusting to one's sexuality. The typical high school environment may not be tolerant of alternative lifestyles. This situation can be the source of considerable distress for some adolescents.

Adolescents may also suffer anxiety or depression due to problems that are situational in origin. Developmental blows such as the death of a parent, divorce, a breakup, rape, pregnancy, a mentally or physically ill parent, or parental financial problems can all cause mental health problems for adolescents. Frequently, adolescents are required to cope with multiple stressors simultaneously, such as a single and depressed parent, neg-

Rapid Reference 3.1
Adolescent Mental Health Problems

- The most common mental health problems of adolescents are anxiety, depression, and conduct disorders. Suicide is also a serious concern.
- Adolescent mental health problems may be secondary to normal development, biological in origin, or situational.
- An understanding of normal and troubled adolescents is essential to appropriate assessment.

lect, financial problems, and separation from the other parent. In theory, the adolescent who has to deal with multiple stressors should be more at risk for mental health problems. However, some adolescents cope very well. Situational supports such as friends and extended family, as well as internal resources such as intelligence, social extraversion, and resilience may help some teens cope with overwhelming circumstances more effectively than can others. Developmental blows are legitimate adolescent problems that have been understudied, but they do not represent mental disorders. Unfortunately, due to the nature of the psychiatric classification system, personality theory, and some assessment tools, adolescent problems of a situational nature are frequently attributed to the adolescent, and an otherwise healthy adolescent is labeled hysterical or dysfunctional.

One of the goals of this book is to help practitioners better understand both normal and troubled adolescents. The previous chapter provided an overview of normal adolescent development, whereas this chapter focuses on mental health problems. Adolescent mental health problems vary in etiology. Some are secondary to normal development, some are biological in origin, and some are situational. However, whatever the origin, when an adolescent problem is diagnosed by a mental health worker, psychiatric categories are used. For this reason, the *DSM-IV-TR* classification system is used in this book.

DSM-IV-TR AND DIAGNOSING ADOLESCENTS

The most widely used U.S. classification scheme for mental disorders is the *DSM-IV-TR* (American Psychiatric Association, 2000). The current version is based on several previous editions. The versions differ by their purpose (e.g., statistical, clinical, phenomenological), and there is considerable disagreement about symptoms, labeling, and prevalence (2000). In fact, the definition of the disorder affects its prevalence. In the United States the first attempt at a classification system of mental disorders was for statistical purposes and based on the 1840 census. It recorded only one category: idiocy-insanity. In 1917, the American Psychiatric Association developed the first plan for medical terminology for mental disorders. The nomenclature was primarily used to diagnose hospital inpatients and for statistical purposes. Major changes in classification schemes were brought about by WWII, the *DSM-I,* and its subsequent revisions. War veterans necessitated a broader nomenclature that included psychophysiological, personality, and acute disorders. At the same time, the World Health Organization (WHO) published the sixth edition of the International Classification of Diseases (ICD), which included mental disorders.

Over the decades, the *DSM* evolved. Attempts were made to make the symptom definitions more reliable and based on empirical evidence. By the time the *DSM-IV* was written (1994), an empirical literature was available for most diagnoses. The recent 2000 text revision of the *DSM-IV* followed very careful and systematic procedures. It was based on a systematic review of the empirical literature, reanalysis of previously collected data sets, and extensive issue-focused field trials (2000).

Although the *DSM-IV-TR* is the most scientifically accurate and widely used psychiatric classification system in the United States, it is still limited. Clinicians differ in their diagnoses and diagnoses are often unreliable. Moreover, the *DSM-IV-TR* does not make implications about etiology or treatment. Mental disorders are not bacterial infections with defined causes and specific treatments. There is no simple one-to-one agreement between adolescent problem, diagnostic category, and prescribed treatment. Furthermore, the *DSM-IV-TR* also states that when it is used in forensic cases, no implications can be made that individuals are responsible for their behavior. Bear in mind that the *DSM-IV-TR* began as a statistical manual. It was designed to count and label mental disorders, not to attribute etiology and guide treatment. In spite of its limitations, the *DSM-IV-TR* represents the best effort of the psychiatric and psychological communities to classify mental disorders at this time.

A *mental disorder* is defined by the *DSM-IV-TR* as "a clinically significant behavioral or psychological syndrome or pattern that occurs in an individual and that is associated with present distress (e.g., a painful symptom) or disability (i.e., impairment in one or more important areas of functioning) or with a significantly increased risk of suffering, death, pain, disability, or an important loss of freedom" (2000, p. xxxi). Furthermore, this syndrome has to be more than a culturally appropriate response to a specific event, such as normal bereavement. The *DSM-IV-TR* also explains that the term *mental disorder* is "a reductionistic anachronism of mind/body dualism" and that there is plenty of "physical" in "mental disorders" and vice-versa (2000, p. 30). Furthermore, somatic symptoms, such as headaches and dizziness, often accompany mental disorders like anxiety.

In the case of adolescent disorders, impairment in functioning can mean failure in school, feelings of sadness, trouble with friends, conflict with parents, or breaking of the law. In general, adolescents are not self-referred; rather, they are referred to the assessment by a parent, counselor, or law enforcement official. This is important to note because their presenting problems are less likely than an adult's to result in personal distress. Their behavior is more likely to be distressing to someone else, as in the case of conduct disorders. Because teenagers are generally being dragged to therapy against their will, clinicians and others are more likely to perceive them as oppositional.

Even a skilled clinician may have difficulty diagnosing adolescent disorders. Diagnosing adolescent disorders is problematic for several reasons. First, adolescent mental disorders do not always present themselves in the same way as adult disorders. For example, a depressed adolescent girl may behave recklessly, a trait shared with conduct disorder. Second, in the past some theorists believed that rebellion was a normal part of adolescent development (Blos, 1989; Freud, 1958; Hall, 1904). Although more recent empirical studies have largely rejected the idea that serious disruptive behaviors are a part of healthy adolescent development, it is still difficult to diagnose a teenager out of context (Petersen et al., 1993). Without knowing a teenager and his or her peer group it is extremely difficult to determine whether the behavior is normal in that context; for example, in some communities teenagers feel required to join gangs for self-protection. Finally, adolescents are more emotional than adults. For example, adolescents are three times more likely than adults to respond positively to the MMPI item *At times I have fits of laughing and crying that I cannot control.*

Normal adolescents' moods fluctuate wildly. In a creative study conducted by Larson and Lampman-Petraitis (1989), 473 children ages 9 to 15 were asked to carry electronic pagers and emotional self-report forms with them for a week. Seven times each day, they were paged and asked to record what they were doing and their mood. Sample data from one teenager, Lorraine Monawski, showed positive and negative mood fluctua-

Rapid Reference 3.2
Diagnosing Adolescent Disorders

When an adolescent problem is diagnosed by a mental health professional, psychiatric categories from the *DSM-IV-TR* are used.

A mental disorder is defined by the *DSM-IV-TR* as a "clinically significant behavioral or psychological syndrome or pattern that occurs in an individual and that is associated with present distress (e.g., a painful symptom) or disability (i.e., impairment in one or more important areas of functioning) or with a significantly increased risk of suffering death, pain, disability, or an important loss of freedom" (2000, p. xxxi).

For an adolescent, impairment in functioning can mean failure in school, feelings of sadness, trouble with friends, conflict with parents or teachers, or problems following the law.

Clinicians who have more experience working with adults tend to over-pathologize adolescent problems.

Personality disorders are very rarely diagnosed in adolescents.

Adolescent problems are generally diagnosed on Axis I only.

tions as often as five out of the seven time samples. All ages showed rapid changes in mood from sadness to happiness and back again. Moreover, as all children became adolescents, they became more introspective, more socially sensitive, and less happy with themselves. Early adolescence, especially, was a period of diminished happiness. To an extent, exaggerated emotionality, mood fluctuations, experimentation, and rebellion are developmentally appropriate adolescent behavior and *not* mental disorders.

Due to the numerous difficulties associated with accurately diagnosing adolescents, clinicians may experience a tendency to overpathologize, especially those who primarily work with adults or administer tools designed for adults. Administering adult measures of psychopathology to adolescents may make normal situational and developmental problems appear more serious. For example, when the same college students were administered both adult and adolescent versions of the MMPI, normal college students looked pathological on the adult version but not on the adolescent version (Gumbiner, 1997). Adolescents routinely score higher on items of mania and schizophrenia, such as *I have strange and peculiar experiences.* During an intake interview at a major medical center, an adolescent girl positively endorsed an item indicating she was hearing voices.

The clinic staff was certain she was schizophrenic. On further interview, it was discovered that she was a very devout Catholic and talked to God in church.

PREVALENCE OF MENTAL DISORDERS

It is estimated that approximately anywhere from 12–41% of adolescents have suffered from a mental disorder during the previous year (National Institute of Mental Health [NIMH], 1990; Olin, 2002; Roberts, Attkisson, & Rosenblatt, 1998); however, accurate prevalence statistics for adolescents are difficult to obtain. Estimates vary depending on the type of research methodology. Data from the Isle of Wight study based on more than 2,000 British 14- and 15-year-olds reported a rate of 21% (Rutter, Graham, Chadwick, & Yule, 1976). Data collected by Kashani et al. (1987) and based on a community sample of 150 adolescents indicated that approximately 41% had at least one *DSM-III* diagnosis. Anxiety disorder (8.7%), conduct disorder (8.7%), and depression (8%) were the three most common specific disorders. Structured interviews conducted with approximately 10,200 fourteen- to 18-year-old high school students in Oregon found that 11.2% of girls and 7.8% of boys met *DSM-III* criteria for psychiatric diagnoses (Petersen et al., 1993). Major depression, unipolar depression, anxiety disorders, and substance abuse disorders were the most commonly diagnosed. Girls were more likely to be diagnosed with unipolar depression, anxiety, eating disorders, and adjustment disorders. Boys were more likely to be diagnosed with disruptive behavior disorders. A study conducted by Achenbach and Edelbrock (1981) indicated that adolescents were most likely to be referred to mental health clinics for unhappiness, sadness, depression, and school problems. In addition, parents and teachers may be unaware of the internal suffering of an adolescent, but a fall in grades is almost always a red flag; thus, clinicians should always be alert to behavioral indicators such as sadness, depression, and falling school grades as potential signs of a mental problem.

The study of suicidal ideation and suicide attempts with adolescents has received special attention (R. P. Archer, 1997; Petersen et al., 1993; Santrock, 2000). Between 1960 and 1975 the rate of adolescent suicide nearly doubled (R. P. Archer, 1997). During the 30-year period from 1957 to 1987, the overall suicide rate for 15- to 19-year-olds quadrupled from 2.5 to 10.3 per 100,000 (Berman & Jobes, 1999). The suicide rate is highest for white boys—18 per 100,000 (Santrock, 2000). Suicide is the third leading cause of death among 15- to 24-year-olds, following accidents and homicide (Berman & Jobes, 1999). Gay and lesbian youth may be at especially high risk. One study reported that gay and lesbian adolescents are 2–6 times more likely to attempt suicide (Berman & Jobes, 1999). Another study conducted by Friedman, Asnis, Boeck, and DiFiore (1987) showed that 53% of the 300 high school students who were sampled reported that they had thought about killing themselves but didn't actually try. When attempts are made, boys are four times more likely to successfully kill themselves than are girls; girls are three times more likely to make a suicide attempt. Adolescent data collected on the MMPI-A normative sample showed that 21% of boys and 38% of girls responded positively to the item *I sometimes think about killing myself.*

Like adult disorders, adolescent mental health disorders tend to cluster together. One large community-based study reported a comorbidity rate of 42% for adolescents with a depressive disorder (Kovacs, 1990). For example, the comorbidity of depression and anxiety disorders is estimated from 30–70%. Depression and conduct disorders also frequently co-occur; estimates range from 10 to 35% in adolescents (Kashani, Reid, & Rosenberg, 1989). Furthermore, eating disorders, substance abuse, and suicide attempts co-occur with depression (Petersen et al., 1993).

GENDER, AGE, AND ETHNICITY

Adolescent girls consistently report more depression than do boys (Nolen-Hoeksema, 1990). The ratio is about 2:1. Kashani et al. (1987) report that 29% of girls as compared to 15% of boys report at least one depressive symptom. Kandel and Davies (1986) found that 23% of 15- to 16-year-old girls claimed to be depressed compared to only 10% of boys. Another study conducted using the BDI found levels of depression as high as 57% in girls and 23% in boys (Albert & Beck, 1975). Moreover, depressed girls are more likely to have eating disorders, whereas depressed boys are more likely to have conduct problems (Petersen et al., 1993).

When girls are assessed on the MMPI-A, they are more likely to show elevated depression scales. Additionally, girls are three times more likely to respond positively to the item *I cry easily* (R. P. Archer, 1997). They are also almost twice as likely to say they are terribly hurt by scolding or criticism. This finding has important implications for parents, teachers, and therapists. Whereas a middle school teacher may find it necessary to apply strict discipline to teaching boys, a softer style may be more effective with girls. In fact, because girls are more likely to run away than to fight back, an overly authoritarian parent might actually encourage a depressed girl to run away from home.

Prior to adolescence, boys are more at risk for nearly every psychological disorder, including adjustment reactions, antisocial disorders, anxiety disorders, learning disorders, and affective disorders (Erme, 1979). Ratios of ADHD range from 2:1 to 9:1, boys to girls. In addition, 60–80% of individuals diagnosed with reading disorders are boys, and stuttering is three times more likely in boys than in girls. Continuing into adolescence, boys are still at greater risk than girls for all disorders except depression and anxiety (Nolen-Hoeksema, 1990).

Research on gender differences using the MMPI-A shows that adolescent boys are more likely to report conduct problems (R. P. Archer, 1997). For example, boys are twice as likely to admit to having been in trouble with the law (R. P. Archer, 1997; Butcher et al., 1992). When specific scales are examined, boys show elevated scores on psychopathic deviance, which measures aggression and conflict with authority. Studies of adult men show higher rates of hostility and antisocial behavior (Gumbiner & Flowers, 1997). Finally, U.S. homicide arrest rates are 10 times higher among adult men than among adult women.

A number of studies of ethnic differences in mental health exist. Most studies involved adult subjects. Research on the MMPI, for example, shows higher rates of somatization in Latino populations (Greene, 1987). Some studies suggest a higher rate of conduct disorders in African American populations (Santrock, 2000). Most of these studies confound socioeconomic status with ethnicity, so it is impossible to tease out whether the problems are due to poverty or ethnicity. To date, no nationally representative research study of mental health disorders in adolescents exists, and exact prevalence rates, ethnic differences, etiology, and family influences remain uncertain. As a result, it is premature to claim that specific disorders are related to ethnic background.

There is a serious and immediate need for more research on adolescent mental health. Compared to adults and children, adolescents are a neglected population (Williams, Butcher, Ben-Porath, & Graham, 1992). When previous U.S. Surgeon General Everett Koop traveled across the United States and interviewed hundreds of adolescents, he concluded that rescuing adolescents should be America's number one priority.

Only the most likely presenting problems of adolescence are reviewed in this book. These problems include anxiety, conduct disorders and delinquency, depression, eating disorders, oppositional defiant disorder, sexual abuse, substance abuse, and suicide. Often, these disorders first become a problem during adolescence. Adolescent mental health disorders differ from childhood and adult disorders. Children are more likely to be diagnosed with enuresis, encopresis, ADHD, learning disabilities, and phobias than are adolescents (Achenbach & Edelbrock, 1981). Adults are more likely to be diagnosed with personality disorders or psychoses (R. P. Archer, 1997).

Some important disorders that occur during adolescence are not included here. ADHD and learning disabilities are prevalent in teens but generally come to the attention of teachers, parents, and clinicians in childhood. Finally, personality disorders are very rarely diagnosed in adolescents—particularly younger adolescents. Most personality disorders are believed to begin in early adulthood. For this reason, adolescent problems are generally diagnosed on Axis I only. For disorders that may occur in adolescence but are not reviewed in this book, the reader is directed to the *DSM-IV-TR*.

As stated earlier, anxiety, conduct disorder and delinquency, eating disorders, family-peer problems, sexual adjustment problems, school problems, substance abuse, and suicidal ideation are the most prevalent mental health problems of adolescents. These problems can be difficult for a practitioner to assess due to the unique developmental characteristics of adolescents. In order to assist practitioners, the following sections provide an overview of the most prevalent disorders, as well as their symptoms, frequency, and diagnostic suggestions.

ANXIETY DISORDERS

Anxiety is the "apprehensive anticipation of future danger or misfortune accompanied by a feeling of dysphoria or somatic symptoms of tension. The focus of anticipated danger may be internal or external" (*DSM-IV-TR*, 2000, p. 820).

Anxiety is not necessarily maladaptive. Some anxiety in life is inevitable and may even be helpful. Anxiety may drive adolescents to study and get good grades. Anxiety only becomes maladaptive when it is frequent, intense, and long in duration. It is also a problem when it interferes with social and occupational functioning. If anxiety is preventing a young person from going to school or social functions, then it is a problem. Some anxieties common to adolescents include worries about body image, acceptance by peers, sexuality, independence from parents, and achievement.

ETIOLOGY

Anxiety is common in the United States. Among adults, it is estimated that in a given year, approximately 13.3% experience anxiety that is so debilitating as to be labeled an anxiety disorder. Accurate statistics for adolescents are difficult to obtain. One study reported that 8.7% of adolescents had anxiety disorders (Kashani et al., 1987). In adults, it is known that women are about twice as likely to suffer from most forms of anxiety. Only two forms of anxiety, obsessive-compulsive disorder and social phobia, seem to be as common in men as in women (NIMH, 2001). The *DSM-IV-TR* lists 11 types of anxiety disorders, and an individual can suffer from more than one type of anxiety. Those anxiety disorders most problematic to adolescents are specific phobia, social phobia, obsessive-compulsive disorder, and posttraumatic stress disorder. For more complete information on other anxiety disorders and differential diagnosis, consult the *DSM-IV-TR*.

Little has been published about anxiety in adolescents. In fact, considerable confusion exists about the prevalence and severity of anxiety during adolescence. Worries and stressors related to normal development are common. Nearly every teenager feels anxious initiating intimate relationships, which encourages the use or abuse of substances at parties to relax. Although anxiety is common in adolescents and may cause distress or self-medication, it rarely is life threatening and can even be helpful. Anxiety may motivate teens to study or to avoid reckless behavior. It may be for these reasons that adolescent anxiety has received less attention than have conduct disorders, depression, eating disorders, or suicide. Nevertheless, one research study estimated that close to 10% of adolescents suffer from anxiety severe enough to be diagnosed as a mental disorder.

SYMPTOMS

- Excessive fear
- Anxiety aroused by a specific phobic object or situation, such as school or peers
- Awareness that the fear is excessive

- Avoidance of the phobic situation
- Intense discomfort or dread in the phobic situation
- Motor tension, muscular tension, or fatigue
- Rapid heartbeat, shortness of breath, dizziness, nausea, or diarrhea
- Hypervigilance such as irritability, startle response, and problems sleeping
- Concentration problems

SUGGESTED PSYCHOLOGICAL TESTS

- Child Behavior Checklist (CBCL)
- Conners' Rating Scales–Revised (CRS-R)
- Millon Adolescent Clinical Inventory (MACI)
- Minnesota Multiphasic Personality Inventory–Adolescent (MMPI-A)

DIAGNOSTIC SUGGESTIONS

Axis I

- 300.29 Specific phobia
- 300.23 Social phobia
- 300.3 Obsessive-compulsive disorder
- 309.81 Posttraumatic stress disorder
- 300.02 Generalized anxiety disorder
- 293.84 Anxiety disorder due to a general medical condition
- ___.___ Substance-induced anxiety disorder
- 300.0 Anxiety disorder not otherwise specified (NOS)

CONDUCT DISORDER AND DELINQUENCY

Conduct disorder is one of the most frequently diagnosed adolescent disorders. It often comes to the attention of the mental health community through the juvenile justice system. When adolescents commit an illegal act, they are called juvenile delinquents. The accompanying psychiatric diagnosis is frequently conduct disorder. Estimates of the rate of conduct disorder vary with the type of research. Depending on the type of population and assessment tool, estimates of conduct disorder range from 1 to

19%. One community sample of 150 adolescents, for example, found a rate of 8.7% (Kashani et al., 1987).

ETIOLOGY

The major symptom of conduct disorder is the "repetitive and persistent pattern" of the violation of rights of others and the violation of societal rules (APA, 2000, p. 93). Excessive fighting, cruelty to people or animals, stealing, destruction of property, theft, and serious violations of rules are all symptoms of conduct disorder. Learning disability, substance abuse, and sexual recklessness often accompany these disruptive behaviors, as do accidents, suicide, and suicide attempts. Children with a history of bullying, threatening, and physical fighting are diagnosed with childhood-onset conduct disorder. After the age of 10, adolescent-onset conduct disorder is diagnosed. Oppositional defiant disorder diagnosis is a related but less serious disruptive disorder. Although the oppositional defiant disorder diagnosis is characterized by disruptive behavior and fighting, the persistent and repetitive violation of others' rights and breaking of rules is less serious.

Boys are more likely than are girls to be diagnosed with conduct disorder, although the *DSM-IV-TR* does not offer specific rates. Boys with conduct disorder engage in more fighting, stealing, and assault, whereas girls with conduct disorder are more likely to run away. Data based on the Unified Crime Reports indicate that 3% of 10- to 14-year-olds and 11% of 15- to 17-year-olds are arrested for criminal offenses (Santrock, 2000), including larceny, assault, vandalism, liquor law violations, drug abuse, disorderly conduct, and running away. Most of these offenders are boys, and this trend continues into adulthood. For example, the adult male-to-female arrest rate is 10:1 for murder and 5:1 for assault in the United States (Myers, 1999). Furthermore, when murder rates are compared, men are 20 times more likely to murder other men than women are to murder women. The government, the media, and citizens seem especially troubled by the rising rates of violent crimes among juveniles. Between the 1960s and 1990s, the juvenile arrest rate increased sixfold (Myers, 1999). Moreover, this rate is known to be an underestimate because up to 20% of adolescents report committing crimes for which they could have been arrested but were not (Santrock, 2000).

Very aggressive children at risk for conduct disorder have been observed as early as preschool (Berger, 2000). Clinicians report 4-year-old fire starters and preschool bullies (Gumbiner, 1996). One extremely aggressive 4-year-old boy organized a group of three other preschoolers to surround, push face down, and step on the back of a more timid boy. They were fighting over a toy shovel in the sandbox. This same preschool boy tied a balloon string around the neck of a little girl. When the preschool director asked the boy what he thought would happen to the girl, he responded without emotion and said, "She would die." Approximately half of these extremely aggressive boys become criminals (Berger, 2000).

Aggressive behavior tends to follow a developmental pattern. Usually the less severe symptoms, such as lying, shoplifting, and physical fighting, are first observable. With age, more serious symptoms develop, such as burglary, rape, and theft while the offender is confronting a victim. Conduct disorders in adolescence are more violent than aggression in elementary school; however, early onset of aggression is more likely to predict adult disorders (R. P. Archer, 1997). For example, many children with conduct disorders are later diagnosed with antisocial personality disorders, substance abuse, and other disorders as adults. The prognosis for milder cases of ADHD and impulsivity is better. Milder cases may improve by adulthood, depending on parenting and other situational variables.

Considerable research has been conducted attempting to understand violent behavior. According to Monahan and Steadman (1994), there are only two certain predictors of violent behavior: sex and age. Criminals are most likely to be men between 18 and 55 years old. Effects of temperament, hormones, parenting, peer group, and television on violent behavior have all been studied (Myers, 1999). Several lines of research point to a biological basis for aggression. For example, children of antisocial parents are more likely to be diagnosed with conduct disorder (*DSM-IV-TR*, 2000). Likewise, children with certain temperaments, such as a low frustration threshold, poor impulse control, and a hot temper are more at risk for violent behavior (APA, 1993). The male hormone, testosterone, is also believed to be related to aggressive behavior. Some studies have found that teenage boys with high levels of testosterone are more prone to delinquency (J. Archer, 1991; Myers, 1999).

Many studies have focused on environmental variables, such as family, peer group, and television, related to youth violence (Myers, 1999). Studies of abused children indicate that they were more likely to have abusive parents than were nonabused children. Most abused children do not become criminals or abuse their own children. However, when abused and nonabused children are compared, abused children are 4 times more likely to have parents who were abused themselves (Myers, 1999). Statistics from the U.S. Bureau of Justice report that 70% of juveniles in detention did not grow up in two-parent families (Myers, 1999). Single-parent families are often faced with more social stressors, such as economic problems and role overload. Their children may receive less supervision after school. Although adolescents from single-parent families are more at risk for mental health problems, most do become healthy adults (Myers, 1999).

The relationship between television and violence has been heavily studied (Myers, 1999). The results indicate that TV provides violent plots and role models to already violent people. Nonviolent people do not become violent by watching TV. However, the greater danger of TV is insensitivity to violence (Berger, 2000). Frequent watchers of TV come to tolerate very high levels of violence; thus, TV can lead children and teens to think that it is normal to carry guns and to be shot.

The final area of promising research is the relationship of violence to group behavior. Although most clinicians focus on individuals, social psychologists have known for some time that certain group variables can increase or decrease aggressive behavior (Myers, 1999). Violence often takes place in groups. Some characteristics of groups, such as diffusion of responsibility, peer pressure, belonging needs, and leadership styles may make it easier for groups such as teen gangs to act aggressively toward others. Given the high rate of violent acts committed in groups, clinicians should always consider the social context of aggressive behavior. An adolescent's friends and peer group may play an important role in stimulating aggressive behavior.

SYMPTOMS

- Aggression to people and animals, excessive fighting
- Destruction of property
- Deceitfulness or theft
- Serious violations of rules in home, school, or community
- Little empathy for others
- Lack of remorse for hurting others
- Conflict with authority at school, home, or community
- Failure to accept responsibility for actions

SUGGESTED PSYCHOLOGICAL TESTS

- Child Behavior Checklist (CBCL)
- Conners' Rating Scales–Revised (CRS-R)

- Millon Adolescent Clinical Inventory (MACI)
- Minnesota Multiphasic Personality Inventory–Adolescent (MMPI-A)

DIAGNOSTIC SUGGESTIONS

Axis I

- 312.82 Conduct disorder/adolescent-onset type
- 313.81 Oppositional defiant disorder
- 312.9 Disruptive behavior disorder NOS
- 314.01 Attention-deficit/hyperactive-impulsive type
- 312.34 Intermittent explosive disorder
- 315.0 Reading disorder
- Substance-related disorders
- V71.02 Child or adolescent antisocial behavior
- V61.20 Parent-child relational problem
- V61.21 Physical abuse of child
- V61.21 Sexual abuse of child
- V61.21 Neglect of child

Axis II

- V71.09 No diagnosis on Axis II
- 799.9 Diagnosis deferred

DEPRESSION

ETIOLOGY

Depressive symptoms are common in adolescents, especially girls. However, depressive symptoms and a diagnosable depressive disorder are two different things. To qualify as a mental disorder, the depression must cause social or occupational impairment or serious distress. Many adolescents are able to function successfully with depressive symptoms. For these reasons, Petersen et al. (1993) suggest distinguishing among *depressed mood, depressive syndromes,* and *clinical depression. Depressed mood* refers to sadness or unhappy mood related to loss or failure. It may be brief or extended. *Depressive syndromes* are a cluster of symptoms including depression and anxiety—for example, loneliness, crying, fear of doing bad things, perfectionism, feelings of being unloved, feelings of worthlessness, guilt, sadness, and worry. *Clinical depression* is a *DSM*-diagnosable disorder such as major depressive disorder or dysthymia.

Estimates of depression in adolescents are based on a growing body of separate research studies. No nationally representative epidemiological study exists. The rate of depressive symptoms increases substantially from childhood to adolescence, and the rate is higher for girls than for boys (Achenbach, Howell, Quay, & Conners, 1991; Costello & Stone (1994); Nolen-Hoeksema, 1990). There is a wide range of statistical estimates of the rate of depression in suicide. The rates vary depending on the type of research tool and the populations. Rates of depression in the general population of adolescents range from 7 to 21% (Kandel & Davies, 1986; Kashani et al., 1987; Petersen et al., 1993). In clinical populations, the rates run as high as 42–57% (Albert & Beck, 1975; Petersen et al., 1993).

Girls are more at risk for depression than are boys: 25–40% of adolescent girls reported depressive mood in the past 6 months as compared to 15–20% in boys (Achenbach et al., 1991). It is not known why girls and women suffer from more depression than do boys or men. Although no conclusive research study exists, several explanations have been proposed. For example, there is some evidence that girls become more depressed with the onset of puberty (Nolen-Hoeksema, 1990). It has also been proposed that an overemphasis on thinness is a cause of depression and eating disorders in adolescent girls (Nolen-Hoeksema, 1990; Santrock, 2000). In other words, many girls are more likely to think that they have to be thin and beautiful to be accepted by others; this leads to dieting and dissatisfaction with body image. Discrimination may also account for depressive symptoms in adult women.

Other factors related to depression in both boys and girls are parental problems and peer problems. Parental divorce often increases depressive symptoms in adolescents. Similarly, a depressed parent, an unavailable or distant parent, marital conflict, and economic problems can lead to depression in adolescence (Santrock, 2000). Peer rejection in adolescence is very serious (Vernberg, 1990). High schools are generally not very tolerant environments, and adolescents who do not fit the accepted or popular mold suffer. In recent years, more attention has been paid to depression among gay and lesbian adolescents (Santrock, 2000).

Learned helplessness is another useful theory for understanding depression. Learned helplessness occurs when individuals are exposed to continued stress or pain over which they have no control. Over time, individuals develop a sense of helplessness, hopelessness, or both, and these individuals feel like giving up. Many adolescents are victims of events over which they have no control. For example, they may be forced to live with negligent or abusive parents because they are unable to support themselves and move out. They may have experienced rape. A majority are subjected to passive confinement, a highly structured regimen, arbitrary content, occasional insults, and age segregation in the educational system. Many adolescents feel that long hours of sitting still, constant lectures, and arbitrary grading from teachers in school are akin to prison. Many schools encourage passivity and helplessness. Adolescents are often not encouraged to be creative and show initiative; few receive recognition. Martin Seligman (1992), who developed the theory of learned helplessness, believes that depression is so common in adolescents because of the hopelessness caused by an overemphasis on the self, independence, and individualism combined with a decreased emphasis on feeling connected to friends, family, community, and religion.

Depression in adolescence is serious and should not be overlooked; however, it may present differently in adolescents from that in adults. Instead of expressing sadness, the adolescent may be irritable or even hostile. Cultural differences also exist in the expression of depression. Members of some cultures are more likely to experience and focus on somatic symptoms such as headaches, stomachaches, and back pain. Other cultures may emphasize feelings of weakness, tiredness, or imbalance. Longitudinal studies suggest that depression often reappears in adulthood. Moreover, depressed individuals are at greater risk for suicide (Santrock, 2000). Furthermore, depression in adolescents is often accompanied by other problems, such as ADHD, anxiety, substance abuse disorders, and eating disorders.

SYMPTOMS

- Depressed mood, sadness
- Loss of interest or pleasure in nearly all activities
- Indifference, apathy, not caring anymore
- Drop in grades
- Thoughts of death, suicidal ideation, suicide attempts
- Isolation from family, friends, or both
- Withdrawal, refusal to talk openly

- Low energy, motor retardation, slowed movements
- Low self-esteem
- Changes in appetite, weight loss or weight gain
- Changes in sleep, sleeping too much or too little
- Feelings of hopelessness, worthlessness, or inappropriate guilt
- Grief issues, loss of family or friends by death, divorce, moving
- Use of alcohol or drugs to feel better

SUGGESTED PSYCHOLOGICAL TESTS

- Beck Depression Inventory–Second Edition (BDI-II)
- Child Behavior Checklist (CBCL)
- Millon Adolescent Clinical Inventory (MACI)
- Minnesota Multiphasic Personality Inventory–Adolescent (MMPI-A)

DIAGNOSTIC SUGGESTIONS

Axis I

- 296.2x Major depressive disorder, single episode
- 296.3x Major depressive disorder, recurrent
- 300.4 Dysthymic disorder
- 296.89 Bipolar II disorder
- 296.xx Bipolar I disorder
- 301.13 Cyclothymic disorder
- 309.0 Adjustment disorder with depressed mood
- 310.1 Personality change due to Axis III disorder
- V62.82 Bereavement

EATING DISORDERS

ETIOLOGY

Eating disorders are severe disturbances in eating behavior, resulting in body weight significantly lower or higher than the recommended weight range for an individual's height. Two of the most prevalent eating disorders in teens are anorexia nervosa and bulimia. Individuals with eating disorders refuse to eat, refuse to maintain a healthy weight, have distorted body images, and may use vomiting and laxatives to prevent weight gain. In serious cases, amenorrhea or starvation may result. Some research suggests that the normal physical changes of puberty decrease girls' satisfaction with their bodies as compared to boys, who gain confidence with the development of muscles (American Psychiatric Association, 1997). Feeling pretty, looking thin, and feeling confident seem to be related to self-esteem and mood in girls. Whereas boys are more likely to emphasize their accomplishments, girls tend to measure their self-worth by some idealized, cultural standard of beauty. Research reviewed by McCarthy (1989) on cultural differences in images of the ideal body shape, sex differences in depression, and rates of eating disorders found that cultures that idealized the extremely thin female had higher rates of eating disorders and depression in women. For adolescent girls, feeling loved, accepted, and popular with peers is often equated with being thin and beautiful. Unfortunately, TV and magazines capitalize on this unrealistic ideal. Furthermore, it may be that with the onset of puberty, girls want to feel sexually attractive; in Western societies, this often equates to being very thin. In an attempt to be thin, they try to diet. Many fail at their diets and become depressed. Others develop eating disorders.

Anorexia Nervosa

Anorexia nervosa is characterized by an intense fear of gaining weight, refusal to eat, a distorted body image, and a refusal to maintain a minimum body weight: typically, 85% of normal weight. Some girls with anorexia also develop amenorrhea. Weight loss is maintained by eating a very restricted diet consisting of usually only a few foods. Individuals with anorexia may spend a lot of time staring at themselves in the mirror and thinking they are fat. The restricted diet and low weight do not improve the distorted body image. Self-esteem of girls with anorexia is often closely related to body shape and weight. Perfectionism and depression are also frequently observed. When the anorexia is severe, hospitalization, starvation, and electrolyte imbalance may result.

The prevalence of anorexia nervosa is approximately 0.5% among girls and women (*DSM-IV-TR*, 2000). It is predominantly a female disorder and rare among men; more than 90% of the cases occur in women. Subclinical cases of the disorder are also common and more likely to be encountered by clinicians. The age of onset is typically mid- to late adolescence or ages 14–18. Anorexia is often triggered by a stressful event such as the adjustment to a new school or the loss of a boyfriend. Some theorists believe that the overemphasis on appearance for girls and the role of the media have caused an increase in the rate of eating disorders in Western countries (Nolen-Hoeksema, 1990). The course of anorexia nervosa differs for each individual. Some individuals have a complete recovery, some struggle with anorexia over a lifetime, and some deteriorate. In general, when the disorder begins in early adolescence (13–18 years) as compared to adulthood, the prognosis is better (*DSM-IV-TR,* 2000).

Bulimia Nervosa

Bulimia nervosa is characterized by binging and purging. Binge eating is defined as consuming large amounts of food in a discrete amount of time, usually 2 hours (*DSM-IV-TR,* 2000). A large celebration meal or continuous snacking during the day is not considered binging. Binge eating often occurs in secret because binge eaters try to hide their eating. Some stressors that trigger binge eating are low mood, interpersonal conflicts, feelings about body image and food, or hunger when dieting. Binging temporarily improves mood but in the long run creates more dissatisfaction with the self and body image. Binge eating is described as taking place in a frenzied state in which the individual often feels out of control. Another important characteristic of bulimia is the use of inappropriate means such as vomiting and laxatives to control weight. The most common technique is vomiting after eating. Eighty to 90% of girls with bulimia induce vomiting by putting their fingers down their throats. Vomiting provides a relief from overeating and fear of weight gain. Laxatives, fasting, and excessive exercise are also used to control weight but are less frequent. Like individuals with anorexia, individuals with bulimia are extremely concerned with body image and not being fat. Confidence, self-esteem, and depression may all be closely related to body image, and this body image is often distorted.

Approximately 1–3% of women experience bulimia nervosa during their lifetime (American Psychological Association, 2000); the prevalence in men is about .1 of this rate. Bulimia nervosa often begins in adolescence or young adulthood. It is more common in families with a history of eating disorders, mood disorders, and substance abuse. Bulimia nervosa has been reported at about the same rate in most developed countries such as the United States, Canada, Europe, Australia, Japan, New Zealand, and

South Africa. Within the United States, bulimia nervosa has been reported primarily among Euro-Americans but has been reported in other ethnic groups as well.

SYMPTOMS

- Refusal to maintain normal body weight or make expected weight gain (e.g., 85% of expected weight)
- Intense fear of gaining weight or becoming fat, even though underweight
- Unrealistic body image, perception of self as fat, even though underweight
- Extreme weight loss
- Amenorrhea
- Binge eating (eating large amounts of food in a small amount of time), followed by purging
- A feeling of lack of control over the eating
- Self-induced vomiting, use of laxatives, fasting, or excessive exercise to avoid weight gain

SUGGESTED PSYCHOLOGICAL TESTS

- Millon Adolescent Clinical Inventory (MACI)

DIAGNOSTIC SUGGESTIONS

Axis I

- 307.1 Anorexia nervosa
- 307.51 Bulimia nervosa
- 307.50 Eating disorder NOS
- 300.4 Dysthymic disorder

Axis II

- 799.9 Diagnosis deferred
- V71.09 No diagnosis

OPPOSITIONAL DEFIANT DISORDER

ETIOLOGY

The *DSM-IV-TR* (2000) estimates that the prevalence of oppositional defiant disorder is 2–16%. It is characterized by a pattern of hostile and defiant behavior toward authority figures for at least 6 months. It also involves frequently losing one's temper; refusing to comply with adults' rules; intentionally annoying other people; blaming others for one's own mistakes; and being touchy, resentful, or vindictive. Prior to puberty, oppositional defiant disorder is more common in boys. Following puberty, the rates are about equal for girls and boys. This disorder is common in adolescents with ADHD and learning disabilities.

Oppositional defiant disorder is not well understood, and research reviews describe considerable overlap between oppositional defiant and conduct disorder diagnostic categories (American Psychiatric Association, 1997). Several symptoms are correlated. Fighting, bullying, and lying tend to be symptoms of *both* oppositional defiant and conduct disorders. Stubborn, defiant, irritable, argumentative, and provocative behaviors tend to be characteristic of oppositional defiant behavior *only*. Stealing, truancy, and running away are specific to conduct disorder. One way of discriminating between the two disorders is by severity. Oppositional defiant disorder is less serious than conduct disorder (American Psychiatric Association, 1997).

Oppositional defiant disorder is difficult to diagnose. First, the oppositional behavior may be displayed only at home and not with friends or at school. Furthermore, the adolescent may deny the behavior, claiming that the parents' rules are unfair. The clinician will be forced to rely on parent report. Second, oppositional defiant disorder diagnosis must be differentiated from conduct disorder and normal adolescent rebellion. Although oppositional defiant disorder is a disruptive behavior, it usually is not as physically aggressive as conduct disorder (American Psychiatric Association, 2000).

Distinguishing between oppositional defiant disorder and normal adolescent rebellion is difficult. Some theorists believe that rebellion is a normal—even necessary—part of adolescent development (Freud, 1958). Talking back to parents and teachers, not doing homework, and having temper tantrums are likely to be interpreted differently by different people. For example, a more authoritative parent is likely to consider acting-out behavior more serious than is a more permissive parent. If he or she responds too strictly, this reaction may encourage defiant behavior in the adolescent. The *DSM-IV-TR* (2000) cautions that the oppositional defiant disorder diagnosis should only be made when the behaviors occur more frequently than observed in individuals of comparable age and developmental level and when the disruptive behavior is causing significant impairment in social, academic, or occupational functioning (p. 100). Again, this disorder is difficult for clinicians to diagnose because they rarely see adolescents in context and may not be familiar with normal adolescent behavior. It may be helpful for clinicians to contact teachers and to obtain data from observational inventories such as the CBCL.

SYMPTOMS

- Frequent loss of temper, screaming, throwing things
- Consistently defiant and hostile to adults
- Deliberately annoys others frequently
- Very argumentative with adults
- Frequently blames others for one's own mistakes
- Frequently angry and resentful
- Frequently spiteful or vindictive
- Touchy, easily annoyed by others

SUGGESTED PSYCHOLOGICAL TESTS

- Child Behavior Checklist (CBCL)
- Conners' Rating Scales–Revised (CRS-R)
- Millon Adolescent Clinical Inventory (MACI)
- Minnesota Multiphasic Personality Inventory–Adolescent (MMPI-A)

DIAGNOSTIC SUGGESTIONS

Axis I

- 313.81 Oppositional defiant disorder
- 312.82 Conduct disorder/adolescent-onset type
- 312.9 Disruptive behavior disorder NOS

- 314.01 Attention-deficit/hyperactivity disorder, predominantly impulsive type

Axis II

- V62.81 Relational problem
- 799.9 Diagnosis deferred
- V71.09 No diagnosis

SEXUAL ABUSE

ETIOLOGY

Sexual abuse is a broad category. It includes seduction, molestation, incest, rape, stalking, and even sexual harassment. Date rape is a growing concern on high school and college campuses (Santrock, 2000). Sexual abuse can be performed by a stranger, an acquaintance, or a family member. Rape is forcible and usually against women, but a growing literature is documenting rape of men (Koss, 2002). Sexual abuse is often referred to as a nonconsensual act imposed on a minor. However, even this definition is problematic because the legal age of majority varies from state to state. Furthermore, sexual abuse of an adolescent does not have to be violent or nonconsensual. A gentle seduction in the form of a developmentally inappropriate sexual experience can be traumatic for a teenager.

The *DSM-IV-TR* provides little help with a definition of sexual abuse. It provides no specific diagnostic category for sexual abuse. Apparently even the psychiatric community disagrees (Kaplan & Pelcovitz, 1997). Sexual abuse of a child is currently considered a V code (V61.21). V codes refer to "conditions that may be a focus of clinical attention" rather than mental disorders (APA, 2000, p. 731). Kempe and Kempe (1984) define incest as sexual abuse of a child by an adult for the purposes of sexual stimulation. Rape, according to legal definitions, is nonconsensual oral, anal, or vaginal penetration, obtained by force, by threat of bodily harm, or when the victim is incapable of giving consent (Searles & Berger, 1987).

Prevalence rates of sexual abuse also vary widely. First, varying definitions make it difficult to collect accurate statistics. Second, many victims, especially young ones, are afraid to report sexual abuse. Conservative estimates are that between 1/3 to 1/2 of rapes go unreported (Kaplan & Pelcovitz, 1997). However, the rate of unreported rape may be high as 85%

(Koss, 2002). Finally, different agencies (e.g., hospitals or police) vary in their methods of screening, defining, collecting, and reporting statistics. For all of these reasons, the prevalence rates of sexual abuse are assumed to be underestimates.

In one large-scale survey of 2,626 Americans, 16% of men and 27% of women reported being abused as children (Kaplan & Pelcovitz, 1997). In another study based on a probability sample of 2,004 adult women, 33.5% reported sexual assault experiences as children. Estimates of adult women who have been raped range from 14 to 25% (Koss, 1993). Whereas most studies are retrospective studies that ask adults about childhood experiences of sexual abuse, a comprehensive study of child sexual abuse conducted on children indicated that 2.5 per 1,000 children under the age of 18 years were reported as sexually abused. For all of the reasons mentioned previously, these statistics are clearly underestimates, and the actual rate of sexual abuse of children and adolescents is much higher.

In spite of the problems defining and counting the incidence of sexual abuse, it is generally agreed to have severely traumatic aftereffects, and these aftereffects can be long lasting (Koss, 1993). Extreme distress, depression, fear, anxiety, and sexual dysfunction are all symptoms of sexual assault (Koss, 1993). Physical symptoms include sexually transmitted diseases, AIDS, pregnancy, chronic pelvic pain, gastrointestinal disorder, headaches, general pain, psychogenic seizures, and premenstrual symptoms (Koss & Heslet, 1992). Studies indicate that the development of psychological problems is dramatically increased by childhood rape (Saunders, Villeponteauz, & Lipovsky, 1992). Campbell and Soeken (1999) found that sexually assaulted women report more depression, more general health problems, more gynecological symptoms, low self-esteem, poor body image, and even increased risk of homicidal victimization. In an attempt to identify those specific characteristics of rape related to chronic Post Traumatic Stress Disorder (PTSD) Darves-Bornoz et al. (1998) found that intrafamily rape, physical violence, low self-esteem, agoraphobia, and depression are all linked to chronic PTSD following rape.

Immediately following rape, victims evaluated at trauma centers are generally given the diagnosis of PTSD (Koss, 1993). Donaldson and Gardner (1985) found 96% of their sample of sexually abused women to have PTSD. Similarly, Lindberg and Distad (1985) found PTSD in all of their 17 patients who were survivors of incest. Norris (1992) states that rape is more likely than robbery, physical assault, tragic death of a close friend or family member, or natural disaster to bring on PTSD. Ninety-four percent of victims still meet the criteria for PTSD 12 days after the assault, and 46% meet the criteria 3 months later (Rothbaum, Foa, Riggs, Murdock, & Walsh, 1992). Furthermore, symptoms may last up to 18 months, and studies conducted years later show symptoms of depression, alcohol abuse and dependence, drug abuse and dependence, generalized anxiety, obsessive-compulsive disorder, and PTSD (Koss, 1993).

PTSD is an anxiety disorder diagnosis that first became widely used with problems experienced by Vietnam veterans. Years after having served in Vietnam, veterans were having recurrent dreams of the war. PTSD consists of the development of anxiety symptoms (e.g., hypervigilance, increased arousal, avoidance, etc.). Example of traumatic events include military combat, violent personal assault (e.g., sexual or physical attack), kidnapping, natural and manmade disasters, automobile accidents, and life-threatening illnesses.

SYMPTOMS OF PTSD

- Exposure to a traumatic event, such as a life-threatening event, natural disaster, or serious injury to self or others
- Intense fear, helplessness, horror
- Persistent reexperiencing of the traumatic event in thoughts, dreams, sensations, or in response to internal or external cues
- Avoidance of stimuli associated with the traumatic event (e.g., thoughts or places)
- Numbing of general responsiveness or amnesia, feelings of detachment, sense of foreshortened future, or inability to recall important aspects of the trauma
- Symptoms of persistent arousal, such as difficulty falling asleep, outbursts of anger, difficulty concentrating, hypervigilance, exaggerated startle response
- Duration of the disturbance is more than 1 month

It is important to emphasize that PTSD is not the only appropriate diagnosis for sexual abuse; depression often accompanies sexual abuse. Furthermore, if the abuse is not traumatic, other indicators such as physical signs of sexual abuse, sophisticated knowledge of sexuality, seductive behavior, and so on may be indicators of developmentally inappropriate sexual experience.

SUGGESTED PSYCHOLOGICAL TESTS

- Millon Adolescent Clinical Inventory (MACI)—Expressed Concerns Scale B: Self-Devaluation, Scale D: Sexual Discomfort, Scale G: Family Discord, Scale H: Childhood Abuse, Clinical Syndromes, Scale EE: Anxious Feeling, Scale FF: Depressive Affect
- Minnesota Multiphasic Personality Inventory (MMPI-A)—Scales 1, 2, 3, 9; Content scales: *A-anx* (Adolescent-Anxiety), *A-dep* (Adolescent-Depression), *A-hea* (Adolescent-Health Concerns), *A-ang* (Adolescent-Anger), *A-lse* (Adolescent-Low Self-Esteem), *A-fam* (Adolescent-Family Problems)

DIAGNOSTIC SUGGESTIONS

Axis I

- 309.81 Posttraumatic stress disorder
- 308.3 Acute stress disorder
- 296.xx Major depressive disorder
- 307.47 Nightmare disorder
- 300.6 Depersonalization disorder
- 300.15 Dissociative disorder NOS

Axis II

- 799.9 Diagnosis deferred

SUBSTANCE-RELATED DISORDERS

The best statistics available on drug use by adolescents in the United States come from the University of Michigan's Institute for Social Research. Every year since 1975 the Institute for Social Research has conducted a study of drug abuse, called Monitoring the Future ([MTF]; National Institute on Drug Abuse [NIDA], 2001). At first the survey sampled only 12th graders, but beginning in 1991 the survey expanded to include 8th and 10th graders. The year 2000 study was based on 45,173 students from 435 public and private schools across the country and featured an 86% response rate. One major limitation of this study is that it is a community sample based on teenagers who are attending school. Many of the most serious users are not in school. Also, the results are based on self-report data, so teenagers may underreport their usage rates.

Illicit substance use is common among adolescents. The most widely used substances are alcohol, cigarettes, and marijuana. Up to 50% of 12th graders and 41% of 10th graders have used alcohol in the last month (NIDA, 2001). Eleven percent of seniors smoke half a pack or more of cigarettes per day, and approximately 20% of 10th and 12th graders have used marijuana in the past month. Two substances, ecstasy or methylenedioxy-n-methylamphetamine (MDMA) and heroin, are growing in popularity among adolescents. These two drugs, although less commonly used, are a focus of concern because of their potency. Data from the MTF study do suggest a developmental trend in the use of substances. As might be expected, older adolescents try and use more drugs than do younger ones. For most drugs—alcohol, marijuana, cigarettes, MDMA, and heroin—use is lighter among 8th graders and increases in 10th and 12th grades. Cigarette smoking is likely to accompany other substance abuse disorders and mental health problems such as oppositional defiant disorder, conduct disorder, and depression. Because cigarette smoking is rarely a presenting problem on its own, it is not covered in this book.

Results of the year 2000 MTF study indicate that illicit drug use among adolescents either remained stable or decreased for the 4th consecutive year. Only three substances increased in use. The use of ecstasy increased among 8th, 10th, and 12th graders. Anabolic-androgenic steroids use increased among 10th graders, and heroin use increased among 12th graders. Several substances decreased in use. For example, cigarette smoking is decreasing in all three age groups. Heroin and inhalants are decreasing among younger adolescents, whereas use of cocaine, crack, and hallucinogens are decreasing among older adolescents. Unfortunately, individuals using one substance are usually using several substances. Use of alcohol is often associated with use of other substances such as cigarettes, marijuana, cocaine, heroin, amphetamines, or pills (*DSM-IV-TR*, 2000). Polysubstance abuse is more likely the rule than the exception.

ETIOLOGY

The *DSM-IV-TR* makes a distinction between *substance abuse* and *substance dependence*. Criteria for substance dependence include tolerance, withdrawal, and the continued use of the substance despite substance-related problems. Tolerance means that over time an individual must use more and more of the substance in order to get high. In other words, the drug seems to have diminished effect with continued use. Withdrawal refers to physical symptoms, such as anxiety, psychomotor agitation, seizures, tremors, insomnia, nausea, and vomiting when the user tries to stop or reduce the use of the substance. Unlike substance dependence, the diagnosis of substance abuse does not require tolerance, dependence, or compulsive use. The main criterion for substance abuse is repeated substance use that results in failure to fulfill major role obligations; for teens, this may mean failure to do schoolwork, truancy, inability to hold down a job, or operation of a car under the influence.

WHO USES AND WHY

Adolescents use drugs for many different reasons (Santrock, 2000). Some use drugs for adventure, excitement, and exploration. Some use drugs for escape, some use drugs to fit in, and some are pressured by peers to use drugs. An adolescent may start by experimenting and become addicted. Others start using, and drug use becomes a way of life necessary for daily coping. Some adolescents are first given alcoholic drinks by their parents as children and later develop daily habits of serious alcoholism.

Research conducted by Johnston, O'Malley, and Bachman (1995) at the Institute for Social Research found that perceived harm and peer norms are related to substance abuse. In recent years, adolescents have reported very little perceived harm from drinking. Only about 6.4% of 12th graders view one or two drinks as potentially harmful. On the other hand, 53% of 12th graders disapproved of people's trying marijuana. In other words, attitudes toward the risks involved with drugs and peer norms may influence substance abuse among teens.

Type of substance abuse varies by availability. Teenagers in different schools have access to different types of drugs. Students in more affluent schools have wider access to more expensive drugs like marijuana, ecstasy, and heroin, whereas teens in less affluent schools use less expensive drugs such as alcohol, inhalants, and crack.

ALCOHOL

Alcohol use is very common among high school students. Based on the MTF study, 50% of 12th graders report having used alcohol in the past month, and 32% report having been drunk (NIDA, 2001). Twenty-four percent of 10th graders and 8% of 8th graders report having been drunk in the last month; this is the highest percentage of 10th-grade drinking ever reported. Binge drinking is also a serious problem. Binge drinking is defined as consuming five or more drinks in a row. In 2000, 30% of 12th graders, 26% of 10th graders, and 14% of 8th graders reported binge drinking (NIDA, 2001). These statistics are based on a community sample of students who are in high school. Although accurate statistics for dropouts are unavailable, the use of alcohol among dropouts and homeless teens is assumed to be much higher.

Binge drinking is also receiving serious attention by college administrators. Drinking and related problems (e.g., accidents and date rape) have a significant presence on college campuses. A recent study conducted by Wechsler at the Harvard School of Public Health found that 44% of college students reported drinking five or more bottles of beer, glasses of wine, or cocktails in a row within the past 2 weeks. The 9-year study was based on the reports of 10,000 full-time undergraduates at 119 4-year colleges. Wechsler is quoted as saying, "this is not having a beer with a pizza" (Lord, 2001). Drinking alcohol is potentially very serious because of the accidents associated with it.

Alcohol intoxication causes maladaptive behavioral, cognitive, and psychological changes. They include inappropriate sexual or aggressive behavior, mood lability, impaired judgment, and impaired social or occupational functioning. Also, slurred speech, loss of coordination, unsteady gait, nystagmus, and impairment in attention or memory can result from intoxication. In extreme cases, drinking can cause a coma (American Psychiatric Association, 2000). With the first drinks, an individual may become talkative, feel good, and become expansive. With too many drinks, some nontolerant individuals will fall asleep. In general, the body is able to metabolize about one drink per hour. The *DSM-IV-TR* provides 16 different diagnostic categories for alcohol-related disorders. Among them are alcohol dependence, alcohol withdrawal, alcohol intoxication, and several other alcohol-induced disorders.

Alcohol causes a loosening of inhibitions and impaired judgment. Adolescents frequently drink at parties to relax and socialize. This situation becomes potentially life threatening when these adolescents get behind the wheel of a motor vehicle while intoxicated. Approximately 25,000 people are killed and another 1.5 million are injured each year by drunk drivers (Santrock, 2000). Alcohol is associated with an increased risk of accidents, violence, and suicide. Up to 40% of people experience an alcohol-related accident, such as drunk driving, during their lifetimes and 20% of intensive care unit admissions are related to alcohol use (*DSM-IV-TR,* 2000). Feelings of sadness and irritability may become more apparent and defenses are let down, leading to fights, suicide attempts, and completed suicides. In addition, depression and anxiety often accompany drinking. Among adolescents, conduct disorder and antisocial behavior often co-exist with alcohol problems.

Alcoholism risk factors include sex, heredity, family influences, peer relations, and personality characteristics. Men are five times as likely to have drinking problems as women. Individuals whose close relatives suffer from alcoholism are three to four times as likely to develop alcohol dependency (*DSM-IV-TR,* 2000). Some studies suggest that family environment can either increase or decrease alcoholism risk. For example, studies suggest that parents who sanction drinking, fail to supervise their children, and drink heavily themselves are likely to increase the chances that their offspring will have drinking problems (Santrock, 2000). Parental support, supervision, and good communication seem to reduce the chances of alcohol problems (Barnes, Farrell, & Banerjee, 1994). Peer use, peer norms, and having older friends also seem to be related to alcohol drinking patterns in teens (NIDA, 2001; Santrock, 2000). Even personality characteristics have been suggested to be related to drinking. For example, Cloninger's (1991) research suggests that easily bored, avoidant, and impatient teens are more at risk for alcoholism than are others.

MARIJUANA

After alcohol and cigarettes, marijuana is the most popular drug among teens. About 20% of 10th graders and 22% of 12th graders report having used marijuana in the last month (NIDA, 2001). Marijuana use is more common among men than among women (*DSM-IV-TR,* 2000). Marijuana comes from the hemp plant *cannabis sativa.* The plant originated in central Asia but is grown all over the world now. Tetrahydrocannabinol (THC) is the active ingredient in marijuana. The legal status of marijuana is controversial. Laws regulating the use of marijuana vary by state. In California before 1976, possession of marijuana was a felony and punishable by up to 10 years in prison. After 1976, a new law reduced the possession of an ounce or less to a misdemeanor with a maximum fine of $100

(Santrock, 2000). Some groups advocate the use of marijuana to control pain associated with cancer and other illnesses. Attempts have been made to legalize marijuana for medical purposes.

Marijuana intoxication produces a sense of feeling high followed by euphoria, laughter, grandiosity, and lethargy. It can produce altered perceptions of time and place, increased sensitivity to sounds and light, and relaxation. In some individuals, marijuana causes intense anxiety and social withdrawal. Impaired judgment may result in physically hazardous situations (e.g., driving a car). Physical effects of marijuana include reddening of the eyes, coughing, and dryness of the mouth. When marijuana is smoked, its effects develop within minutes. When the substance is ingested orally, its effects take longer to develop.

ECSTASY AND OTHER DRUGS

Trends in substance use among adolescents change over the years. During the 1960s and 1970s, LSD was an experimental, recreational drug used by some adolescents and college students. Since the late 1990s, ecstasy and heroin have become established party drugs. Although they are not as common as cigarettes, alcohol, or marijuana, ecstasy and heroin are both increasing in popularity. Eleven percent of high school seniors report having tried ecstasy, and less than 2% of high school seniors report having tried heroin (NIDA, 2001). The prevalence rates are believed to be higher on college campuses. Other drugs of concern are inhalants, cocaine, crack cocaine, LSD, other hallucinogens, and amphetamines, specifically methamphetamine. The presence of these drugs on high school and college campuses is alarming because of their potency. They can seriously impair social and occupational functioning. For more in-depth information on substance abuse, the reader is directed to NIDA and the *DSM-IV-TR.*

SUGGESTED PSYCHOLOGICAL TESTS

- MacAndrew Alcoholism Scale–Revised (MAC-R)
- Millon Adolescent Clinical Inventory (MACI)
- Minnesota Multiphasic Personality Inventory–Adolescent (MMPI-A)

DIAGNOSTIC SUGGESTIONS

Axis I

- 303.00 Alcohol intoxication
- 305.00 Alcohol abuse
- 303.90 Alcohol dependence
- 305.20 Cannabis abuse
- 304.30 Cannabis dependence
- 304.20 Cocaine dependence
- 304.50 Hallucinogen dependence
- 305.30 Hallucinogen abuse
- 304.60 Inhalant dependence
- 305.90 Inhalant abuse
- 304.80 Polysubstance dependence
- 304.90 Other (or unknown) substance dependence
- 305.90 Other (or unknown) substance abuse
- 292.89 Other (or unknown) substance intoxication
- 313.81 Oppositional defiant disorder
- 312.82 Conduct disorder/adolescent-onset type
- 300.4 Dysthymic disorder
- 309.4 Adjustment disorder with mixed disturbance of emotions and conduct

Axis II

- 799.9 Diagnosis deferred
- V71.09 No diagnosis

SUICIDE RISK

The study of suicidal ideation and suicide attempts in adolescents has received special attention (R. P. Archer, 1997; Petersen et al., 1993; Santrock, 2000). Between 1960 and 1975 the rate of adolescent suicide nearly doubled (R. P. Archer, 1997). During the 30-year period from 1957 to 1987, the overall suicide rate of 15- to 19-year-olds quadrupled from 2.5 to 10.3 per 100,000 (Berman & Jobes, 1999). Suicide is the third leading cause of death in 15- to 24-year-olds, following accidents and homicide (Berman & Jobes, 1999).

Some groups are at greater risk than others. The suicide rate is highest for white boys: 18 per 100,000 (Santrock, 2000). When attempts are made, boys are four times more likely to successfully kill themselves than are girls. Girls are three times more likely to make suicide attempts. Gay and lesbian youth may be at especially high risk. One study found that gay and lesbian youth are at 2–6 times greater risk for suicide (Berman & Jobes, 1999).

Thoughts of suicide are fairly common among adolescents. In a study conducted by J. M. H. Friedman et al. (1987), 53% of the 300 high school students who were sampled reported that they had thought about killing themselves but didn't actually try. Adolescent data collected on the MMPI-A normative sample showed that 21% of boys and 38% of girls responded positively to the item *I sometimes think about killing myself.*

In their book, *Adolescent Suicide: Assessment and Intervention,* Berman and Jobes (1999) stated that numerous problems are associated with assessing suicide risk. First, there is no common nomenclature. Different therapists and different researchers use different terms. Second, most assessment tools used to assess suicide lack sufficient reliability and validity. Third, these tools result in an unacceptable rate of false positives. Fourth, the study of suicide depends on unreliable forms of data such as coroner's reports and death certificates. Finally, the suicidal individual is not available for follow-up interviews after a successful attempt. Because there are so many problems with suicide assessment tools, Berman and Jobes recommend evaluating common themes of suicide rather than relying on a psychological test.

SUICIDE THEMES

Some of the research-based common themes in suicide risk are childhood problems, psychopathology, stress, breakdown of defenses, social withdrawal, low self-worth, suicidal ideation, and accessibility of a means (Berman & Jobes, 1999). Childhood problems include prior self-harm, social skill deficits, biochemical vulnerability, poor parental role models, parental psychopathology, and a family history of suicidality. Examples of psychopathology include Axis I or Axis II disorders, especially disruptive disorders, depression, poor impulse control, social withdrawal, and a low frustration threshold combined with substance abuse. Stress, such as rejection, humiliation, or fear of punishment can trigger attempts.

When defenses break down in the form of irrational thinking, intense anxiety, panic, loss of reality testing, acute behavioral change, or rage, the teen may be at risk. Social withdrawal in the form of pulling away from friends, spending a lot of time alone, or becoming antagonistic toward authority can be risk factors. Self-demeaning attitudes, pessimism, feelings of worthlessness, hopelessness, and death-related and suicidal fantasies can be a source of concern. Finally, method availability, accessibility, and knowledgeability are risk factors. Thus, a teen who is lonely, frustrated, depressed, with poor impulse control and a history of previous attempts combined with alcohol use and access to a gun is at high risk.

Assessment of suicide is extremely difficult; a very high rate of false positives is obtained with adolescents. Nevertheless, most experts agree that it is better to be conservative—better to overdiagnose than to miss a possible suicide. No teen in distress should ever be ignored. On the other hand, just because some of the risk factors are present does not mean that a teen is going to make an attempt. Furthermore, there are social expectation and labeling effects. For example, a young, vulnerable, and confused person could be led to believe that his or her condition is more serious than it is. Because the assessment of suicide is so delicate, clinicians should make sure they are comfortable with the challenge.

SUICIDE RISK FACTORS

- Childhood problems, family history of suicide
- Psychopathology, anger, depression, self-destructive behavior
- Breakdown of defenses
- Social withdrawal
- Suicidal ideation, previous attempts
- Low self-worth
- Access to means

SUGGESTED PSYCHOLOGICAL TESTS

Due to the aforementioned limitations of psychological tests, experts recommend assessing research based suicide themes and risk factors rather than relying solely on testing.

Research based suicide themes include: childhood problems, psychopathology, stress, breakdown of defenses, social withdrawal, low self worth, suicidal ideation, and accessibility of means.

DIAGNOSTIC SUGGESTIONS

Axis I

- 296.2x Major depression, single episode
- 296.3x Major depression, recurrent
- 300.4.1.1 Dysthymic disorder
- 296.xx Bipolar I disorder
- 296.89 Bipolar II disorder, depressed
- 309.81 Depressive disorder NOS
- 309.81 Posttraumatic stress disorder

Axis II

- 799.9 Diagnosis deferred
- V71.09 No diagnosis

CONCLUSION

Common mental health problems of adolescents are anxiety, depression, conduct disorder and juvenile delinquency, eating disorders, family-peer problems, school problems, sexual issues, substance abuse, and suicidal ideation. Adolescents also suffer from psychoses, but these problems are more rare. Some disorders, such as ADHD and learning disabilities, have probably already been diagnosed in childhood but continue into adolescence. According to the *DSM-IV-TR* (2000), adolescents are very rarely diagnosed with personality disorders on Axis II.

Adolescent problems are particularly difficult to diagnose because they often are not mental disorders but rather developmental or situational in origin (e.g., problems resulting from parental divorce). In spite of the difficulties of diagnosis, it is estimated that between 12 and 41% of adolescents are diagnosed with a mental disorder each year (NIMH, 1990; Olin, 2002; Roberts et al., 1998). Accurate statistics on the prevalence of mental disorders in adolescents are extremely difficult to obtain. The existing statistics are estimates based on a collection of small studies. More comprehensive data collected by the NIMH (2001) estimate the prevalence of mental disorders in adults (over 18 years) to be 22%. The actual rate of adolescent disorders is probably very close to or higher than this statistic.

Given the high rate of mental health problems among adolescents, there is an urgent need for accurate assessment and treatment. This chapter reviews the most common adolescent mental health problems and provides a brief research description, etiology, prevalence, symptom list, suggested *DSM-IV-TR* diagnoses, and suggested psychological tests for assessment of each disorder. Mental health problems included in the overview are anxiety, conduct disorder and delinquency, depression, eating disorder, oppositional defiant disorder, sexual abuse, substance-related disorders, and suicide risk.

Four

— ♦ —

Diversity

— ♦ —

The Ethics Code requires that "psychologists take into account the purpose of the assessment as well as the various test factors, test taking abilities, and other characteristics of the person being assessed, such as situational, personal, linguistic, and cultural differences, that might affect psychologists' judgments or reduce the accuracy of their interpretations" (APA, 2002, p. 14). Specific guidelines for ethical assessments can be found in the APA Ethics Code (2002), the *Standards for Educational and Psychological Testing* (APA, 1999), and appendix D. Assistance with diagnosis can be found in the *DSM-IV-TR*, which offers an introductory section, discussions in each diagnostic category, and an appendix dealing with cultural issues. The *DSM-IV-TR* appendix includes an outline of cultural formations in diagnoses and culture-bound syndromes. Age and gender are also addressed in each diagnostic category of the *DSM-IV-TR*. In this chapter I consider how differences in gender, age, culture, and disability affect assessment.

Each human being is unique. It is estimated that at birth there are trillions of possible combinations of the chromosomes from the mother and father (Berger, 2000). Each person has a unique genotype and personal history. Furthermore, each individual organizes his or her own experience in a unique cognitive manner. At the same time, we as social beings all belong to groups. These groups are defined by gender, culture, language, religion, and other factors. Both unique individual differences and group membership influence psychological assessment. For example, group membership affects psychological assessment when individuals speak a lan-

Rapid Reference 4.1
Diversity

- The APA Ethics Code requires that psychologists take into account test factors; test-taking abilities; and personal, linguistic, situational, and cultural differences affecting assessments.
- The United States of America is a country of immigrants. More than 30 million Americans have a dominant language other than English. More than half of these speak Spanish. Chinese, Korean, and Vietnamese are also common.
- 2000 U.S. Census data indicate that 12.3% of the national population considers themselves African American, 3.6% Asian, and 12.5% Latino. These percentages translate to about 80 million people.
- Test examiners are ethically responsible for considering the effect of culture on test administration and interpretation.
- Considerable research has examined test fairness for special populations.
- Some differences in test performance do exist for special populations. The examiner should be familiar with the psychological literature and test manual for the specific special populations.
- When outside their area of competence, the test examiner should refer the client to a specialist.
- Many tests have separate norms for boys and girls. It is important that the test examiner use female norms with girls and male norms with boys.
- When gender differences exist, girls are more likely to be depressed or have eating disorders. Boys are more likely to have conduct problems.
- In general, tests should be administered to the age group on which they were normed. Administering tests to other groups may invalidate test interpretations.

guage other than English and identify themselves with a specific ethnicity. Furthermore, each ethnic group is heterogeneous; thus, within the ethnic group, each person is unique. An Israeli and an Orthodox Jew may both speak Hebrew and identify themselves as Jewish, but their beliefs may be very different.

One of the objectives of scientific psychology is to formulate universal laws of human behavior; this is accomplished through theory and experimentation. Psychological tests are developed and normed on large cohorts of subjects, generally Euro-American men and women. Large groups are needed for statistical purposes such as standardization, reliability, and validity. At times, some entire groups score differently from the norm group. For example, women tend to score higher on depression than do men. Latinos score higher than do others on the L scale of the MMPI. When group differences are known to apply to psychological assessment, they should be considered.

Specific guidelines on how to assess the influence of such factors as gender, culture, age, or disability on testing do not exist. A thorough clinical assessment focuses on one individual, but the interaction of gender, culture, and test fairness can influence the outcome of the assessment. The problems are multifold. For example, a test normed on Euro-American adult men may need to be adjusted for interpretation with Latino adolescent women. Furthermore, each teen is unique and brings a unique history to the assessment situation. For example, one teen may be Latino and not speak Spanish. Another may be less acculturated and need an assessment in his or her native tongue. Because of the complexity of these issues, each is addressed in a separate section of this chapter. Even though there are no definitive black-and-white answers, it is the responsibility of the test examiner to select appropriate assessment tools, to adjust them when necessary, and to seek outside consultation if it is needed. Some guidelines for appropriate assessment are included in this section. The *Standards* state very clearly that when a test user is faced with a test taker whose special characteristics are outside the range of his or her professional experience, the test user should seek consultation from a professional who possesses relevant experience (Standards, 1999).

CULTURE

The United States of America is a country of immigrants. Many of the original settlers, Pilgrims and Puritans, left their homes in England because they were victims of religious persecution. Others were forced to emigrate because they were debtors. In the late 19th and early 20th centuries, waves of immigrants came from Ireland, Italy, and Eastern Europe. Many of these immigrants, such as Eastern European Jews, were victims of poverty, war, and religious pogroms. Chinese immigrants came to the United States and eventually helped build the transcontinental railroad.

More recent waves of immigrants have been victims of war-torn countries, corrupt governments, and poverty. They have come from Asia, Central and South America, and they speak many Asian and Spanish dialects. According to the 1990 U.S. Census, 31,844,976 people older than 5 years were living in the United States whose dominant language was not English (Sandoval et al., 1998; U.S. Bureau of Census, 1990); that was 14% of the country at the time—more than a decade ago. The number has increased since that time. More than half of those individuals were Spanish-language–dominant. Other prevalent languages were Chinese, Korean, Vietnamese, French, German, and Italian. In some states, such as California, one third of all students in kindergarten through 12th grade enter school as limited English proficient or LEP. New York, New Jersey, Texas, Arizona, and New Mexico have similar situations.

Although the idea of the melting pot has largely been rejected, the United States is definitely multicultural. U.S. Census data from the year 2000 indicated that 12.3% of the country identifies themselves as African American, 3.6% as Asian, and 12.5% as Latino (U.S. Census, 2002). Numerically, these percentages translate to approximately 80 million people. These statistics represent the country at large, but minorities are concentrated more heavily in certain geographic areas such as California. It is estimated that Latinos will comprise 50% of the population of Los Angeles by 2005 (U.S. Census, 2002). Moreover, these statistics are most likely underestimates. Prior to the year 2000, Latinos were considered Whites and counted as part of the White population. In addition, many non–English-speaking residents go uncounted.

Immigrants face dramatic cultural adjustments. Some come from rural villages where they were surrounded by family and traditions. Their new lives bring challenges of culture shock, difficulty communicating in a new language, acculturation to a very different society, and conflict between generations. According to Padilla and Medina (1996), some of the problems that affect psychological assessment of immigrant groups include level of formal education, English language proficiency, length of residence in the United States, level of acculturation, family income, cultural values, and family values. Because important life decisions can hinge on the results of psychological assessments, test results may accidentally harm individuals of different backgrounds in ways never intended by test makers.

Culture is extremely difficult to define, and multiple definitions exist. In fact, social and behavioral scientists have reached little consensus regarding a universal definition of culture. Furthermore, every cultural group is heterogeneous; within each group, individuals differ enormously in values and in attitudes. Triandis and Brislin (1984) observed that culture is "often used in a vague manner and refers to some combination of differences in skin color, country of origin, language, customs, socialization priorities, and sometimes socioeconomic class" (p. 1007). D. W. Sue and Sue

(1990) defined culture as "all those things that people have learned to do, believe, skills, tools, customs, and institutions into which each member of a society is born" (p. 35).

In spite of a lack of agreement on a definition of culture or on specific assessment guidelines, the test examiner is ethically responsible for being sensitive to cultural differences. According to Frisby (2001), guidelines by the APA's Office of Ethnic Minority Affairs encourage psychologists to "consider the validity of a given instrument or procedure and interpret resulting data, keeping in mind the cultural . . . characteristics of the person being assessed" (p. 51). Padilla and Medina (1996) state that assessment is made culturally sensitive by meshing "the process of assessment and evaluation with the cultural characteristics of the group being studied" (p. 4). This type of evaluation is done with a series of insertions and adaptions in the assessment process, including the development of instruments, test administration, analysis of scoring, and test interpretation.

Cultural differences in the recognition and reporting of symptoms have been documented for decades (Zola, 1966). On the MMPI, for example, Hispanics tend to score higher on the *L* scale and occasionally on Scales 1 and 3. Rather than lying, the elevated scores on *L* may indicate an eagerness to please or to be *muy amable,* which is a cultural value. Scales 1 and 3 measure somatic complaints. Some authors suggest that these groups show greater somatization tendencies (Greene, 1980). At any rate, cultural differences in emotional expression do exist and have been measured by psychological tests. Most of these differences have been addressed as issues of test fairness.

TEST FAIRNESS

Researchers have long debated the bias of Eurocentric approaches to testing (Suzuki, Ponterotto, & Meller, 2001)—that is, the tendency for instruments normed on majority populations to discriminate against nonmajority populations. The reason tests have been questioned for cultural bias is that the reliability and validity of tests are standardized on different cultural or linguistic groups. Sanchez first raised questions about lack of cultural sensitivity 70 years ago (Sandoval et al., 1998). Later, Jensen (1980) followed by delineating "culturally loaded" and "culturally reduced" dimensions of testing. Culturally loaded dimensions include paper-pencil tests, printed instructions, reading, written responses, speed tests, and specific factual knowledge. Culturally reduced dimensions include performance tests, pictures, oral responses, and abstract reasoning. During the 1970s, Mercer (1979) developed a pluralistic means of assessment. The System of Multicultural Pluralistic Assessment (SOMPA) contains four sociocultural scales (urban acculturation, socioeconomic status, family structure, and family size) combined with the WISC-R to determine IQ scores for minority children.

One extensively researched example of test fairness is the MMPI. Early studies conducted by McDonald and Gynther (1963) indicated that African-American students produced higher scores than did their Euro-American peers on Scales *L, F, K, Hs, D,* and *Ma.* Concluding that the test was culturally biased, Gynther (1972) called for the development of new MMPI norms. Further study by Dahlstrom, Lachar, and Dahlstrom (1986) and Greene (1987) argued that the differences are too small to be clinically meaningful or to justify specialized norms. More recently, Gynther (1989) repeated his warning that Scales *F,* 8, and 9 overpathologize for African Americans.

In 1989, Campos published a meta-analytic review of 16 studies that compared Euro-Americans and Hispanics on the adult version of the MMPI (Campos, 1989). He found that Hispanics scored higher than did Euro-Americans on one scale only (*L*), and this was only by 4 *T*-score points. Campos concluded that the MMPI predicts job performance equally well for Hispanic and Euro-American police officers. Comparisons of college students' responses on the MMPI-2 demonstrated that Euro-American students scored higher on Scales *K,* 3, and 4 and Hispanic students in Scale L even though none of the differences exceeded 5 *T*-score points. When administering both English and Spanish versions to bilingual college students, Karle and Velasquez (1996) found no differences. They concluded that *acculturation,* not culture, is the meaningful variable. In one of the few studies focused specifically on Hispanic adolescents, Gumbiner (1998) found elevated *T*-scores on seven MMPI-A clinical scales and six content scales. Scales *F, L, Hs, D,* and *Sc* were all elevated, as were low self-esteem, low aspirations, and school problems for boys. No MMPI-A scores were elevated for Hispanic adolescent girls. When they are found, cultural differences are generally small and still warrant more research with teens. For the present, the test examiner should assume that the MMPI is basically valid for Hispanic populations. Only the *L* scales seem to be consistently elevated, a finding that appears to demonstrate the culturally valued eagerness among Hispanics to please.

Research with Asians and other cultural groups on the MMPI is rela-

> ### *Rapid Reference 4.2*
> ## Guidelines for Culturally Sensitive Assessments
>
> - The test examiner is ethically responsible for selecting, administering, and interpreting appropriate psychological tests.
> - Examiners are responsible for practicing within their area of competence as qualified by education, training, or experience.
> - Be thoroughly familiar with the test and test manual.
> - Be aware of the groups on which the test was normed and profile patterns of diverse groups.
> - Have a sound rationale for the selection of each test.
> - Select tests that are appropriate for the individual and referral.
> - Establish rapport with the examinee.
> - Make sure the examinee understands and follows the directions.
> - Be sure to include cultural and socioeconomic context in the written report.
> - Give reading, acculturation, or language tests when appropriate.
> - Hire an interpreter if necessary.
> - No decision should be based on a single test score. A multimethod assessment battery strengthens validity.
> - Obtain informed consent (see Appendix D).

tively scarce. Sue and Sue (1974) compared MMPI elevations between Asian-American and non-Asian college students at a psychological services center and found more elevated scales of L and F for Asian men. Among women, Asian Americans had higher scores on Scales L, F, and 0. In general, Asian-American students scored higher on items measuring somatic and family problems; according to Greene (1987), this is a consistent finding in the MMPI and in the psychological and anthropological literature. Consistent with the work of Karle and Velasquez (1996) with Hispanics, degrees of acculturation tend to be related to MMPI scores. Studies conducted by Keefe, Sue, Enomoto, Durvasula, and Chao (1994) indicate that less acculturated Asians show higher degrees of distress.

In sum, most of the research related to cultural differences on the MMPI has been conducted with adults on the original version of the test. Some small differences have been found, but they are not sufficient to justify new norms. A paucity of research exists for adolescents and with the newer MMPI-A. What research does exist shows that profiles on the normative sample of the MMPI-A indicate ethnic differences of about 3–5 *T*-score points across clinical Scales L, F, 4, 6, 7, 8, and 9 (R. P. Archer, 1997). However, the ethnic sample on the MMPI-A was small and awaits replication.

Many testing experts believe that the problems are not with test construction but rather with inequities in society. According to Anastasi and Urbina (1997) the answers to social inequities lie not in statistical adjustments to test scores, cutoffs, or subgroup norming. Because the inequities are due to society, societal changes—not testing changes—are called for. For the present, it can be assumed that most tests are valid for diverse groups. However, when differences exist it is the examiner's responsibility to be familiar with the differences and to make adjustments. It is recommended that the examiner proceed in a "culturally sensitive" manner as suggested by Padilla (Sandoval et al., 1998).

LANGUAGE

For at least 14% of the U.S. population, English is a second language (Sandoval et al., 1998). All tests normed on English speakers test language proficiency to an extent. The first challenge facing the examiner is assessing how well non-English speakers communicate in English. Unfortunately, very little empirical evidence is available to help the professional decide when it is appropriate to test a nonnative English speaker on a test standardized in English. A very thorough discussion of the role of language in psychological assessment can be found in the chapter on language written by Sandoval and Duran in *Test Interpretation and Diversity* (Sandoval et al., 1998). Some helpful guidelines for testing a nonnative English speaker include allowing extra time to take a test, using a version of the test standardized in the tester's native tongue, using a translator, administering the test orally with a translator, test adaptation to culture and language, and using nonverbal tests or performance tests. Further guidelines for test adaptation or translation, including back translation and review of the test by a panel of experts, are presented by Geisinger (Sandoval et al., 1998).

ACCULTURATION

Acculturation refers to the degree to which an individual has adopted the beliefs, values, culture, and practices of the host culture (Sandoval et al., 1998). Some authors argue that it is essential to measure acculturation when conducting psychological assessments. Acculturation factors that can influence psychological assessment are age at migration, years of residence in the United States, educational and occupational status, ethnic identity, gender roles, relationships with extended family and other ethnic group members, frequency of trips to homeland, and language preference. Language preference is very important. One way to assess language preference is with the Short Acculturation Scale (Sandoval et al., 1998). The Short Acculturation Scale asks respondents the degree to which they prefer to speak their native tongue (e.g., Spanish only, Spanish better than English, Spanish and English equally, etc.) in different contexts: at home, at work, in thinking, or with friends. Another easy measure of acculturation is to ask the examinee with whom they socialize. For example, do they socialize with Latinos only or do they go out with members of other ethnic groups? Many other scales also measure acculturation. Most of these scales have been used for research purposes and are discussed in greater detail in Sandoval et al. (1998).

GENDER

Men and women, boys and girls perform differently on psychological tests. Because gender differences exist, tests are normed separately for boys and girls. It is critical that test examiners compare boys' scores to male norms and girls' scores to female norms.

Gender differences have been found in studies of intellectual functioning, personality, depression, and interests. When present, however, the differences may be small and do not universally apply to all boys and girls. For this reason, generalizations about gender differences must be made cautiously.

Some of the first investigations of sex differences in intellectual functioning were reviewed by Maccoby and Jacklin (Maccoby, 1966; Maccoby & Jacklin, 1974). As early as 1966, Maccoby reported that girls exceeded boys in most aspects of verbal performance. Arithmetic ability is the same for boys and girls in elementary school, but by high school, college, and adulthood, boys generally surpass girls. Boys also do better overall in spatial reasoning. It is interesting to note that Maccoby reported that although boys may score higher on standard achievement tests, girls generally get better grades. Maccoby concludes that it is difficult to know the exact magnitude of the sex differences due to differences in research methods between studies.

Gender differences in intellectual functioning are difficult to study and document. There is also considerable overlap between boys and girls; some individual girls excel at math and surpass boys. Maccoby's early work states that differences in general intelligence between boys and girls are due to item selection on tests. Her more recent reviews (1987) report that verbal differences have disappeared. It is interesting to note that at the same time, SAT scores have changed. Girls used to have higher verbal scores but no longer do. As the SAT has come under attack for gender and cultural bias over the years, test items have been dropped and changed. It is difficult to know whether the changes in verbal performance are true differences between boys and girls or an artifact of testing methodology.

Gender differences in personality and mood have also been studied for decades. Generally speaking, psychologists refer to girls as nurturant and boys as aggressive. Broverman's classic 1970s study of stereotypes found that boys were more likely to be labeled "instrumental" and girls "expressive." In other words, boys were the doers and girls the feelers. Sandra Bem's (1974) work on androgyny theorized that each individual possess both masculine and feminine characteristics; boys can be loving and girls can be aggressive. More recent work from the 1980s and 1990s has confirmed some of these stereotypes (Eagly, 1995). Women in general do seem to be more empathic, better readers of nonverbal communication, and more caring toward others. Men, on the other hand, are overall more socially dominant and aggressive.

The state of research on gender is in flux. There is so much disagreement and debate that Anastasi and Urbina (1997) omitted a review of gender research in their most recent edition of *Psychological Testing.* They also refer to Betz as saying that the study of gender is in "conceptual disarray." The field needs more work on logical explanatory theories and empirical support. Nevertheless, specific results related to psychological testing can still be reviewed here.

Normative research on the MMPI-A, for example, indicates gender differences in profiles and code types. On the MMPI-A, close to 100 items showed a differential endorsement rate of at least 10% between boys and girls. Some items, such as reading love stories and keeping a diary, were endorsed by more than 70% of girls as compared to 20% of boys. Girls also tend to cry more easily, be more sensitive to criticism, and like poetry (R. P. Archer, 1997).

Psychological test results indicate that teenage and adult women score higher than do men on *depression* and *somatic concerns* (Gumbiner & Flowers, 1997; Nolen-Hoeksema, 1990; Taylor, 1998). Men tend to score higher on measures of antisocial behaviors and conduct disorders (Gumbiner & Flowers, 1997). Adolescent boys score significantly higher than do girls on every scale of the CRS-R except Anxious-Shy and Psychosomatic. Boys score higher on Oppositional, Cognitive Problems/Inattention, Hyperactivity, ADHD Index, Conners' Global Index-Restless-Impulsive and other related scales. That females are more sensitive to somatic states has long been reported in the health psychology literature (Taylor, 1998). Women report more somatic symptoms and go to doctors more often. Women are also at greater risk for depression, which first emerges in early adolescence. Results of the BDI found that by age 13, 57% of girls but only 23% of boys reported moderate to severe depression (Albert & Beck, 1975).

In general, before adolescence, boys are at greater risk than are girls for all types of psychological symptomology, including depression. Boys are more likely to have conduct disorders, attention deficit disorders, and learning disabilities. Entering adolescence, girls begin to express more anxiety and affective disorders than do boys (Nolen-Hoeksema, 1990).

It is not clearly understood why teenage girls and women experience more depression than do boys or men. Biological, social, and psychological theories have all been proposed (Nolen-Hoeksema, 1990). Biologists favor biological explanations, such as hormones and genetics. If the explanation were purely biological, postpubertal women of all ages should experience more depression than do men. However, female college students do not experience more depression than do their male cohorts (Nolen-Hoeksema, 1990). Differential gender rates for depression can perhaps best be explained by a complex interplay of social, cultural, psychological, and biological influences. During adolescence, teenagers are changing very rapidly. They are also facing many difficult and complex social expectations. At the same time, they are adjusting to their changing bodies, moving away from their parents, and facing increasing peer and vocational demands. Most likely, hormones increase the sensitivity to psychosocial stressors, which make both normative and nonnormative events more challenging to deal with.

Results of psychological tests indicate gender differences not only in intellectual functioning, personality, and depression, but also in interests. As early as the 1930s, E. K. Strong observed differences in the patterns of item responses between men and women. Even the 1994 version of the Strong Interest Inventory (SII) demonstrated large differences between men's and women's preferences for decorating, shopping, danger, and enterprising activities. Overall, women and men respond differently to approximately one fourth to one third of the SII items. The differences are so great that for years the SII consisted of two forms—a men's form and a women's form (Harmon, Hansen, Bogen, & Hammer, 1994).

Not only do women and men have different interests, they also often choose different careers and have different career paths. Women often enter and leave the workforce at different stages in their lives. Whereas a man's career may be linear, a woman's may be interrupted by childbirth and raising children. Women may choose careers that allow them to balance multiple roles such as mother, wife, and career woman. In the past, women selected careers traditionally viewed as feminine (e.g., teaching and nursing), and social interests seemed to be more important to women than to men. These trends may be changing, however. Research by Marshall (1989) points to the importance of recognizing diversity in career paths and flexible work environments that can accommodate the needs of careers, relationships, family, and self. More and more women are seeking entrepreneurial ventures for the flexibility these careers offer.

To reiterate, boys and girls score differently on psychological tests. For this reason, most tests are normed separately for each gender. It is very important that test examiners compare girls' scores to female norms and boys' scores to male norms. As a result, a section on gender differences is included as part of the review of each test discussed in this book.

AGE

Adolescence has been defined as the stage of development between childhood and adulthood. But when does childhood end? And, when does adulthood begin? These are complicated questions that bear on psychological assessment and cannot be easily answered with a chronological age such as 13 or 18. Growth and development are slow and gradual. Young people do not instantly transform from children into adults on their 18th birthdays. The transition from childhood to adulthood involves the complex interplay of biological, social, and psychological changes.

From a biological perspective, adolescence begins with puberty. Puberty is gradual and varies from child to child, although girls typically reach puberty before boys do. If adolescence is measured by the onset of puberty, it can be concluded that adolescence begins at a different age for each girl or boy. In other words, there is no single clearly defined chronological age that universally marks the beginning of adolescence.

If the beginning of adolescence is not clearly defined, its ending is even more ambiguous. When does a youth become an adult? Unlike puberty, there is no biological turning point from adolescence to adulthood. Adolescents can buy alcohol at 21, be drafted and vote at 18, and drive a car at 16; these are legal limits and somewhat arbitrary. When asked, very few college students consider themselves adults. They think of their parents as adults because they hold down jobs, pay taxes, and support families. With the extended educational demands of a highly technological society, many young people are not self-sufficient until their mid- or late 20s. Marriage and children may come even later. This long period of dependency on parents and teachers extends adolescence.

The age dilemma presents special problems for test examiners. It cannot be automatically assumed that tests of adolescent development must be given to all teens ages 13 through 17. In theory, the ideal practice should be to administer each test to the age group on which it was normed. However, each test is normed on a different age group and some related tests overlap. For example, the WISC-III was normed on children ages 6 through 16. The WAIS-III, or the adult version of the Wechsler test, was normed on adults ages 16–89.

Some tests are designed specifically for adolescents. The MACI was normed on 13- to 19-year-olds and the MMPI-A was normed on 14- to 18-year olds. The self-report scales of the CRS-R can be administered to 12- through 17-year-olds. Other tests begin in childhood and end with adolescence, such as the Goodenough-Harris Drawing Test, which is recommended for ages 3 through 15. Still other tests begin with childhood and extend through late adulthood, such as the WRAT3, which has extensive norms for individuals from 5 years through 74 years. Finally, other tests refer not to ages, but rather grade levels. The SII, for example, begins with eighth graders.

Each test is written and standardized on a different age group. For this reason, it is critical that the examiner read the manual carefully. The recommended age and a description of the standardization population for each test can also be found in chapter 6. Still, the situation is problematic. Perhaps an especially precocious 12-year-old can read well enough to take a test standardized on 13-year-olds. On the other hand, an immature 18-year-old may present a more accurate profile on an adolescent version of a test instead of an adult version. Although administering these tests to individuals of ages other than the normative age group risks invalidating the test, it is still common practice. Many tools designed for adults have been widely used with adolescents, especially the BDI and the MMPI.

Prior to the development of the adolescent version of the MMPI, the adult test was frequently used with adolescents (R. P. Archer, 1997). When tested on the adult version, adolescents looked more pathological than they really were. Behaviors that are considered normal for adolescents, such as seeking excitement, are abnormal for adults. One specific scale, the F scale, has always been problematic for teens (Butcher, Graham, Dahlstrom, & Bowman, 1990).

Questions also arise regarding administration of tests to youths at both the lower and upper age limits. For example, during the standardization phase of the MMPI-A, subjects as young as 12 were included in the normative and clinical studies. Based on a small sample of 13-year-olds, it was found that the 13-year-old group produced higher F and Sc scores than did the 14- through 18-year-old group. For this reason, the MMPI-A norms were limited to the age categories of 14 through 18 (Butcher et al., 1992). In spite of this limitation, R. P. Archer (1997) presents a set of MMPI-A norms for 13-year-old boys and girls and recommends using the test with certain 12- and 13-year-old adolescents.

At the upper age limit, it is hard to know whether 18- and 19-year-olds should be tested with the adult or adolescent version of the MMPI. When college students were administered both versions, they looked more normal on the adolescent version (Gumbiner, 1997). The same male college students who were 18 and 19 years of age obtained higher F, Pa, and Sc scores and looked pathological when tested on the adult version. This finding poses a potentially very serious problem. If the MMPI age norms are strictly followed and 18-year-old boys are routinely administered the adult version, there may be an unwarranted number of false positives. In an extreme case, an adventurous 18-year-old adolescent could be misdiagnosed with a very serious disorder such as schizophrenia. To an inexperienced or hasty examiner, an adolescent with a vivid imagination may be labeled with a thought disorder. To deal with this problem, Butcher et al. (1990) recommended a case-by-case decision for 18-year-olds. If the 18-year-old is living independently, the adult test may be more appropriate. On the other hand, if the 18-year-old is immature, the adolescent version may be more appropriate.

Furthermore, administering the test to the age group on which it was standardized may not always be the most appropriate practice. For some tests, such as the WISC-III and WAIS-III, there is considerable overlap for young adults. For example, the WISC-III was normed on children aged from 6 through 16. The test manual states that it was designed to be used with teens up to 16 years and 11 months of age. Because the WAIS-III can also be administered to 16-year-olds, it is recommended that 16-year-olds with below-average cognitive ability be tested on the WISC-III and those of average and above-average cognitive abilities be tested on the WAIS-III (Kaufman & Lichtenberger, 1999; Wechsler, 1991). Although the tests are normed on large groups of individuals of specific ages, sometimes the most appropriate practice is to adjust the age range expectations to the ability and maturation of the adolescent rather than strictly to chronological age. Nevertheless, determining the maturation level of adolescents is also difficult.

Each adolescent is unique. The test examiner is in the special situation of applying test theory standardized on large cohorts of individuals to a specific individual. Special characteristics of that individual may necessitate that the test examiner adjust the testing method. One special characteristic is maturation. Some teens are intellectually and socially precocious at a young age, and others mature later. Maturation cannot be measured by chronological age. When in doubt, the most conservative policy is to follow the directions in the test manual. Read the test manual carefully. Administer the test to the ages recommended by the publisher. The examiner should also be familiar with the ages of the norm group and accommodations for early or late bloomers. Because each teen is unique, a case-by-case decision should be made based on the unique abilities of each adolescent. When it is necessary to make adjustments, the examiner should be sure that the adjustments are described and justified in the written report.

LEARNING DISABILITIES

No consistent definition of learning disability exists. According to Cunningham (1998) *learning disability* (LD) is a "catch-all" term used by school districts for funding purposes. Approximately 5–15% of school-age children have problems in reading, writing, arithmetic, or classroom conduct, yet do not fit into routine categories of exceptionality. Children diagnosed with learning disabilities are more likely to be male than female and may exhibit everything from dyslexia to attention problems. Approximately 40% of adolescents with learning disorders drop out of school (*DSM-IV-TR,* 2000). The main purpose of identifying young people with LD is to help them perform better in school.

Teachers and schools are usually the first to call attention to a suspected learning disability. Most schools rely on the definition of a learning dis-

Rapid Reference 4.3
Learning Disabilities

- A learning disability is defined by federal law as a severe discrepancy between intellectual ability and academic achievement.
- The *DSM-IV-TR* refers to a discrepancy of more than 2 standard deviations between achievement and IQ as a *learning disorder.*
- The *DSM-IV-TR* has diagnostic categories for reading disorders, mathematics disorders, disorders of written expression, and learning disorder not otherwise specified.
- Demoralization, low self-esteem, social skill deficits, conduct problems, and high school dropout rates are frequently related to learning disorders.
- *Reliable* and *valid* tests that assess reading, mathematics, and spelling are essential tools in assessing learning disabilities.
- The diagnosis of a learning disability must be based on many variables, including developmental history, medical history, family history, academic achievement, standardized tests, and behavioral observations.

ability supplied by federal law in the Education for All Handicapped Children Act (Sandoval et al., 1998). This federal law refers to a severe discrepancy between intellectual ability and academic achievement. However, each state differs in its interpretation of *severe discrepancy.* Many different types of quantitative methods are used to measure severe discrepancy. Statistical methods include expectancy formulas, standard score comparison, grade level deviations, and regression formulas.

HISTORY OF LEARNING DISABILITIES

Learning disabilities have been studied by researchers and doctors as early as the 1800s (Cunningham, 1998). Certain individuals were observed to possess disorders in spoken language, written language, and perceptual-motor processes. During the 1930s and 1940s, these differences were attributed to neurological causes and labeled *minimal brain damage* and later *minimal brain dysfunction* (MBD). In the 1960s, the diagnosis and treatment of LDs took two parallel paths. One path resulted in a classification system by the medical community and the other by the educational community. The medical community focused on behavioral problems, such as hyperactivity, distractibility, and impulsivity. The term *MBD* was replaced with *hyperkinesis* and treated with stimulant medications. More recently, hyperkinesis has been relabed *attention deficit hyperactivity disorder* (ADHD).

At the same time, the field of education focused on observable learning disabilities, and the learning disabilities movement emerged. Individual Education Plans (IEPs) were developed, special schools and classrooms were built, and teachers were trained in special education. Children were tested in schools and teachers were required to help them learn. Even though the classification of LDs emerged as disorders separate from ADHD, considerable confusion between the two classifications still exists today. In addition, learning disabilities, attention problems, and conduct disorders frequently cluster together in individuals and families. The confusion regarding classification systems and diagnoses may be traced to the historical definition of MBD, the parallel evolution of separate medical and educational treatments, the difficulty of diagnosis, and a still relatively young scientific body of knowledge (Cunningham, 1998).

INFORMATION PROCESSING

A useful model for organizing observations of a learning disability is the four-stage information processing model (see diagram). *Information processing* compares cognitive development to a computer with steps of sorting, categorizing, storing, and retrieving (Berger, 2000). In this model, learning is broken down into specific tasks and diagrammed with a flowchart (see Figure 4.1). The first step is the *sensory register.* In this stage, short-term memory registers a perceptual image for a split second. Most of the information coming in is discarded. Only meaningful information is transferred to the next stage. In this first stage, a child with a learning disability may not register the information properly. A *d* may be encoded as a *b.* Step 2 involves *working memory.* It is here that comprehension and conscious mental activity take place. A word, sentence, or paragraph takes on meaning. Some meaningful memories are retained, and many are discarded. A child with a learning disability may not attend to the relevant stimuli and discard important information.

The third step in an information processing model is *long-term memory.* Long-term memory organizes and analyzes responses to stimuli. Information can be stored in long-term memory for days, months, or even

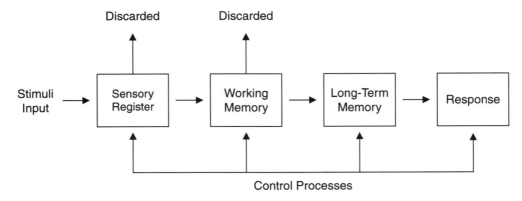

Figure 4.1.   Information processing. (Adapted from Shiffrin and Atkinson, 1969)

years. Dyslexic children are known to have trouble remembering phonetics such as *at, cat, sat, rat,* and so on over the long term.

Step 4 is the *response* or *output* stage. In this stage, the child relies on the previous stages of input and memory to produce a response. The response may require pronouncing a new word based on a memory of sensory stimuli or phonetics. If these stimuli were not encoded, stored, or combined properly, the child may respond with an incorrect pronunciation.

Finally, the control processes put everything together. *Control processes* are involved with selective attention, emotional regulation, and strategic thinking. Control processes help retrieve and organize information from long-term memory. Children with learning disabilities are known to have problems with skills such as filtering out information and using mnemonic strategies. For example, a noisy, cluttered, open-space classroom may make it difficult for a child to focus. He or she may be more successful in a smaller group with fewer social distractions.

The information processing model has been successfully applied by educators to observe and work with learning disabilities. According to this model, individuals with learning disabilities have difficulty with information processing. They do not use strategies such as chunking, mnemonics, and rehearsal as effectively as their peers. They do not remember content, and they do not scan for relevant details. People with reading disabilities may have deficits encoding phonological information and storing it in long-term memory. Educational programs that apply direct instruction of mnemonic strategies individually and in small groups can be very successful with students who have learning disabilities. Many other suggestions for step-by-step remediation strategies can be found in Sattler (2001).

DEVELOPMENT OF LEARNING DISABILITIES

Early intervention is always the most effective strategy. An experienced first-grade teacher will be able to identify a possible reading disability. In the best possible scenario, a 6-year-old diagnosed with mild dyslexia can receive extra outside tutoring and maintain grade-level work. Pullout, small group instruction at the school or individual tutoring at home may help the student function in a regular classroom and stay with peers. In some cases, a private school with smaller classes may be necessary. Many individuals who struggled with dyslexia in elementary school have overcome their disabilities and gone on to become teachers, doctors, and corporate executives.

On the other hand, learning problems can snowball if they are not caught early. A child with reading difficulties often becomes frustrated. This frustration can result in classroom conduct problems. The child may not get the extra help he or she needs and may become isolated from friends. Reading problems, attention problems, poor self-control, and poor social skills frequently cluster together. By the time such children reach middle school, they may be 2–3 years behind their peers. If the student is not treated until middle or high school, a poor academic history combined with conduct problems can be very serious and much more difficult to reverse. Many of the adolescents in special placements are there due to a combination of learning disabilities, school failure, and social and conduct problems.

It is interesting to note that if adolescents with learning disabilities can survive high school and make it to college, the scenario often improves. Although very little empirical research with LD adolescent and adult populations exists, studies of college students show a reversal of the typical pattern. In general, students with learning disabilities tend to score higher on IQ scales of performance than they do verbal scales. However, research with college students indicates that they score higher on verbal scales than they do performance scales. Kaufman (1990) attributes this finding to such students' success in school. He believes that LD students have learned compensatory strategies that have allowed them to acquire academic knowledge of the type tested on intelligence tests. In addition, community colleges and many private universities offer special help for college students with learning disabilities. Thus, if students with learning disabilities can get assistance through elementary and high school, many will succeed in college.

TYPES OF LEARNING DISABILITIES

Many types of learning disabilities have been documented. The *DSM-IV-TR* calls them "learning disorders" and defines them as achievement that is substantially below expectations for age, schooling, and level of intelligence on standardized tests in reading, mathematics, or written expression. According to the *DSM-IV-TR, substantially below* generally refers to a discrepancy of more than 2 standard deviations between achievement and IQ. The *DSM-IV-TR* goes on to say that demoralization, low self-esteem, and deficits in social skills can be related to learning disorders. The school dropout rate for adolescents with learning disorders is 40%. The *DSM-IV-TR* has diagnostic categories for reading disorders, mathematics disorders, disorders of written expression, and learning disorders not otherwise specified. Of those diagnosed with reading disorders, 60–80% are boys.

Dyslexia and Reading Ability

Most psychological tests require at least a sixth-grade reading level. Most tests reviewed in this book mention the required reading level, and more information can be found in the test manuals. For some preteens and teens, reading will be a problem. To assure test validity, reading comprehension should be evaluated before the examiner administers a test.

According to the *DSM-IV-TR,* a reading disorder is characterized by reading accuracy, speed, or comprehension substantially below chronological age and intelligence. Oral reading contains distortions, substitutions, or omissions. Both oral and silent reading are slow. Comprehension is poor. Reading disorder, also called dyslexia, tends to be more common in boys than in girls and runs in families.

The diagnosis of a reading disorder is not simple. The same steps should be followed as for a learning disability. The WISC-III, WAIS-III, WRAT3, WIAT II, WJ III, or the Kaufman Test of Educational Achievement (K-TEA) can be used along with an informal assessment by the student's teacher.

For purposes of administering a psychological test, a brief assessment of the examinee's reading comprehension may be necessary. It is essential that the test taker not only be able to decode words but also can understand the meaning of test items. To demonstrate comprehension to the test examiner, it may be helpful if the test taker reads some items aloud and paraphrases them.

At other times, poor reading or limited English proficiency may interfere with the administration of a psychological test. In some cases, it is necessary for the examiner to read the test aloud to the test taker. Because this procedure may alter test validity, the manual should be consulted and the adjustments recorded in the written report. When it is necessary to estimate IQ independent of reading level, a nonverbal test such as the Peabody Picture Vocabulary Test–Revised or the Columbia Mental Measurement Scale may be helpful.

ASSESSING A LEARNING DISABILITY

Determining whether a child or teen has a learning disability is not an easy task. By the time a preteen gets to a therapist, there is probably a documented history of academic failure. However, it is still likely that the preteen or teen never received a thorough psychological assessment. One rich source of data can be found in teachers and parents. Still, test examiners are cautioned to wait to collect these data until after they form a hypothesis. Although teachers are a rich source of information that should always be included in a complete assessment, the examiner should attempt to remain unbiased during the testing phase.

Assessing a learning disability requires a thorough evaluation. Guidelines are provided by the U.S. Office of Education as part of Public Law 94-142. A team evaluation is required, and the team may determine that a specific learning disability is present if they find a "severe discrepancy between achievement and intellectual ability" in one or more of the following areas: oral expression, listening, written expression, basic reading skills, reading comprehension, mathematics calculation, or mathematics reasoning. A child may not be identified as having a specific learning disability if the severe discrepancy between ability and achievement is primarily due to a visual, hearing, or motor handicap; mental retardation; emotional disturbance; or environmental, cultural, or economic disadvantage (Sattler, 2002).

Many tests can be used to assess learning disabilities. Both a formal assessment with a standardized test and an informal assessment of reading errors are recommended. *Reliable* and *valid* tests that assess reading, mathematics, and spelling are essential tools in assessing learning disabilities. Because a learning disability is defined as a severe discrepancy between aptitude and achievement, intelligence and achievement tests are frequently used to assess learning disabilities. Two well-researched tests

Rapid Reference 4.4
Public Law 94-142

Public Law 94-142 (PL 94-142) was designed by the federal government to ensure the right to education for all persons.

Some important stipulations of PL 94-142 as they pertain to assessment and testing are that

- Tests and evaluation be provided in a child's native language unless clearly not possible.
- Tests have been validated for the specific purpose used.
- Tests are administered by trained personnel consistent with test publishers' guidelines.
- Tests assess the specific educational need and not just a general IQ.
- No single test is ever used as the sole criterion for placement.
- Evaluations are conducted by teams.
- The student is assessed in all appropriate areas, including vision, language, and so forth.

include the WISC-III and the WAIS-III. As noted earlier, individuals with learning disabilities often display Performance greater than Verbal (Performance > Verbal) profiles on Wechsler instruments (Kaufman & Lichtenberger, 1999). In general, studies of adolescents and adults with learning disabilities show a difference of 7–19 points between Performance IQ and Verbal IQ; Kaufman and Lichtenberger (1999) explain that this is because Verbal subscales test school knowledge (i.e., academic achievement), which seems to be weak in the LD population.

Bannatyne (1974) and Sattler (1992) have proposed hueristics by which to assist with the diagnosis of learning disabilities. Bannatyne used WISC scales to describe a common pattern found among learning disabilities; that is, spatial scales are higher than conceptual scales, which are higher than sequential scales, or Spatial > Conceptual > Sequential. Picture Completion, Block Design, and Object Assembly are spatial scales. Comprehension, Similarities, and Vocabulary are conceptual scales. Arithmetic, Digit Span, and Coding are the sequential scales. Information, arithmetic, and vocabulary are the acquired knowledge scales. For example, an adolescent with an LD should show the strongest performance on Picture Completion, Block Design, and Object Assembly, which make up Bannatyne's Spatial Ability factor. Lower performance is expected on Arithmetic, Digit Span, and Coding subscales, which comprise Bannatyne's Sequential Ability subtests. Sattler (1992) rank orders the WISC subtests from easiest to hardest as follows:

1. Picture Completion
2. Picture Arrangement
3. Block Design
4. Object Assembly
5. Similarities
6. Comprehension
7. Vocabulary
8. Coding
9. Digit Span
10. Arithmetic
11. Information

The four subscales that seem to be the most difficult for students with learning disabilities are Arithmetic, Coding, Information, and Digit Span. This profile is commonly referred to as *ACID*. After examining six studies of the ACID profile, Kaufman (1990) concluded that the "ACID profile did not contribute anything over and above the Bannatyne groupings" (p. 452). Kaufman and Lichtenberger (2000) also emphasized that although these patterns of subtest scores are common in LD populations, the presence of ACID, for example, is not sufficient evidence to diagnose a learning disability. The diagnosis of a learning disability must be based on many variables including developmental history, medical history, family history, academic achievement, standardized tests, and behavioral observations.

In his most recent version of *Assessment of Children,* Sattler (2002) offers a revised opinion of WISC-III discrepancy scores. He states very clearly that there is no evidence Verbal-Performance discrepancies, ACID, SCAD, or Bannatyne profiles can reliably identify children with learning disabilities. Sattler continues to say that children with leaning disabilities are a heterogeneous group which cannot be defined by a common Wechsler profile and he suggests using the WISC-III to assess intelligence and cognitive patterns only. However, the examiner should still be aware of these heuristics because they are widely used. The diagnosis of a learning disability is a complex and controversial procedure. Techniques that are used in practice may conflict with legal definitions and/or the most recent scientific evidence.

Other tools can be used to assess learning disabilities. The WJ III is frequently used. The WISC-III can be compared to the WRAT3 to judge the aptitude-achievement discrepancy. The WRAT3 provides a reliable assessment of academic codes, such as word recognition, spelling, and writing. It was designed to be used in conjunction with the Wechsler tests. Whereas the WISC-III measures comprehension, the WRAT3 measures word decoding. By observing spelling errors, the test examiner may gain insight into reading problems. A comparison of the two tests can help identify the specific reading problems a teen is having. Work samples from teachers can be also very helpful in identifying patterns and developing educational plans for remediation. Additional informal assessment tools are suggested by Sattler (2002), who provides a method for examining reading errors.

In sum, the most widely used definition of a learning disability is *a severe discrepancy between achievement and intellectual ability* in one or more of the following areas: oral expression, listening, written expression, basic reading skills, reading comprehension, mathematics calculation, or mathematical reasoning (Cunningham, 1998). Various statistical methods are used to measure severe discrepancy, including regression equations, standard deviations, and expectancy formulas.

Many formal and informal assessment tools can be used to diagnose learning disabilities. Valid and reliable psychological tests are necessary. The WISC-III, WAIS-III, WRAT3, and WJ III have all been used. However, the assessment of a learning disability must be based on more than a single psychological test. It is a team decision that should include the student's developmental history, medical history, family history, academic achievement, standardized test scores, and behavioral observations.

PHYSICAL DISABILITIES

HISTORY OF PHYSICAL DISABILITIES

Legislation stipulating the appropriate testing procedures for persons with disabilities began in the 1970s with Public Law 94-142 (PL 94-142), the Education for All Handicapped Children Act. This law was designed to ensure that all children received the education they deserved. It had widespread implications for both ethics and testing. Among other things, PL 94-142 required that tests be carefully selected and tailored to reflect the aptitude of handicapped or language-limited children. Tests could be administered only by trained personnel and used for the purpose of their validation sample. Team evaluations, multimethod testing batteries, and IEPs were required. Parents also had the right to see the test results.

More recent laws have expanded and ensured the rights of physically disabled individuals. More specifically, civil rights laws and the Americans With Disabilities Act (ADA) of 1990 prohibit discrimination. Discrimination is prohibited in the areas of employment practices; accessibility to physical facilities; preschool, elementary, and secondary education; post-secondary education; and health, welfare, and social services. Although the law has been applied primarily to elementary education and employment practices, it also applies to adolescents in secondary education.

TESTING ACCOMMODATIONS

As noted earlier, the goal of psychological assessment is to obtain the optimal performance of the test taker. For some individuals with visual, auditory, or motor disabilities, reaching this goal requires adjusting the testing situation. The test examiner must carefully consider the type of limitation and how it interferes with the measurement of the desired characteristic. For example, if a teen has an LD and is being tested for intelligence, special care should be taken to provide a quiet room that is free of distractions and perhaps an extended time limit. Although adjustments may be required to administer the test, they may also compromise the reliability of the results. The test manual should be read very carefully for guidance as to what kinds of adjustments are acceptable or appropriate, and the examiner should document in the written report any deviations from the standard administration procedures.

In the most ideal assessment situation, individuals with particular disabilities would be administered standardized tests, and their scores would be compared to norms based on similar populations; unfortunately, from a practical perspective this is nearly impossible. Norms appropriate for individuals with particular disabilities often do not exist. Although the law requires adjusting testing procedures to accommodate physical disabilities, it is not known how these adjustments affect test reliability and validity. It may be that minor changes in wording or time limits have a small effect on the reliability of test scores. However, because the effects of test adjustments on reliability and validity are unknown, test scores based on adjusted procedures should be interpreted with caution.

Selecting tests for individuals with handicapping conditions should be done carefully because the tests may require skills that are beyond the examinee's ability (e.g., reading, concentration, or motor skills). Testing such individuals with tools that require abilities they lack seriously confounds their test results. Some tests can be modified to accommodate individuals. One modification for testing individuals with motor handicaps, for example, is to eliminate performance tests and use only verbal tests. Because vocabulary scales generally correlate highly with overall IQ, the vocabulary scales will provide a fairly accurate estimate of the total test score. It is important to remember, however, that such scores represent only an estimate and should be used cautiously.

HEARING IMPAIRMENT

A growing body of literature documents the test performance of individuals with impairments on several psychological tests. Although it was standardized on hearing persons, the WISC-R has been widely used with hearing impaired children (Anastasi & Urbina, 1997). Special adaptations of the WISC were made to accommodate deaf children, including printing oral questions on cards. The Hiskey-Nebraska Test of Learning Aptitude (Hiskey, 1966) was developed and standardized specifically for deaf and hearing impaired children and can be used with young people aged 3–17 years. Speed was eliminated and pantomime and practice exercise are used to communicate instructions. One large scale study conducted by Educational Testing Services (ETS) compared standard and nonstandard versions of the SAT and Graduate Record Examination (GRE) on hearing impaired, visually impaired, learning disabled, and physically impaired adolescents. For the most part, reliability, validity, item meaning, and administration adjustments were comparable (Willingham et al., 1988).

VISUAL IMPAIRMENT

For individuals with visual impairments, performance tests are less useful than are verbal tests. Verbal items can be read aloud. Adaptations of both Binet tests and Wechsler tests exist for blind individuals. Adaptations of the Wechsler scales include omitting performance tests and relying on verbal tests. The Perkins-Binet Test of Intelligence for the Blind was standardized on and has separate forms for visually impaired children. Global IQ measures cannot be relied on as accurate measures of intellectual functioning of visually impaired children. However, a WISC-III administered by a skilled clinician can provide a valuable profile of strengths and weaknesses.

OTHER IMPAIRMENTS

When oral and written responses are difficult, tests are available that require no reading, verbal responses, or fine motor skills—only pointing. Two examples are the Raven's Progressive Matrices and the Peabody Picture Vocabulary Test–Revised. In both tests, the test taker is presented with pictures on cards and communicates by pointing. The Raven Standard Progressive Matrices and the Coloured Progressive Matrices measure spatial aptitude, visual discrimination, and perceptual accuracy and can be used by individuals with many handicapping conditions. Raven's Progressive Matrices has no time limit and can be responded to orally, in writing, by pointing, or by nodding. It is flexible and has a high ceiling. Raven's Progressive Matrices has been used very successfully with individuals with cerebral palsy and other motor disorders (Anastasi & Urbina, 1997).

The Peabody Picture Vocabulary Test–Revised (PPVT-R; Dunn & Dunn, 1981) test is a quick screening for vocabulary. It is appropriate for individuals who cannot vocalize well or who are deaf. Consisting of 175 plates, it is easy to administer and can be completed in 15 min. The test examiner presents a word orally, and the respondent is asked to point to the correct picture. Extensive psychometric research has been conducted on the PPVT-R. The test was originally standardized on 4,200 children between the ages of 2.5 and 18 years. Recent research indicates that results tend to correlate highly with those obtained on other vocabulary tests.

Some tests also have alternate forms useful for individuals with handicapping conditions. For example, the modified WAIS (WAIS-M) allows higher starting points on five of the subtests and reduces administration time by one fourth. Also available are modified versions of the MMPI and the Sixteen Personality Factor Questionnaire for individuals with reading problems.

Both the ADA and professional organizations provide guidelines for adjusting traditional tests to assist individuals with handicapping conditions. Legal requirements of the ADA include (a) an accessible examination site, (b) test selection that reflects aptitude and achievement rather than impairments, and (c) changes in the length of time. The *Standards* (1999) suggest test adjustments through the use of extra-large type, audiotaped administrations, qualified readers, extended time limits, frequent breaks, and help with administration. The testing area may need special chairs, lighting, or space to obtain optimal test performance. Regarding interpretation, the *Standards* (1999) state the test score interpretation must include the effect of modifications on test results. Similarly, the APA requires that psychologists consider all test factors and characteristics of the examinee influencing assessment results. For more suggestions on accommodations for specific populations, the reader is directed to Pratt and Moreland's (1998) chapter entitled "Individuals With Other Characteristics."

Five

— ◆ —

Psychometric Review

— ◆ —

A good test is standardized on a large, representative sample, is reliable, and is valid. Measurement principles and statistical concepts (e.g., reliability and validity) that are used to quantify psychological characteristics are called *psychometrics*. This section on basic psychometrics explains test standardization, norms, reliability, and validity. It also explains why it is critical that a psychological test be psychometrically sound. This section is not intended to replace a psychological testing course or textbook. It is assumed that the reader has taken at least one course in testing and statistics. However, the material is presented in a way intended to be accessible to students and nonpsychologists, such as attorneys, judges, and parents. Readers who would like to refresh their general testing knowledge should refer to Anastasi and Urbina's *Psychological Testing* (1997) and Sattler's *Assessment of Children* (2001, 2002).

Without norms, reliability, and validity, it is practically impossible to know exactly what a test score means. For example, when a mother takes a child's temperature and the thermometer says 102°, she knows that the child is sick. This analogy does not always apply to psychology. Just because a teen scores high on a test of suicidal tendency does not mean that the teen is suicidal (although he or she should be monitored closely). It could mean that the test was wrong. The test score could be due to error in the testing tool. In theory, each test score is the result of a true psychological characteristic, like depression, plus error in measurement. In psychology, it is difficult to separate the illness from the measurement of the illness due to the possibility of error in our measurement tools.

119

Some measurement tools have more error and some have less. For example, therapists and teachers often use checklists to assess behavior. Many checklists are neither reliable nor valid. Results of unreliable and invalid checklists should not be presented to parents as truth. More than one parent have been told their children have ADHD because of an unreliable test. Such practices are unethical and cause considerable heartbreak to the family of the child being tested. Checklists should be used very cautiously if at all. Other tools, such as specific intelligence tests, are more reliable but still contain error. Fortunately, there are ways to measure error with statistics. Correlation coefficients are the most widely used statistical techniques for measuring reliability and validity.

CORRELATION COEFFICIENT

A correlation coefficient measures the strength and direction of an association between two variables, such as intelligence and achievement. A correlation coefficient ranges in size from –1 to +1. A perfect positive correlation is summarized by $r = 1$. A perfect negative correlation is equal to –1. When there is no relationship between two variables, $r = 0$. Most correlations range from 0 to 1. A commonly used guideline to determine the strength of an association was suggested by Cohen (1988). According to Cohen, $r \approx \pm .10$ is small, $r \approx \pm .30$ is medium, and $r \approx \pm .50$ is large. More recent guidelines endorsed by the APA Psychological Assessment Work Group (PAWG; Meyer et al., 2001) support the recommendations of Rosenthal, which encourage using the actual correlation as a benchmark. Thus, for example, because average correlations between the WISC-R and the WRAT reading scores across studies were .57 for the Verbal Scale and .56 for the Full Scale, it can be concluded that these measures of intelligence and achievement are highly correlated (Wechsler, 1991).

According to the APA 2002 Ethical Code "psychologists administer, adapt, score, interpret, or use assessment techniques, interviews, tests, or instruments in a manner and for purposes that are appropriate in light of the research on or evidence of the usefulness and proper application of the techniques." Psychologists should also recognize the limits to the certainty of judgments based on these techniques. In other words, it is *unethical* for a psychologist to administer, score, and interpret a test without knowing the reliability and validity of that test. *The Standards for Educational and Psychological Testing* (1999), which is published jointly by the AERA,

Rapid Reference 5.1
Correlation

- A correlation measures the strength and direction of an association between two variables, such as intelligence and achievement.
- A correlation coefficient ranges in size from –1 to +1.
- A perfect positive correlation is symbolized by $r = 1$.
- A perfect negative correlation is symbolized by $r = -1$.
- When there is no relationship between two variables, $r = 0$.
- According to Cohen (1988),
  - $r \approx \pm .10$ is small.
  - $r \approx \pm .30$ is medium.
  - $r \approx \pm .50$ is large.
- The PAWG (APA, 2001) recommends reporting the actual magnitude (e.g., $r = .57$) of the correlation rather than just saying whether the correlation is large or small.

APA, and NCME, also provides important guidelines for the use of psychological tests. According to *The Standards* (p. 41) "the principal questions to be asked in evaluating test use are whether or not the test is appropriate (valid) for its specific role in the larger assessment process and whether or not the test user has accurately described the extent to which the score supports any decision made or administrative action taken." In order to evaluate the psychometric properties of a test, the examiner needs to be familiar with basic measurement concepts.

STANDARDIZATION AND NORMS

Standardization refers to *uniformity* of administration and scoring. For accurate interpretation of a test, uniform methods of administration and scoring must be followed. Test manuals include specific guidelines for administration, including wording. Scoring follows uniform steps. The reason for these guidelines is to reduce bias, to reduce error, and to be as scientific as possible. To compare a teenager in California to a teen in the Midwest, the test must be administered in exactly the same way. Unless the test is administered exactly according to the specific procedures documented in the test manual, the examiner introduces bias. This bias can invalidate test results and test interpretations, making norms meaningless.

NORMS

During the test construction phase, the test is administered to a large representative group of individuals, referred to as subjects. This group is called the standardization sample or norm group. Norms are derived from this sample. Norms are percentiles, standard scores, and other scores derived from the standardization sample. They indicate test performance relative to other peers in the norm group. Norm does *not* mean normal; it is a statistical term. Most tests have a very wide range of normal scores. Normal can mean anything from the 40th percentile to the 80th percentile. Average, on the other hand, is usually the 50th percentile, right in the middle of the distribution. The average score is simply a benchmark for comparison. As the middle score, it helps to determine how extreme an individual score may be. This point of reference helps the test examiner know, for example, whether a teen is mildly depressed or extremely depressed compared to other teens.

It is important for the reader to be aware that what is average for adolescents is very different from what is average for adults. Adolescents commonly have wide mood swings and seek out excitement. For decades, teenagers were tested on the adult version of the MMPI even though it was known to overpathologize for teens. When adolescents are tested with tools standardized on adults and compared to adult norms, teens appear to be more distressed than they really are. This situation is potentially serious because it results in a high rate of false positives. Teens can be incorrectly diagnosed as sick when they are expressing normal adolescent angst. For this reason, it is critical that adolescents are tested on developmentally appropriate instruments and compared to adolescent norms, *not* adult norms. At the very least, if a test examiner is going to use an adult instrument with an adolescent, *Standards* (1999) state that the "ultimate responsibility for appropriate test use lies with the test user." A test examiner who uses an adult test with an adolescent should be prepared to provide a sound rationale and defend his or her decision.

As stated previously, the purpose of norms is to allow an examiner to compare a teen to an appropriate peer group—that is, norms help the clinician understand teens in the context of their peers. Simply knowing a teen's score on a WRAT, for example, is not as helpful as knowing that the score is equivalent to seventh-grade work on a national sample. A good norm sample should be representative and sufficiently large.

REPRESENTATIVENESS

The ideal normative sample is as representative of the population under study as possible. Thus, the ideal normative sample of U.S. teens should adequately reflect U.S. census figures. For example, the normative sample should contain the same proportion of adolescent, Latina girls as the U.S. population in general. Important demographic characteristics that should be considered in a norm group are age, grade level, gender, geographic region, ethnicity, and SES.

SIZE

In general, a larger sample is more stable than a smaller sample. When several grade levels are administered a test, approximately 100 subjects should represent each grade level. Unfortunately, many tests don't meet the standard of size. It is extremely difficult to obtain data on adolescents for several reasons. First, they are minors, and informed consent must be obtained from both teens and their parents. Second, most teens are congregated in schools, and in recent years schools have become increasingly resistant to scientific research. Finally, until recently very little research was conducted on adolescents at all. Adolescents were generally given tests developed for adults. For these reasons, the field of psychological assessment of adolescents is in its infancy. Scientists are just beginning to study and design developmentally appropriate tests for this group.

Representativeness and sample size influence the interpretation of test results. An examiner can have more confidence in the interpretation of a test standardized on a large and representative sample than one on a small and nonrepresentative sample. Unfortunately, very few tests meet the standard of representativeness. In reality, nearly all psychological tests are standardized on predominantly Euro-American adolescent populations; however, this does not necessarily invalidate their use with other groups. Cultural bias of psychological tests has been the subject of heated debate over the past 3 decades. This topic has also been investigated empirically.

Rapid Reference 5.2
Standardization and Norms

....

- Tests have strict guidelines for administration, scoring, and interpretation.
- Standardization, or uniformity, reduces test bias and allows the comparison of an adolescent's test score to those of his or her normative group.
- Failing to follow standard test procedures can invalidate a test.
- During the construction phase of a test, the test is administered to a large group of representative individuals. This group is called the *standardization sample* or *norm group.*
- Norms are percentiles, standard scores, and other scores derived from the standardization sample. They indicate test performance relative to others in the group.
- The ideal norm group is representative of the population under study. Age, grade level, gender, geographic region, ethnicity, and SES should all be considered.
- In classical testing theory, a larger sample is more stable than a smaller one.
- Ethically, adolescents should be administered tests normed on adolescents; in most cases, this is the appropriate norm group.

One example of an in-depth study of cultural bias in personality assessment is the MMPI. Research indicates that the MMPI, like most tests, performs slightly differently on minority populations. For example, Hispanic populations tend to score higher on Scales *L* and 1. However, the differences are not sufficient to invalidate scale interpretation or to justify designing new tests (Greene, 1987). However, the test examiner should always consider the socioeconomic and cultural contexts of testing and include this information in the test interpretation (Gumbiner, 1998). When norms for specific populations are available, as in the case of the African American norms for the CRS-R, it is the responsibility of the test examiner to use them (Standards, 1999).

THE NORMAL PROBABILITY CURVE, STANDARD DEVIATIONS, AND PERCENTILES

The normal probability curve is frequently used for test interpretation. It is assumed that many psychological characteristics, such as intelligence,

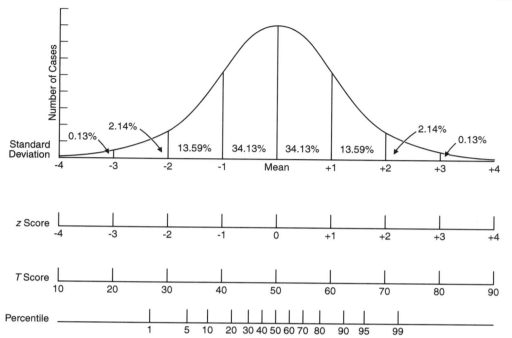

Figure 5.1. The normal probability curve.

when measured on large samples, fall into a normal or bell-shaped curve. For example, when hundreds of intelligence test scores are sampled, most of them fall near the center of the curve. The mean falls in the middle of the curve, and extreme scores fall at the two ends (see Figure 5.1).

The normal curve is very useful for understanding *standard deviations* (SD) and *percentiles.* The SD is a measure of variability. It is represented by the mathematical equation

$$SD = \sqrt{\frac{\sum X^2 - \left(\sum X\right)^2 / n}{(n - 1)}}$$

and represents the dispersion of test scores. Approximately 68% of test scores fall within 1 SD above or below the mean. Approximately 95% of all test scores fall within 2 SDs above or below the mean (see Figure 5.1). Thus, for example, when a child scores 2 SDs above the mean on an intelligence test, he or she ranks in the top 2.5 percentile of his or her peers; this is generally defined as gifted by most school districts.

Rapid Reference 5.3
The Normal Probability Curve, SD, and Percentiles

- It is *assumed* that psychological characteristics such as intelligence scores fall into a normal distribution or probability curve when they are measured on large samples.
- The SD is a measure of variability. It represents the dispersion of the test scores.
- Approximately 68% of test scores fall within 1 SD above or below the mean on a normal distribution.
- Approximately 95% of all test scores fall within 2 SDs above or below the mean.

RELIABILITY

The Standards (1999) state that estimates of reliability and standard errors of measurement should be provided for each score reported in order to judge the accuracy of the test scores for their intended use. Reporting reliabilities is essential but not simple. Test manuals report different types of reliabilities, which can be confusing.

Reliability means consistency. Reliability coefficients tell the test users how reproducible a test score is likely to be. Several different types of reliability exist. The most commonly reported reliabilities are measures of internal consistency (usually, Cronbach's alpha) and test-retest reliability. *Internal consistency* is a statistical technique for determining how well test items correlate with each other. It is based on one administration of the test. Cronbach's alpha measures the homogeneity of test items or how well a test hangs together. Tests with items that are similar and test one dimension (e.g., depression) often report high internal consistency reliabilities.

To a test examiner, test-retest reliability is often more important. *Test-retest reliability* measures the stability of a test over time. It measures the likelihood of obtaining the same results if the same person tests again in 6 months with the same test. To obtain test-retest reliability, a test is administered at least twice. Two factors that influence reliability are the duration of time between test intervals and the length of the test. The shorter the amount of time between testing intervals (e.g., 3 weeks), the higher the reliability. Also, a longer test is likely to be more reliable than a shorter one.

Test manuals frequently report high internal consistency correlations as measures of reliability and fail to report test-retest reliabilities or report test-retest reliabilities based on small samples. This practice is misleading. Knowing the stability of a test can be more important than knowing its internal consistency. For example, if a teen is given a test prior to treatment and then again following treatment, a test with high test-retest reliability will provide a more accurate estimate of treatment effectiveness. If the test has a low test-retest reliability and hence more error, it will be difficult to determine whether change was due to the treatment or due to error in measurement.

How high of a reliability coefficient is sufficient? There is no clear-cut answer to this question. Some researchers set an arbitrary level of .7. Many measurement textbooks set no cutoff level as acceptable or unacceptable (Anastasi & Urbina, 1997; Kerlinger & Lee, 2000). The opinion of the PAWG group at APA is that the actual relationship should be reported, and some theorists believe that an acceptable reliability level depends on the use of the measure (Meyer et al., 2001).

STANDARD ERROR OF MEASUREMENT

All measurement contains error. The *standard error of measurement* (*SEM*), or standard error of a score, is an estimate of error in an individual's score that can be derived from an estimate of reliability. The standard error of measurement is simply the SD of error scores. In other words, it tells how variable the error scores are. A test with a small standard error of measurement will be less variable, have less error, and be more reliable than one with a high standard error. *The Standards* (1999) recommends that the standard error be reported along with reliability coefficients because it helps judge the precision of a test. The standard error tells test users how little or how much confidence they can have in test results. Standard errors are presented in this book when they are made available by the test publishers.

VALIDITY

Validity addresses the question of whether a test measures what it purports to measure. There are several different types of validity, including face validity, content validity, construct validity, and predictive validity. Validity is generally reported in the form of correlation coefficients.

Rapid Reference 5.4
Reliability and Standard Error of Measurement

- Ethically, test examiners are expected to report reliability estimates and standard errors of measurement.
- *Reliability* means consistency. Reliability coefficients tell test users how reproducible a test score is likely to be.
- *Test-retest reliability* measures the stability of a test over time.
- The *standard error of measurement (SEM)* is an estimate of error in an individual's score that can be derived from an estimate of reliability.
- A test with a small standard error is less variable and has less error than does one with a large standard error.

FACE VALIDITY

Face validity means that a test looks as though it measures what it is supposed to measure. The test may not actually measure the desired characteristic; it just looks like it. For example, many people assume that if someone drives an expensive car, he or she is wealthy. In reality, that person may be heavily in debt: He or she only looks rich. Tests with face validity look as though they are valid.

CONTENT VALIDITY

Content validity refers to the degree that a test is a good representative sample of the domain of the purported characteristic—that is, do test items represent the domain of that characteristic? For example, a test that purports to measure third-grade arithmetic should include addition, subtraction, and multiplication, but not geometry.

CONSTRUCT VALIDITY

Construct validity tells the examiner the degree to which a test is a good measure of the construct or trait it is trying to assess. The construct validity of depression can be measured by correlating one scale of depression with another. It can also be determined by comparing depressed and non-

Rapid Reference 5.5
Validity

- *Validity* addresses the question of whether a test measures what it purports to measure.
- Ethical standards require *evidence* of validity (Standards, 1999).
- *Construct validity* tells the test examiner the degree to which a test is a good measure of the construct or trait it is trying to measure.
- Generally, short test forms are not recommended. They may compromise validity.

depressed patients on a scale of depression. Another way to measure construct validity is with factor analysis. Factor analysis is a statistical procedure for determining which test items cluster together in factors. Wechsler Scales of Intelligence, for example, show factor loadings on verbal and performance factors. A *factor loading* is the correlation between a test item and a rotated factor in factor analysis. These factor loadings demonstrate that the WISC has a verbal factor and a performance factor. Construct validity is very important because it ensures that a test measures the purported variable (e.g., depression).

The Standards (1999) require evidence of validity. They emphasize that it is the test examiner's responsibility to demonstrate that the test being used is valid and appropriate for the intended purpose. In other words, a test examiner should demonstrate that the test being used to measure depression really does measure depression rather than anxiety or some other construct. Unfortunately, tests that have face validity but are weak in construct validity are still relied on for important decisions such as school placements. A school psychologist with a heavy caseload and a weak testing background may fail to consult a test manual to verify construct validity. Similar problems may arise in professional settings. For example, an executive in a municipal fire department may assume that because a company calls its test a management ability inventory that it is a valid measurement of the construct *management ability*. He then promotes someone to management based on that person's inventory scores. Later, it is discovered that the test lacked reliability and construct validity. These types of hasty decisions can result in irresponsible decision making, unethical placement, serious errors of judgment, and costly lawsuits.

PREDICTIVE VALIDITY

Predictive validity measures how well a test predicts a criterion variable. Consider, for example, that colleges want to select the best prepared high school students because they want the students most likely to succeed in college. In theory, the SAT or other standardized test(s) used for selection should have high predictive validity of college grades.

Validity is important because major life decisions are made on the basis of tests and psychological assessment batteries. Tests are used to make decisions on special education placements, college placements, jail sentences, treatment interventions, and countless other decisions of huge impact.

Occasionally, it is assumed that psychological tests are less valid than medical ones. In a recent large-scale investigation of psychological test validity, Meyer et al. (2001) demonstrated that this is *not* the case. Data from more than 125 meta-analyses on test validity and 800 samples demonstrated that psychological test validity is strong. For example, MMPI validity scales provide better predictions of malingering than electrocardiogram (ECG) predictions of coronary artery disease. Moreover, MMPI scales detect depression and psychotic disorders better than mammogram results predict breast cancer.

When used carefully and as part of an assessment battery, tests can be very helpful. However, when tests with questionable reliability and validity are used to make hasty decisions, the consequences to individuals and society can be costly. *The Standards* clearly state that "the ultimate responsibility for appropriate test use lies with the test user," "it is appropriate to ask a test user to ascertain that procedures result in adequately valid predictions or reliable classifications," and "the greater the potential impact, the greater the need to satisfy relevant standards" (*Standards,* 1999, p. 41). *The Standards* also state that evidence of validity "should be presented for the major types of inferences for which the use of a test is recommended" (1999, p. 13).

Unfortunately, there exists a major discrepancy between *The Standards* and the data available to the practitioner. Very few test manuals provide acceptable reports of validity data. Generally, sections on validity are glossed over or the reader is directed to other research; several possible explanations for this can be offered. The validity correlates may be so low that the authors don't publish them in the manual, the test authors may be unfamiliar with statistical analyses, or they may think that construct validity is insignificant. This state of affairs is unfortunate. If psychology is to advance as a discipline and if practitioners are going to uphold the highest standard of care, then test authors should collect and report construct validity in their manuals.

SHORT FORMS

To save administration time, attempts have been made to design brief tests or shorter versions of existing tests. Kaufman designed the Kaufman Brief Intelligence Test (K-BIT) as a quick screening for intelligence. Advocates of Millon tests claim they have an advantage over the MMPI-A because the MACI is quicker to administer. The CRS-R has both long and short versions of the same test. Tests are usually shortened by eliminating scales or by designing newer, briefer tests. In general, tests with fewer test items are less reliable than longer tests. Longer tests provide more quantitative and more qualitative information about the examinee. A well-researched, longer test is also more likely to have better construct validity.

Shortcuts can lead to costly mistakes. One school psychologist who was in a hurry gave a fifth-grade boy a brief intelligence test because it only took a few minutes. Without consulting the boy's teachers or cumulative file and basing his decision solely on the brief test score, the psychologist decided the boy was of average intelligence and denied him placement in the school gifted program. When this same boy was later given a Full Scale WISC-III, he scored in the gifted range. He went on to conquer advanced calculus, obtain a 4.2 high school GPA, and be admitted to one of the most prestigious universities in the country. This school psychologist obviously made a serious mistake because he was in a hurry. He relied on one single, brief test instead of a multimethod assessment battery. His mistake resulted in a faulty educational placement and considerable confusion and anxiety to the boy's family.

Although a single, quick test may seem more convenient in the short run, it is often foolhardy in the long run. Relying on any one sole means of assessment is unethical and unwise. Furthermore, an abbreviated assessment is more likely to be inaccurate. In a recent review of over 125 meta-analyses of test validity, the PAWG of APA (2001) concluded that relying on only one technique leads to "incomplete or biased understandings" (p. 150). Not only is this practice unfair to the adolescent and his or her family, but a biased assessment also places the examiner at risk. Given that *The Standards* (1999) state that "test users evaluate the available written documentation on the validity and reliability of tests," a test examiner may be held legally liable if he or she fails to do so.

Even though a complete assessment is more time consuming initially, it is more ethical and more cost-effective. More appropriate, useful, and accurate information can be gained from 4 hours of testing than will ever be extracted from 4 hours of interviews. On MACIs, for example, teenage girls have been known to disclose eating disorders that both therapists and parents overlooked during the interview. Furthermore, self-report testing items are often linked to *DSM* diagnostic criteria and treatment suggestions. A test is nothing more than a structured interview. It is a sample of behavior and should always be combined with clinical interviews, parent-teacher observations, and a thorough assessment.

Six

— ◆ —

Test Reviews

—— ◆ ——

ACHENBACH SYSTEM OF EMPIRICALLY BASED ASSESSMENT (ASEBA)

PURPOSE, USE, AND BRIEF DESCRIPTION

The Child Behavior Checklist (CBCL) is a standardized rating scale designed by Achenbach (1966, 1978, 1991). Since the mid-1960s, considerable empirical research has been conducted on this rating scale. The most recent version, 2001, combines the CBCL along with two other scales designed by Achenbach—the Youth Self-Report (YSR) form and Teacher's Report Form (TRF)—into the Achenbach System of Empirically Based Assessment or ASEBA (Achenbach & Rescorla, 2001).

The purpose of the CBCL is to obtain observational data from a parent or parent surrogate on a broad range of a child's or adolescent's (6–18) competencies, adaptive functioning, and problems. In addition, the CBCL can be scored for empirically based syndromes and *DSM-IV* oriented diagnoses. There are eight syndrome scales. They are anxious-depressed, withdrawn-depressed, somatic complaints, social problems, thought problems, attention problems, rule-breaking behavior, and aggressive behavior. The *DSM*-oriented scales include affective problems, anxiety problems, attention-deficit/hyperactivity problems, conduct problems, oppositional defiant problems, and somatic problems. The *DSM*-oriented scales represent clusters of items that are consistent with psychiatric diagnoses. For several reasons explained in the ASEBA manual, the *DSM*-oriented scales

133

Rapid Reference 6.1
ASEBA

- The Child Behavior Checklist (CBCL) is part of a larger assessment package that includes the Youth Self-Report (YSR) and the Teacher's Report Form (TRF). The complete assessment package is currently referred to as the Achenbach System of Empirically Based Assessment (ASEBA; Achenbach & Rescorla, 2001).
- The CBCL, YSR, and TRF are standardized ratings of child and adolescent functioning viewed from the perspective of parents, parent surrogates, teachers, and the youth him- or herself.
- The CBCL can be scored for eight empirically based syndromes and six *DSM*-oriented scales.
- The eight syndrome scales are anxious-depressed, withdrawn-depressed, somatic complaints, social problems, thought problems, attention problems, rule-breaking behavior, and aggressive behavior.
- The *DSM*-oriented scales include affective problems, anxiety problems, somatic problems, attention-deficit/hyperactivity problems, oppositional defiant problems, and conduct problems.

are consistent with but *not* directly equivalent to *DSM* diagnoses. They are best used for assistance with diagnostic hypotheses (Achenbach & Rescorla, 2001).

To complete the CBCL, a parent or parent surrogate is asked to rate the child or adolescent on more than 100 items such as extracurricular activities, school performance, social skills, and mental-physical symptoms. Children are rated on a 0- to 2-point scale relative to their peers. The YSR form is a similar rating scale that is completed by the young persons themselves. The third rating scale in the ASEBA system is the TRF, which is completed by the teacher. Taken together, the three rating scales provide a standardized, empirically based, and multiple-method assessment system. These checklists are part of an ongoing research effort by Achenbach (1966, 1993) to create an empirical taxonomy of behavioral problems and related syndromes.

ADMINISTRATION, SCORING, AND INTERPRETATION

Administration

The CBCL is completed by a parent or parent surrogate for a child or adolescent aged 6–18 years. The rating scale takes about 15–20 min to complete. The parent is asked to complete a section on his or her son or daughter's sports, activities, and academic performance. This section is followed by a list of items describing mental and physical symptoms. The parent is asked to describe his or her child's behavior now or within the last 6 months on a 0- to 2-point scale, with 0 representing *not true,* 1 equal to *somewhat true,* and 2 equal to *very true* or *often true.* There are two open-ended questions. They are *What concerns you most about your child?* and *Please describe the best things about your child.*

The YSR is completed by the youth him- or herself between the ages of 11 and 18 and the TRF is completed by the teacher. They also take about 15–20 minutes to complete. These two forms were designed with items that parallel the CBCL and are very similar in content to the CBCL.

These three scales—CBCL, YSR, and TRF—also referred to as ASEBA are available in 61 languages and require about a fifth-grade reading level. If necessary, the rating scales can be read aloud to examinees.

Scoring

ASEBA forms are scored separately for boys and girls in two age groups, 6–11 and 12–18. It is absolutely essential that the age and gender appropriate form be used. A very helpful website is available at www.ASEBA.org.

Scoring of the ASEBA forms can be completed by hand or computer. Appendix A in the ASEBA manual provides instructions on hand scoring. Hand scoring is a bit confusing at first but becomes easier with practice. The real advantage of the computerized scoring is comprehensive graphs and tables. The computerized form comes with item totals, scale totals, histograms, and graphs. Also included are concordance correlations between parent, teacher, and self. The computerized scoring system provides the test examiner with considerable useful information.

On both the hand-scored version and the computer-scored form, raw scale scores are converted to *T* scores. *T* scores allow the examiner to compare a particular adolescent's score to normative data on thousands of peers. *T* scores provide the examiner with cutoffs for normal, borderline, and clinical behavior ranges. Furthermore, the CBCL contains 12 critical

Rapid Reference 6.2
ASEBA Administration, Scoring, and Interpretation

- Each ASEBA rating scale takes 15–20 min to complete.
- The CBCL is completed by a parent or parent surrogate and is appropriate for children and adolescents from 6 to 18 years.
- The TRF is completed by a teacher and is designed for 6- to 18-year-olds.
- The YSR is completed by the adolescent him- or herself between the ages of 11 and 18.
- ASEBA forms are scored separately for boys and girls in two age groups, 6–11 and 12–18.
- Scoring can be completed by hand or by computer. The computerized report offers considerable valuable information, including item totals; scale totals; histograms; graphs; a critical item list; and concordance correlations between parent, teacher, and adolescent. The computerized narrative report is neither overly general nor overly inferential.
- Interpretation is straightforward, and profiles are easy to read.
- *T* scores indicate normal, borderline, or clinical-range behaviors.

items such as harming self, attempting suicide, setting fires, and committing cruelty to animals. A considerable amount of information can be derived from the combination of the forms, including competence scales of activities, social performance, and school performance as rated by a parent with a total competence scale. A syndrome profile is derived from the CBCL that covers parent observations of clinical problems such as anxiety, depression, thought, attention, and conduct problems and is totaled for total scales of internalizing, externalizing, and total problem score. Adaptive functioning in the areas of academic performance, working hard, behaving appropriately, learning, happy, and total scale by teacher is computed. Finally, *DSM*-oriented scales can be obtained. A major attribute of this system is the multiple-method approach.

Interpretation

Interpretation is fairly straightforward and profiles are easy to read. The manual is very clearly written and easy to follow. *T* scores indicate whether behavior is in a normal, borderline, or clinical range. *DSM*-oriented scales help the clinician decide whether to pursue a clinical diagnosis, and critical items point to adolescents at risk. The computerized narrative report is descriptive of test results without being overly general or too inferential.

ETHNIC AND GENDER DIFFERENCES

In general, ethnic groups and geographic regions are well represented in the normative sample. Gender differences are dealt with by having two separate sets of norms, one for boys and one for girls. There are also two sets of norms for separate age groups, 6–11 and 12–18. In spite of these strengths, some potential sources of bias are worth noting. The South is overrepresented and the West is underrepresented in the normative data. Also, Latinos are slightly underrepresented. Furthermore, most of the respondents were middle- or upper middle-class. These three factors—a slight underrepresentation of Latinos, a slight underrepresentation of the Western geographic region, and a possible underrepresentation of lower SES—could be problematic for test users in highly concentrated areas of Latinos (e.g., California), especially because SES is frequently confounded with ethnicity and has been found to influence test performance on some psychological tests, such as the MMPI-A (Gumbiner, 1998).

Also worth noting is that 72% of the respondents on the CBCL were mothers. It is known that depressed mothers are likely to rate their children differently from nondepressed mothers (Achenbach & Rescorla, 2001). For this reason, Achenbach and Rescorla (2001) recommend evaluating the youth on all three forms (i.e., the CBCL, YSR, and TRF), as well as collecting other forms of data such as psychological tests and clinical interviews. A multimethod approach is always likely to result in a less biased and more thorough assessment.

PSYCHOMETRIC PROPERTIES

Research conducted on the ASEBA forms and profiles is impressive. Norms, validity, and reliability data have been collected since the 1960s. More than 4,000 studies have been published in 50 countries (Berube & Achenbach, 2001). Over the years, ongoing empirical research continually refines and improves the tests. The most recent revision, published in 2001, builds on the strengths of previous versions, improves weaknesses, and includes some important innovations. Compared to the 1991 version,

2001 innovations include a changed age range for the CBCL and TRF (now 6–18 years), new national samples, revised syndrome scales, *DSM*-oriented scales, narrative reports with critical items, and new software.

Standardization Sample and Norms

Nonreferred Sample   Two national samples were used in order to compare checklist items between a healthy nonreferred sample and a clinically referred one. Demographic data describing the two populations is presented in the manual. The nonreferred group consisted of 1,753 children and adolescents, ages 6–18, for the CBCL sample. The sample was approximately half boys (52%) and half girls (48%). Sixty percent of this sample was non-Latino White, 20% African American, 9% Latino, and 12% mixed. These ethnic demographics are more representative than those offered by most tests and are a reasonable approximation to the 2000 U.S. Census (see chapter 4). Seventeen percent of the respondents came from the Northeast, 20% from the Midwest, 40% from the South, and 24% from the West. Regarding SES, 84% came from upper- and middle-class families as categorized by the father's occupation. The remaining 16% came from lower socioeconomic brackets. Finally, 72% of the checklists were completed by mothers, 23% by fathers, and 5% by others.

The standardization sample for the YSR form consisted of 1,057 youths aged 11–18 whose parents had completed the CBCL. The sample for the TRF was made up of 2,319 teachers by combining 1989 and 1999 samples of teachers. Other demographic characteristics of the YSR and TRF samples are similar to those of the CBCL.

Referred Sample   A second normative sample was made up of children and adolescents referred for mental health services. These young people resided in 40 U.S. states, the District of Columbia, 1 Australian state, and England. There are 1,651 boys aged 6–11, 1,447 boys aged 12–18, 870 girls aged 6–11, and 1,026 girls aged 12–18, to total CBCL $N = 4,994$. To ensure high problem scores, subjects were included whose scores were at or above the gender-specific median for the healthy population. Data for the referred sample came from the 1999 National Survey and from 20 outpatient and inpatient mental health services. Compared to the referred population, the mean SES is similar, as are the ethnicity data for the TRF. However, the CBCL and YSR samples are less non-Latino White and contain a higher percentage of Latinos than does the healthy group;

this may be insignificant because matched samples were used in the validity tests. Unfortunately, the ASEBA manual does not explain the type of mental health facilities, mental health problems, or diagnoses of the population.

Reliability

Several types of reliability are reported in the ASEBA manual (Achenbach & Rescorla, 2001). In fact, an entire chapter is devoted to the topic of reliability. Data are presented for internal consistency, test-retest reliability, and cross-informant reliabilities. Internal consistency as measured by Chronbach's alpha is high. Alphas on the CBCL range from .63 to .97. Alphas on the YSR range from .55 to .95, and alphas on the TRF range from .72 to .95.

Test-retest reliabilities, in general, are good. Test-retest reliabilities on the CBCL are based on 75 children and sampled at 12 and 24 months. The resulting Pearson r correlations range from .31 to .81, with most in the .60s and .70s. The most stable scales are Total Problems and scales concerning conduct-attention problems.

Test-retest reliabilities on the YSR are based on 144 children and sampled at 7 months. They range from .36 to .63, with most of them in the .50s; this really is not surprising that children and adolescents would fluctuate in their self-assessment over a 7-month period. It is interesting to note that test-retest correlations on the YSR for a shorter period of time (i.e., 8 days) are higher and in the .70s and .80s.

Test-retest reliabilities on the TRF are based on 22 teachers and sampled at 2 and 4 months. The correlations range from .17 to .85. The strongest correlations are on scales of Anxious-Depressed, Hyperactivity-Impulsivity, Attention Problems, and Total Problems. The lowest correlations are on the Somatic Complaints scale. For most of the remaining scales, the correlations were in .70s and .60s.

Validity

The Achenbach scales are very well researched and rest on an impressive foundation of empiricism. An entire chapter in the ASEBA manual is devoted to validity studies. It covers content validity, criterion validity, and construct validity.

Content validity was established in the 1960s and 1970s through the procedures used for item selection (Achenbach & Rescorla, 2001). Extensive literature reviews; consultation with mental health professionals and educators; and pilot testing with parents, youth, and teachers were all used to carefully select the most appropriate test items for the CBCL, YSR, and TRF. In the following decades, feedback and continuing research were used to further refine test items.

Several methods of criterion validity were presented in the ASEBA manual (Achenbach & Rescorla, 2001). One method was by selecting items that discriminated significantly ($p < .01$) between referred and nonreferred children and adolescents. Referred and nonreferred children and adolescents were matched on demographic factors (e.g., age, gender, SES, and ethnicity), and analyses of variance were conducted to ensure that items discriminated between the two groups (referred and nonreferred) at a statistically significant level ($p < .01$). Next, multiple regression analyses were conducted using referral status and demographic variables as the independent variables and raw scale scores as the dependent variable. Results of the regression analyses indicate that referral status accounts for a large portion of variance in the competence and adaptive scales of the CBCL, YSR, and TRF. Effect size was largest for CBCL Attention Problems (30%), Aggressive Behavior (33%), Externalizing (33%), Total Problems (36%), *DSM*-Oriented Affective Problems (29%), and *DSM*-Oriented Conduct Problems (39%) scales.

Construct validity of ASEBA scales is supported by evidence from correlations with analogous scales, correlations with *DSM* criteria, factor analytic studies, and cross-cultural replications of ASEBA syndromes (Achenbach & Rescorla, 2001). One method of establishing construct validity reported in the manual is by correlating ASEBA scales with *DSM-IV* checklists and *DSM* clinician diagnoses. Although they are based on a small sample ($N = 65$), some of these correlations are especially noteworthy. The empirically based CBCL scale of Attention Problems correlated .80 with the *DSM-IV* criteria, and the *DSM*-oriented scale ADH Problems correlated .80. Several scales of aggressive behavior or conduct-related problems correlated with *DSM-IV* criteria in the .60 range.

The ASEBA scales also correlate nicely with other analogous scales such as the CRS and Behavior Assessment System for Children (BASC) Scales. The ADHD Index on the CRS correlates .77 with parent ratings of attention problems and .88 with teacher ratings. Convergent correlations for oppositional behavior are also very strong (e.g., $r = .79$ and .81).

Rapid Reference 6.3
Psychometric Properties

Empirical research has been conducted on the ASEBA scales since the 1960s and over 4000 studies have been published in 50 countries (Berube & Achenbach, 2001).

The 2001 version is based on new national normative samples.

A "healthy" sample and a clinically referred sample were compared to determine discriminant validity of test items.

Test re-test reliabilities on all of the subscales of the CBCL ($n = 75$), YSR ($n = 144$), and TRF ($n = 22$) are good and generally in the .50s, .60s, and .70s. However, the samples are small and more data would be helpful.

The ASEBA manual contains a very thorough presentation of validity data. Content, criterion, and construct validity are all good.

To ensure content validity and criterion validity, test items were written by professionals and were selected that discriminated significantly ($p < .01$) between clinically referred and non-referred children/adolescents.

Construct validity was established by correlating ASEBA scales with analogous scales and DSM criteria.

The empirically based CBCL scale of Attention Problems correlated .80 with the *DSM-IV* criteria. Several scales of aggressive behavior or conduct-related problems correlated with DSM-IV criteria in the .60 range.

Convergent correlations between the ASEBA scales and the Conners Rating Scales or Behavior Assessment System for Children (BASC) are very good.

Validity data on attention problems and conduct related problems are especially strong.

Correlations between ASEBA and Behavior Assessment for Children (BASC) scales range from .38 to .89. The highest correlations are on the Internalizing, Externalizing, and Total Problems scales, ranging from .74 to .89.

SUMMARY

In sum, the CBCL, TRF, and YSR forms are reliable and valid measures of child and adolescent behavior. They rest on a solid scientific foundation and many years of ongoing research. The ASEBA system represents the

Rapid Reference 6.4
Strengths and Weaknesses of ASEBA

Strengths

The ASEBA scales are reliable and valid.

Decades of empirical research have been conducted on the CBCL, YSR, and the TRF.

The ASEBA system is multimethod, containing observations from parents, teachers, and the youth him- or herself.

The ASEBA checklists are quick to administer.

The computerized profile offers considerable useful clinical information.

The CBCL is especially strong for assessing conduct and attention problems.

DSM-IV oriented scales are on the CBCL.

Weaknesses

There are no response style scales.

Social desirability and lying are hard to detect.

More test-retest reliability data would be useful.

lifetime work of Achenbach aimed at understanding the empirical nature of child and adolescent behaviors. Thousands of research studies have been conducted investigating these scales. An important innovation of the 2001 version is scales that are consistent with *DSM-IV* diagnoses to assist clinicians. The ASEBA scales are especially useful for identifying children and adolescents with attention and conduct problems.

BECK DEPRESSION INVENTORY–SECOND EDITION (BDI-II)

PURPOSE, USE, AND BRIEF DESCRIPTION

Published in 1996 by Beck, Steer, and Brown, the BDI-II aims to measure the severity of depression. Originally based on patients' verbal descriptions of depression, the BDI-II test items correspond with *DSM-IV-TR* diagnostic criteria for depressive disorders. The test consists of 21 items labeled *sadness, pessimism, past failure, loss of pleasure, guilty feelings, punishment feelings, self-dislike, self-criticalness, suicidal thoughts or wishes, crying, agitation, loss of interest, indecisiveness, worthlessness, loss of energy, changes in sleeping pattern, irritability, changes in appetite, concentration difficulty, tiredness or fatigue,* and *loss of interest in sex.*

ADMINISTRATION, SCORING, AND INTERPRETATION

Administration

The BDI-II can be administered individually or in a group and in written or oral format. Self-administration takes 5–10 min. Directions ask patients to assess their depression over a 2-week period in order to be compatible with *DSM-IV-TR* criteria for major depression. The patient rates each of 21 items on a scale from 0 to 3. No age requirement is mentioned in the manual.

The reading requirement is elementary, but the clinician should ensure that the client is fluent in English, can concentrate, and has basic reading ability. If these criteria cannot be met, the test may be read aloud to the client.

Scoring

Scoring is straightforward. A total score is derived by adding up item values. The patient rates each of these items on a scale from 0 to 3. For most of the items, 3 represents a greater quantity of the symptoms than does 0 or 1. Unfortunately, four of the items (6, punishment feelings; 9, suicidal thoughts or wishes; 11, agitation; and 12, loss of interest) do not seem to represent ordinal ranking. This problem is potentially serious, especially for Item 9, which attempts to measure suicidal ideation (see interpretation section). The maximum score is 63. Severity of depression is assessed based on the following ranges:

Total Scores	Range
0–13	Minimal
14–19	Mild
20–28	Moderate
29–63	Severe

Source: Beck et al., 1996.

A computer scoring program is available from the Psychological Corporation.

Interpretation

The BDI-II measures the severity of depression but is not a diagnosis of depression. A diagnosis should be made by a trained clinician after a thorough examination. Certain test items may be helpful in detecting suicide. For example, patients with scores of 2 or 3 on Item 2 (hopelessness as measured by pessimism) and Item 9 (suicidal ideation) should be monitored closely. However, caution is warranted with Item 9 (suicidal ideation). According to the BDI-II manual, outpatients with severe depression were more likely to endorse the first option of this item (e.g., *I have thoughts of killing myself, but I would not carry them out*) for 1 point than they were to endorse the third option (e.g., *I would kill myself if I had the chance*) for 3 points (Beck et al., 1996). In other words, it cannot be safely assumed that patients with lower scores are less at-risk for suicide. This point is potentially serious because a suicidal patient may obtain a lower score than a nonsuicidal one may obtain.

In the manual, Beck et al. (1996) recommend carefully reviewing specific item content to understand the pattern of depression for each patient. For example, some patients may not express hopelessness or suicidal ideation but have stopped eating. Considerable diagnostic information can be gained from reviewing specific item content. For example, the patient may be fatigued and irritable due to a sleep disorder rather than depression. Finally, because depression frequently occurs concurrently with other disorders such as panic disorders and schizophrenia, the clinician should never rely exclusively on the BDI-II for diagnosis. Combined with other instruments and clinical judgment, the BDI-II can be a useful screening tool for severity of depression.

ETHNIC AND GENDER DIFFERENCES

The BDI-II standardization sample is described as primarily White (91%) and female (63%). No socioeconomic data are offered. It is difficult to know whether all socioeconomic groups are represented. Women tend to score higher on the average ($\bar{X} = 23.61$) than do men ($\bar{X} = 20.44$) on the BDI-II. These three facts need to be considered when interpreting the test results (Beck et al., 1996).

PSYCHOMETRIC PROPERTIES

In general, the presentation of the psychometric properties of the BDI-II in the test manual is weak. The authors direct the readers to other studies rather than reviewing findings directly in the manual. Conclusions are inferential and based on a correlation between the original BDI and the BDI-II. Beck et al. (1996) state that the BDI-IA and the BDI-II are essentially the same instrument and that the original validity research applies to the BDI-II. However, calibration studies show score differences as great as 3 between the BDI-IA and BDI-II near the middle of the distributions. Furthermore, construct validity findings are simply correlations with other Beck tests or closely related psychological tools. In addition, statements about the discriminant validity of the test are misleading and overgeneralize from the data. The reader is cautioned to be skeptical of the interpretation of the statistics presented in the BDI manual.

Standardization Sample and Norms

Four different psychiatric outpatient groups ($n = 500$) and one college student group ($n = 120$) were used to study the psychometric properties of the BDI-II. The psychiatric patients were predominantly from university psychiatry departments. Of the 500 psychiatric patients, 53% were diagnosed with mood disorders, 18% with anxiety disorders, 16% with adjustment disorders, and 14% with various other types of disorders (Beck et al., 1996).

Reliability

The BDI-II manual offers little useful data on reliability. The test appears to have high internal consistency. Internal consistency reliability for the clinical sample equals .92, and for the college sample it equals .93 (Beck et al., 1996). Data on test-retest reliability are scarce. The only test-retest reliability mentioned in the manual is based on a sample of 26 outpatients. The outpatients were administered the BDI-II at their first and second therapy sessions, approximately 1 week apart. The mean at first administration was 20.27 (SD = 10.46) and the second administration was 19.42 (SD = 10.38). The test-retest correlation was .93. Because the sample was small and the time interval short, there is a need for more test-retest reliability data.

Validity

The strongest validity data consist of a comparison of means between outpatients (n = 500) and college students (n = 120) by diagnostic grouping. As would be predicted, the average score on the BDI-II is higher for outpatients ($\bar{X}$ = 22.45, SD = 12.75) than for college students ($\bar{X}$ = 12.56, SD = 9.93; Beck et al., 1996). Among outpatients, the major depression grouping has a higher mean BDI-II score than do anxiety disorders. Also, patients with more serious depressive disorders obtain higher BDI-II scores on average than do patients with less serious depressive disorders. Clearly, more of this type of construct validity work needs to be conducted.

Most of the validity data offered in the BDI-II manual consists of correlating the BDI-II with other tests designed by Beck. The BDI-II correlates .93 and .84 with the BDI-IA on small outpatient samples. The BDI-II is positively correlated with the Beck Hopelessness Scale (r = .68, n = 158). The authors claim that the Beck Hopelessness Scales have been described as positively related to depression yet provide no actual data (Beck et al., 1996). The correlation between the BDI-II and the Beck Anxiety Inventory is .60 (n = 297), suggesting that the BDI-II correlates positively with both depression and anxiety. There also exists a strong correlation (r = .71, n = 87) between the Hamilton Psychiatric Rating Scale for Depression (HRSD) and the BDI-II. It is interesting to note that the relationship between the BDI-II and the Scale for Suicide Ideation (SSI) is only moderate (r = .37, n = 158). This relationship seems small, given the widespread assumption that clients with depression are at risk for suicide and that the BDI-II asks directly about suicidal ideation. Theoretically, depression and suicide should have a stronger relationship.

The test manual presents a moderate correlation between the BDI-II and the Hamilton Rating Scale for Anxiety (HRSA; r = .47) based on a small sample of 87 subjects and using revised scoring procedures (Beck et al., 1996). The authors claim that "these findings indicate a robust discriminant validity between depression and anxiety" (p. 28). This statement is an overgeneralization from their data and potentially misleading to practitioners untrained in testing theory. In general, the BDI-II awaits

---

Rapid Reference 6.5
Beck Depression Inventory–Second Edition (BDI-II)

- This test is a quick screening tool for severity of depression; high scores indicate a more depressed individual.
- Elementary reading level and fluency in English are required.
- Administration time is 5–10 min.
- Item 2 (Pessimism) and Item 9 (Suicidal Thoughts or Wishes) may indicate suicidal risk.
- Test-retest reliability at 1 week equaled .93 ($n = 26$); however, these results were obtained with a very small sample and brief time interval.
- The BDI-II manual offers limited validity data, mostly convergent validity with similar Beck tests.
- Standardization sample was predominantly female (63%) and Euro-American (91%).
- The BDI is not an instrument for clinical diagnosis.
- Factor analyses indicate three factors: negative attitude toward self, performance impairment, and somatic disturbance.

---

further construct validity studies, especially external validity on known groups (e.g., patient populations) rather than simply convergent validity with similar psychological self-inventories written by Beck.

Factor Analyses

Factor analytical data presented in the BDI-II manual may be useful in interpreting the BDI-II. Based on a factor analysis of the 500 psychiatric outpatients, the authors found the BDI-II to load on two factors. Beck et al. (1996) labeled these factors as a somatic-affective factor and a cognitive factor. Test items such as loss of pleasure, crying, agitation, loss of interest, indecisiveness, changes in sleeping pattern, irritability, changes in appetite, problems in concentrating, fatigue, and loss of interest in sex load on the first factor, the somatic-affective factor. Sadness, pessimism, past failure, guilt, punishment feelings, self-dislike, self-criticalness, suicidal thought, and worthlessness load on the second factor, referred to as the cognitive dimension. A separate factor analysis conducted by Brown, Schulberg, and Madonia and reported by Plake and Impara (2001) found three highly intercorrelated factors. These three factors are (a) negative attitudes toward self, (b) performance impairment, and (c) somatic disturbance. These factor analyses are important because they provide

Rapid Reference 6.6
Strengths and Weaknesses of Beck Depression Inventory–Second Edition (BDI-II)

Strengths	Weaknesses
Brief and easy to administer, score, and interpret.	Unidimensional, measures depression only.
Consistent with *DSM-IV-TR*.	Not an instrument for clinical diagnosis.
Items 2 (Pessimism) and Item 9 (Suicidal Thoughts or Wishes) may indicate suicidal risk.	Standardization sample was predominately female and White.
Test-retest reliability at 1 week was .93 ($n = 26$).	Test-retest reliability of BDI-II was based on a very small sample ($n = 26$).
Some evidence exists for convergent validity with similar tests (Beck Hopelessness Scale, $r = .68$, HDRS, $r = .71$).	The BDI-II manual offers limited validity data.
	Lacks response style scales, easy to fake.

Caution
- Depression frequently occurs concurrently with other disorders, such as a panic disorder and schizophrenia. For this reason, the BDI-II should *not* be used as the only instrument in identifying depression.
- Cutoff scores are conservative; this means that there is a low rate of false negatives. Very few patients with depression will be missed. However, some cases of mild depression may appear more severe than they are due to an increased rate of false positives.
- The standardization sample was predominantly Euro-American. The BDI-II manual offers no socioeconomic data. Caution is warranted in interpreting results with different ethnic and socioeconomic groups.
- Four items, Item 6 (Punishment Feelings), Item 9 (Suicidal Thoughts or Wishes), Item 11 (Agitation), and Item 12 (Loss of Interest) do not display ordinal ranking and should be interpreted carefully.

empirical evidence for the underlying nature of the BDI—somatic problems and self-demeaning attitudes.

SUMMARY

The BDI-II is a quick screening tool for severity of depression and is easy to administer, score, and interpret. The test items are designed to be compatible with the *DSM-IV-TR* criteria for depression. Also available is computer scoring and interpretation. The BDI-II seems to be a useful and homogeneous measure of the severity of depression. It is *not* a diagnostic instrument. Any diagnosis of depression should be based on multiple measures, including a thorough clinical evaluation by a trained clinician. Because the test is simple and intuitive, faking is easy. In cases in which the test takers may be motivated to deceive—for example, custody hearings or workers' compensation—the test examiner is advised to use additional measures of assessment. Like many psychological instruments, the BDI-II awaits further psychometric research.

CONNERS' RATING SCALES–REVISED (CRS-R)

PURPOSE, USE, AND BRIEF DESCRIPTION

Published in 1999, the CRS-R assesses ADHD, conduct problems, cognitive problems, family problems, emotional problems, anger control problems, and anxiety problems. The CRS-R is a multimodal assessment tool. It contains rating scales from three different sources: parents, teachers, and the teen. Each version consists of subscales tied to the *DSM-IV-TR*. The self-report version for teens consists of 80 items. The 80 items form the following subscales: oppositional, cognitive problems and inattention, hyperactivity, anxious-shy, perfectionism, social problems, psychosomatic, Conners' ADHD index, Conners' Global Index (CGI): Restless-Impulsive, CGI: Emotional Lability, CGI: Total, *DSM-IV-TR:* Inattentive, *DSM-IV-TR:* Hyperactive-Impulsive, and *DSM-IV-TR:* Total. Conners (1997) describes the adolescent self-report form as a means of obtaining useful information on the teens' self-perception. Parent and teacher versions provide additional perceptions of the teen.

Although the primary use of the CRS-R tends to be the assessment of ADHD, the CRS-R can also be used to assess conduct problems and other comorbid disorders. This test can be helpful with *DSM-IV-TR* diagnoses when used in research, outpatient, residential treatment, forensic, and other clinical settings.

ADMINISTRATION, SCORING, AND INTERPRETATION

Administration

There are both long and short forms of each version of the CRS-R. The long forms take about 15–20 min to administer. The CRS-R for teachers and parents can be used with children aged 3–17. The self-report form for adolescents is designed for ages 12–17. A sixth-grade reading level is required for the adolescent form, and a ninth- to 10th-grade reading level is required for the parent and teacher forms. Administration is easy and straightforward. The parent or teacher completes a Likert-type rating scale covering 80 items such as angry, prone to fights, and irritable. The manual offers clear guidelines on administration. For the adolescent self-report form, individual administration is preferred to group administration; if it is necessary, however, group administration is acceptable.

Scoring

There are several methods of scoring, including computer scoring, MHS mail-in, scantron or fax scoring, and the manual QuikScore format. Scoring directions in the manual are clearly written. The test is given in a multilayered format that makes it easy to score directly from the rating sheet. Raw scores' totals are tallied and transferred to a profile sheet with *T*-score comparisons. Separate profiles exist for boys and girls. The manual contains a table for conversion from *T* scores to percentiles. The profile sheet is well organized and contains useful diagnostic information, including definitions of the subscales.

Interpretation

The CRS-R can be interpreted at several levels: global index, subscale, and profile analysis. The test manual gives clear, in-depth, and easy-to-follow guidelines for interpretation. It also contains helpful case study examples. Conners recommends starting by analyzing the index scores first. The ADHD index score helps identify children at risk for ADHD, and the CGI is sensitive to overall psychopathology.

Following index analysis, the profiles should be analyzed. Profiles with *T* scores above 60 to 65 are considered clinically significant. The manual explains *T* scores and the appendix contains percentile equivalents.

Finally, the clinician combines information from all sources, decides on the appropriate intervention, and gives feedback to the parents, teacher, and adolescent.

Much useful information comes from examining profile patterns of subscales. The QuikScore profile is relatively easy to use with practice. The profile itself contains definitions of the subscales. These subscales, such as oppositional, hyperactivity, and social problems can be useful diagnostic aids. Elevations on the *DSM-IV-TR* symptom subscales are indicative of a *DSM-IV-TR* diagnosis. Further insightful information can be culled from examining individual item responses because these items can be helpful guides for therapy.

The CRS-R forms can also be compared to obtain a more complete understanding of the situation. If the three scales (e.g., parent, teacher, and teen) agree, then the therapist has converging lines of evidence. If they don't agree, then the therapist has additional clinical insight into the complexity of the teen's problems.

ETHNIC, GENDER, AND AGE DIFFERENCES

As with most testing instruments, age, gender, and ethnic differences have been found. CRS-R offers different norms for age, gender, and ethnicity. Scores for boys and girls are interpreted on separate norms, as are age differences. Boys score higher in many areas, including oppositional, cognitive problems and inattention, hyperactivity, ADHD index, and CGI total. Girls score higher on anxious-shy and psychosomatic. The profiles are interpreted by five age categories: ages 3–5, 6–8, 9–11, and 15–17. Extensive data are provided for ethnic groups, including African Americans, Asian Americans, Euro-Americans, Hispanic Americans, and Native Americans. Separate norms are presented for African American adolescents and should be used with this group. Scores of other minority teens should be interpreted cautiously. Conners (1997) states that socioeconomic data were collected but not reported in the manual. Because previous research indicates that SES and ethnicity are confounded, Conners reported ethnic differences may be due to SES rather than ethnicity (Gumbiner, 1998). More data on ethnicity and SES remain to be collected.

PSYCHOMETRIC PROPERTIES

Standardization Sample and Norms

The normative sample of the CRS-R was large, with over 8,000 participants sampled from around the United States (Conners, 1997). The Conners-Wells' Adolescent Self-Report Scale: Long Version (CASS:L) was based on a normative sample of 3,394 adolescents (1,558 males and 1,836 females) between the ages of 12 and 17 years. Most of these individuals were older adolescents in the 15–17 age group. Sixty-two percent of the adolescents were self-identified as Euro-American; 29.9% as African American or Black; 2.3% as Hispanic; 1.6% as Asian; 1.3% as Native American; and 3.1% as other. Because age and gender affect the norms, separate norms are provided for boys and girls in five age groups.

Standard Error of Measurement

A standard error of measurement was calculated for each subscale and each age range. They can be found in the test manual and range from approximately .74 to 2.6.

Reliability

The test-retest reliability coefficients of the CASS-L are high, although they are based on a small sample. Based on a sample of 50 children and adolescents with an average age of 14.84 years, the test-retest reliability coefficients at 6–8 weeks ranged from .73 to .89 (Conners, 1997). In other words, the teens' ratings of themselves on emotional problems, conduct problems, and family problems were quite stable 2 months later. However, the sample is small, combines children and adolescents, and awaits replication.

Validity

Factor analyses seem to support three factors on the CRS-R: Oppositional with Cognitive Problems and Inattention, Oppositional with Hyperactivity, and Cognitive Problems and Inattention with Hyperactivity. The manual presents limited evidence of construct validity. Validity data presented in the manual basically consist of the CRS-R correlated with itself. Very little convergent validity with analogous tests is presented. One study with a very small sample ($N = 29$) is reported correlating the CASS:L with the Children's Depression Inventory (Conners, 1997). In

Rapid Reference 6.7
Conners' Rating Scales–Revised (CRS-R)

- The test aims to assess ADHD, conduct problems, cognitive problems, family problems, emotional problems, anger control problems, and anxiety problems.
- The CRS-R was designed for adolescents ages 12 to 17.
- Sixth-grade reading level is required.
- Administration time is 20 min.
- The CRS-R is a multimodal assessment tool based on observations from parents, teachers, and teens.
- A large standardization sample ($N = 3,394$) was used, approximately half male ($n = 1,558$) and half female ($n = 1,836$), mostly Euro-American (62%) and African American (29.9%). The sample was only 2.3% Hispanic, 1.6% Asian, and 1.3% Native American.
- Separate norms are available for African Americans.
- Standard error of measurement was calculated for each subscale and age range; it ranges from .74 to 2.6.
- Test-retest reliability at 6–8 weeks ranged from .73 to .89 on a small sample ($N = 50$).
- Validity data are still being collected.

general, the correlations are moderate to large, ranging from .38 on the ADHD index to .76 on Emotional Problems. On the other hand, the data supporting discriminant validity are stronger. When Nonclinical, ADHD, and Emotional Problem groups of children are compared, scores on the CASS-L between the three groups tend to be statistically significant. However, these data are based on one small study with young adolescents, and the authors do not report how the ADHD diagnosis was made. In sum, although an impressive amount of data has been collected on CRS-R, research on reliability and validity is still needed. The authors themselves state that additional discriminant validation as well as validation with other instruments and with other ethnic groups would be revealing.

SUMMARY

The CRS-R can be a useful measure of a teen's self-perception and a parent's and teacher's perception of the same teen. The scales are designed to

Rapid Reference 6.8
Strengths and Weaknesses of Conners' Rating Scales–Revised (CRS-R)

Strengths	Weaknesses
Linked to *DSM-IV-TR*.	Needs more research on reliability and validity.
Multimodal assessment tool; includes data from teen, parent, and teacher.	Needs more research on ethnic differences in Hispanic and Asian groups.
Contains an index of ADHD, oppositional behavior and other subscales specific to teens.	Contains no test-taking scales (i.e., social desirability and lying are hard to assess).
Quick, easy administration.	
Relatively easy scoring.	
Profile contains considerable useful diagnostic information.	
Separate norms are available for African Americans.	

Caution
The clinician should consider the cultural and socioeconomic context of the adolescent when interpreting scores.

---

be compatible with the *DSM-IV-TR* and aim to measure ADHD, Oppositional behavior, Cognitive Problems and Inattention, Hyperactivity, Anxious-Shy behavior, Perfectionism, Social Problems, and Psychosomatic Problems. The profile form offers valuable diagnostic information. Separate norms exist for age and gender, with additional norms for African Americans. Considerable data have been collected on the CRS-R, yet reliability and validity studies are still in their early stages. A strength of the CRS-R is its multimethod technique of obtaining observations from the teen, the parent, and the teacher on important diagnostic criteria. Its multimethod nature makes the CRS-R a strong component of a complete assessment battery.

GOODENOUGH-HARRIS DRAWING TEST

PURPOSE, USE, AND BRIEF DESCRIPTION

The Goodenough-Harris Drawing Test, which builds on the original 1920s work of Florence Goodenough, was revised by Harris in 1963 (Harris, 1963). Goodenough (1926) believed that children's mental maturity could be assessed through their drawings. In the current version, children aged 3 to 15 are asked to draw a picture of a man, a woman, and themselves. The drawings are carefully scored to assess their developmental mental maturity and compared to norms of their age group. For example, drawings with more detail, such as fingers and eyelashes, receive more points. There are several different methods of interpreting drawings. Goodenough's goal was to assess intellectual functioning. Machover (1949) offers a psychoanalytic interpretation and Koppitz (1968, 1984) focuses on mental maturity. Koppitz's (1968, 1984) method is the most thorough and empirically based. With time and experience, many clinicians develop their own interpretations.

Koppitz (1968, 1984) describes children's drawings as a form of nonverbal communication between an examiner and a child. The drawings can be analyzed for quality, details, and overall impressions. The drawings may be helpful for forming diagnostic hypotheses but should never be the sole basis for decision making.

Drawing comes naturally to young people and can be thought of as a behavior sample. An astute clinician can gain valuable insights while observing the teen draw. These insights might be about self-concept, family problems, sexual concerns, or test-taking attitudes. Human Figure Drawings (HFDs) can also point the way to important therapeutic issues. Anastasi and Urbina (1997) point out that the qualitative information gained from testing is just as important as the quantitative.

ADMINISTRATION, SCORING, AND INTERPRETATION

Administration

The manual is clearly written and easy to use. The Goodenough-Harris Drawing Test is available in print form and on computer disk. The manual consists of a chapter from Harris's out-of-print book entitled *Chil-*

dren's Drawings as Measures of Intellectual Maturity: A Revision and Extension of the Goodenough Draw-a-Man Test (1963) and contains specific directions for administration and scoring.

For administration, the examinee needs a test booklet and a number two pencil. The use of crayons is not allowed, and the area should be cleared of pictures or drawings to discourage copying. The Goodenough-Harris Drawing Test is an untimed test; however, it normally takes about 10–15 min to administer. The test is normed for ages 3 through 15 and requires no reading. As a result, it is often recommended as a nonverbal assessment of mental maturity. It also may be less culturally biased than verbal tests.

Scoring

Scoring of the Goodenough-Harris Drawing Test is detailed. The manual states that careful study of the manual is imperative and recommends that the examiner follow the guidelines painstakingly. Each drawing is scored for the presence or absence of specific drawing details, and the test booklet contains spaces for scoring. For example, the teen gets 1 point if the drawing contains fingers and an additional point based on the position of the thumb. More detailed drawings receive higher total points. For the drawing of the man, for example, a total raw score of 73 is possible. This raw score is then converted to standard scores by age, gender, and percentile ranks using tables in the manual. The manual contains norms computed by age and gender.

Interpretation

Although Florence Goodenough's original goal was to assess intellectual level, children's drawings have often been used as projective measures of personality. Machover's interpretations are psychoanalytic in nature and emphasize what she called psychic value, the conscious, and unconscious. Koppitz (1968, 1984) believed that HFDs reflect mental maturity. They are developmental in nature, and drawings improve until puberty. Drawings reflect the quality and content of a child's self-concept, attitudes, and conflicts. Koppitz developed and tested the most thorough interpretative system. For that reason, her system is presented here. She recommends that examiners become thoroughly familiar with the drawings of normal children before attempting to analyze those of children with problems. According to Koppitz, HFDs should always be used with another psychological tool or as part of a battery, and drawings should be analyzed on the basis of the child's age, maturation, emotional state, and social and cultural background (Koppitz, 1984).

HFDs change at puberty. The quality of the drawings stabilizes and the content changes. Because of these changes, Koppitz wrote a book entitled *Psychological Evaluation of Human Figure Drawings by Middle School Pupils* (1968). Further assistance with older adolescents can come from Schildkrout, Shenker, and Sonnenblick (1972) in *Human Figure Drawings in Adolescence*. Whereas Koppitz's work focuses on elementary-aged children and preteens, Schildkrout et al. analyzed 1500 drawings of teens aged 12–19 for organicity, neuroses, psychoses, acting out, suicide, homicide, and sexual problems. With preadolescents, Koppitz (1984) uses six methods of interpreting HFDs: observation, overall impression, mental maturity, emotional indicators, content analysis, and organic signs. Observing how the youth takes the test can provide invaluable insights into motivation, impulsivity, compulsivity, and perfectionism. The overall impression of a drawing refers to its emotional tone and provides a general impression as to the happiness or unhappiness of the teen.

Koppitz (1984) describes 15 essential or Expected Items that are relied on to determine mental maturity: head, eyes, nose, mouth, body, legs, arms, feet, arms two-dimensional, legs two-dimensional, hair, neck, arms down, arms at shoulder, and two or more pieces of clothing. She states that the absence of these expected items may reflect limited mental ability or underlying emotional problems. However, she cautions very strongly not to assume that there is a one-to-one relationship between drawings and clinical problems. She cites the example of students who are gifted intellectually but have limited artistic ability.

After obtaining behavior observations, an overall impression, and assessing emotional maturity, Koppitz assesses HFDs for emotional indicators. Emotional indictors are rare clinical signs of impulsivity, insecurity, anxiety, shyness, and anger as indicated by lack of limbs, poor integration of body parts, and other signs. Content analysis of HFDs refers to the identity of the person in the drawing and what that person is doing. Koppitz directly asks the youth who he or she is drawing; how old the person is; and what the person is doing, thinking, and feeling. Content analysis can yield rich insights into self-concept, concerns over sexuality, and family conflicts with teens. Finally, HFDs are analyzed for neurological signs. Some signs such as the omission of neck, arms incorrectly attached, and poor integration can point to the need for more in-depth evaluation, but diagnoses of brain injury should *never* be made on the basis of a drawing test alone (Anastasi & Urbina, 1997).

Koppitz's analyses of human figure drawings are supported by numerous case study examples and empirical comparisons of drawings between clinical subjects and nonclinical ones. Anyone planning to analyze HFDs is strongly urged to review Koppitz's books: *Children's Drawings as Measures of Intellectual Maturity: A Revision and Extension of Goodenough Draw-a-Man Test* (1968) and *Psychological Evaluation of Children's Human Figure Drawings* (1984).

ETHNIC AND GENDER DIFFERENCES

The Goodenough-Harris Drawing Test is normed separately by gender. In other words, there are norms for the drawing of a man by boys and drawing of a man by girls. There are also separate norms for the drawing of a woman by boys and by girls. Research studies conducted in Mexico and Iran demonstrate ethnic differences (Laosa, Swartz, & Diaz-Guerrero, 1974; Mehryar, Tashakkori, Yousefi, & Khajavi, 1987). As would be expected, cultural background seems to influence drawings.

PSYCHOMETRIC PROPERTIES

Reliability and Validity

Because HFDs are projective techniques, it is difficult to apply conventional statistical definitions of reliability and validity. However, in spite of this difficulty, considerable reliability and validity data have been collected on HFDs. In the Goodenough-Harris test manual, Harris mentions that the Goodenough-Harris Drawing Test has good interrater reliability. In terms of validity, Harris states that correlations of Full Scale Intelligence Scale scores and Development scores on HFDs are relatively low for teens and not meaningful for younger youths. He concludes that HFDs are *not* good measures of overall mental maturity (Harris, 1963). Scoring systems are developed and based on 1,856 children aged 5–12.

Koppitz offers extensive case study data and statistical analyses. Each of her interpretive techniques is supported by several case studies. In addition, she conducted statistical validity analyses. For example, she compared the frequency of organic signs such as omission of neck, arms incorrectly attached, and poor integration in boys with and without brain

Rapid Reference 6.9
Goodenough-Harris Drawing Test

- A good rapport builder, this test is a nonthreatening way to begin an assessment.
- The test consists of a behavioral drawing sample of a man, woman, and self.
- Ages 3–15 can be administered this test.
- About 10–15 min administration time is required.
- No reading is required for this nonverbal test.
- Drawings can be analyzed for self-concept, family problems, sexual concerns, or test-taking attitudes.
- Drawings change with development.
- The test was standardized on 1,856 children aged 5–12.

Rapid Reference 6.10
Strengths and Weaknesses of Goodenough-Harris Drawing Test

Strengths

Excellent for clinical observation and rapport

Fun, quick, and nonthreatening

Nonverbal test, which may be less culturally biased

Projective test, which allows qualitative analyses

Weaknesses

Difficult to find data on reliability and validity

Caution

A diagnosis cannot be made from drawings alone. A drawing is a sample of behavior and may indicate the need for a more thorough, in-depth clinical evaluation. A diagnosis must be based on multiple measurements, including self-report, clinical observations, parent and teacher report, and additional assessment tools.

injury. The data indicated statistically significant differences between the two groups. In sum, Anastasi and Urbina (1997) state that Koppitz's uses of HFDs are grounded on a solid empirical base.

SUMMARY

The Goodenough-Harris Drawing Test is a brief projective measure. It takes about 15 min to administer and is usually fun for teenagers. The teen is asked to draw a picture of a man, a woman, and him- or herself. The manual comes with clear guidelines for administration and scoring. Interpretation takes training and experience. There are several methods of interpretation. The most empirically sound interpretative technique was developed by Koppitz (1968, 1984). The best uses of HFDs are as warm-ups to assessment batteries, rapport builders, guides to clinical insight, aids to clinical observations, and components of complete batteries.

MACANDREW ALCOHOLISM SCALE–REVISED (MAC-R)

PURPOSE, USE, AND BRIEF DESCRIPTION

The MacAndrew Alcoholism Scale–Revised (MAC-R) is a widely used and researched test of alcohol and substance abuse with adolescents. For this reason, it is included here as a separate test, although it is really an MMPI-A scale. Readers unfamiliar with the MAC-R are advised to read the MMPI-A section first. The MAC-R consists of 49 MMPI-A items. Sample items are *I am a very sociable person, I can express my true feelings only when I drink,* and *I have some habits that are really harmful.* The complete list of 49 items is printed in the appendix of the MMPI-A. The best use of the MAC-R is as a screening device for substance abuse.

The MAC was written in 1965 by MacAndrew, who contrasted item answers between 300 adult male alcoholics and 300 adult male psychiatric patients (R. P. Archer, 1997). The MAC-R is a revised form of the MAC created along with the revised MMPI-A. The two scales are nearly identical. Forty-five of the original MAC items were retained and four new items were added. Because the two scales are so similar, it is assumed that the interpretation of the MAC applies to the MAC-R, although to date there are no studies on the comparability of the MAC and the MAC-R scales for the MMPI-A. The MAC-R seems to measure antisocial characteristics, including alcohol and polysubstance abuse (Basham, 1992). Some caution should be taken with interpretation because the MAC was developed on adult, white males. The sociocultural context of the teen should always be considered. The MAC-R may also overpathologize for teens, and some evidence suggests that the MAC-R is not appropriate in medical settings (R. P. Archer, 1997).

ADMINISTRATION, SCORING, AND INTERPRETATION

Administration and Scoring

Because the MAC-R is made up of MMPI-A items, the administration and scoring procedures are the same as those for the MMPI-A. Scoring can be completed by hand with templates, by computer, or by mail from National Computer Systems (NCS). The test is appropriate for teens ages 14–18.

Interpretation

For adolescents in psychiatric settings, Ganter, Graham, and Archer (1992) found that scores of 28 or greater for boys and 27 or greater for girls provided the most accurate diagnoses of substance abuse. Among normal high school students, cutoff scores of 26 for boys and 25 for girls proved accurate. Some research suggests that elevated MAC-R scale scores may be related to different adolescent code types (R. P. Archer, 1997). Adolescents with 2-3/3-2 codes are less likely to obtain high MAC-R scale scores than are those with 4-9/9-4 codes. Although this knowledge is useful for interpretation, code types are not currently recommended for diagnostic use with teens (Butcher et al., 1992).

According to R. P. Archer (1997), the following characteristics would describe a boy with a score of 28 or more and a girl of 27 or more on the MAC-R:

- Increased likelihood of alcohol or drug abuse problems
- Interpersonally assertive and dominant
- Self-indulgent and egocentric
- Unconventional and impulsive
- Greater likelihood of conduct disorder diagnosis
- Greater likelihood of legal involvement and violation of social norms

Low-range scores on the MAC-R may indicate dependent, conservative, indecisive, overcontrolled, and sensation-avoidant teens. False negatives, or teens who abuse alcohol but have low MAC-R scores, could be neurotic individuals who self-medicate with alcohol.

ETHNIC AND GENDER DIFFERENCES

Like the MMPI-A, the MAC-R is normed separately on boys and girls because gender differences exist. Boys and girls should always be profiled on the appropriate recording form. Studies conducted on adults suggest that the MAC-R may not be diagnostically useful for African Americans. Because findings from the adult version are often applied to adolescents, the concern may apply to adolescent African Americans as well (R. P. Archer, 1997). Because the MMPI and MMPI-A were standardized on largely Euro-American educated populations, interpretations with non-White groups should be made cautiously.

PSYCHOMETRIC PROPERTIES

Standardization Sample and Norms

The standardization sample for the MAC-R is the same as that for the MMPI-A (Butcher et al., 1992). A more complete description of this population can be found in the MMPI-A manual and in the MMPI-A section of this book. Internal consistency measurement of reliability coefficients was based on a normative sample of 805 boys and 815 girls ages 14–18 and on a clinical sample of 420 boys and 293 girls ages 14–18. The normative sample came from junior high and high schools across the United States. The clinical sample came from inpatient alcohol-and-drug treatment units, inpatient mental health facilities, day-treatment programs, and a special school program. Test-retest reliability data were based on a subsample of the normative group consisting of 45 boys and 109 girls ages 14–18. The teens completed the second administration of the test 1 week after the first administration.

Reliability and Standard Error of Measurement

Internal consistency reliability of the MAC-R at 1 week is .50 and .45 for normative boys and girls, respectively. It is .44 and .55 for clinical boys and

Rapid Reference 6.11
MacAndrew Alcoholism Scale–Revised (MAC-R)

- The MAC-R is a widely used and well-researched test of alcohol and substance abuse with adolescents.
- The MAC-R is an MMPI-A scale.
- Ages 14–18 can be administered this test.
- A sixth-grade reading level is required.
- Normative sample consisted of 805 boys and 815 girls.
- Normative sample was primarily Euro-American with educated and professional parents.
- Caution is warranted interpreting scores of diverse populations.
- Some false positives are obtained among high scorers.
- Test-retest reliability at 1 week is .47 with a standard error of 2.79 ($n = 154$).
- Extensive validity research was conducted on the original adult version (MAC) with adolescents.
- Validity findings on the adult MAC are assumed to apply to the new adolescent MAC-R.
- Adult MAC validity findings indicate increased polysubstance abuse (e.g., alcohol, amphetamines, barbiturates, cocaine, hallucinogens, and marijuana).
- MAC scores are related to conduct disorder diagnoses, low grades, and substance abuse in adolescents.

girls. Test-retest reliability at 1 week is .47 with a standard error of measurement of 2.79 (Butcher et al., 1992).

Validity

The MAC has received extensive empirical investigation with adolescents. Elevated MAC scores are associated with substance abuse in adolescents in several settings including public school settings, hospitals, residential psychiatric settings, and drug treatment settings. Additional research indicated that MAC scale scores seem to be related to polysubstance abuse (e.g., amphetamines, barbiturates, cocaine, hallucinogens, and marijuana), as well as conduct disorders, low grades, and delinquent behaviors (R. P. Archer, 1997). Basham's (1992) study of 326 adolescent inpatients suggests that the MAC measures an antisocial personality dimension.

Rapid Reference 6.12
Characteristics of MAC-R High Scores[a]

- Increased probability of alcohol or drug abuse problems
- Interpersonally assertive and dominant
- Self-indulgent and egocentric
- Unconventional and impulsive
- Increased probability of conduct disorder diagnosis
- Increased probability of legal involvement and violation of social norms

[a]Males ≥ 28, females ≥ 27. From R. P. Archer (1997).

Rapid Reference 6.13
Strengths and Weaknesses of the MAC-R

Strengths	Weaknesses
The MAC-R is a widely used measure of alcohol and substance abuse with teens.	The MAC-R may have a high rate of false positives with teens.
The MAC-R is well researched.	The MAC-R may be sensitive to faking in teens trying to minimize psychopathology.
The MMPI-A has response style scales sensitive to lying, faking, and social desirability.	

Caution

The MAC-R may not be appropriate in medical settings.
Interpretation should consider the sociocultural context of the teen.

SUMMARY

The MAC-R is a widely used and researched test of alcohol and substance abuse with adolescents. The MAC-R is one scale on the MMPI-A and is administered, scored, and interpreted like other MMPI-A scales. For normal high school students, cutoff scores of 26 for boys and 25 for girls indicate substance abuse. For clinical populations, the cutoff scores are 28 for boys and 27 for girls. Because the MAC was developed on adult White males, the cultural and economic context of the adolescent must always be considered in interpretation of test results. The best use of the MAC-R with teens is as a screening device for substance abuse.

MILLON ADOLESCENT CLINICAL INVENTORY (MACI)

PURPOSE, USE, AND BRIEF DESCRIPTION

The Millon Adolescent Clinical Inventory (MACI), designed by Theodore Millon and published in 1993, aims to assess adolescent personality, self-reported concerns, and clinical syndromes. Grounded in Millon's (1990) personality theory as developed in his book, *Toward a New Personology,* the MACI is compatible with the *DSM-IV-TR.* The test consists of 27 component scales and response style scales. The 27 content scales cluster into three main categories: personality patterns, expressed concerns, and clinical syndromes.

The 12 *personality pattern* scales parallel the *DSM-IV-TR* Axis II disorders as follows: Introversive (Schizoid), Inhibited (Avoidant), Doleful (Depressive), Submissive (Dependent), Dramatizing (Histrionic), Egoistic (Narcissistic), Unruly (Antisocial), Forceful (Sadistic), Conforming (Obsessive-Compulsive), Oppositional (Negativistic), Self-Demeaning (Self-Defeating), and Borderline Tendencies.

The cluster of *expressed concerns* scales addresses the phenomenological attitudes of teenagers toward developmental issues such as family problems, peer relations, identity, and body image. There are eight scales in this cluster: Identity Diffusion, Self-Devaluation, Body Disapproval, Sexual Discomfort, Peer Insecurity, Social Insensitivity, Family Discord, and Childhood Abuse.

The *clinical syndrome* scales assess serious behavioral difficulties of adolescents such as Eating Dysfunction, Substance Abuse, Delinquent Predisposition, Impulsive Propensity, Anxious Feelings, Depressive Affect, and Suicidal Tendency. These states are transient and are usually the initial focus of treatment, such as a presenting problem.

The MACI manual describes four response style scales, called modifying indexes, aimed at measuring adolescent test-taking attitudes: Disclosure, Desirability, Debasement, and Reliability. The Disclosure scale measures openness and honesty. The Desirability scale measures social desirability or the patient's ability to present him- or herself in a favorable light. The Debasement scale measures the extent to which the teen devalues him- or herself. The Reliability scale screens for whether the patient read the items. A sample Reliability scale item is *I have not seen a car in the last ten years.* It is interesting to note that the MACI manual refers to four modifying indexes, but a recent version of the computerized interpretive report only contained three: Disclosure, Desirability, and Debasement.

The MACI was designed specifically for troubled adolescents. It is *not* for use with normal adolescents. One of its best uses is for generating diagnostic hypotheses related to DSM-IV-TR Axis I and Axis II disorders. MACI scales parallel DSM-IV-TR diagnostic categories except for paranoia. However, most clinicians are reluctant to diagnose a personality disorder in an individual younger than 18 years old. For further information on the MACI scales and personality theory, the reader is directed to the MACI manual and *Toward a New Personality* (Millon, 1990).

ADMINISTRATION, SCORING, AND INTERPRETATION

Administration

The MACI consists of 160 true-false items and takes approximately 30 min to administer. The test can be administered individually or to a group. A sixth-grade reading level is recommended, but some of the double negatives may be difficult to understand. Certainly, good mastery of the English language and good reading skills are required to self-administer this test.

Millon recommends administering the test to 13- to 19-year-olds. However, the test was normed predominantly on 13- to 17-year-olds, and caution is advised in interpretation of MACIs administered to older adolescents.

Scoring

Hand scoring and computer scoring are available; however, the authors do not recommend hand scoring because it is complex, time consuming, and easy to make an error. Computer scoring is recommended and can either be done by the therapist or by sending the test booklet to NCS. Also available are English and Spanish audiocassettes.

After the MACI is administered and raw scores are obtained, the raw scores are transformed to base rates (BRs) using statistical techniques. Higher BRs indicate more serious personality problems. A BR cutting line of 75 indicates the presence of a problem, and 85 indicates prominence.

BR scores are also valuable for comparing scores in profile coding. The MACI manual offers an excellent explanation of profile coding. Basically, the profile code is divided into three parts, which is indicated by double slashes (//). The first third represents personality patterns, the second third expressed concerns, and the final third clinical syndromes. Only scale scores above BR of 59 are listed in the code, and they are placed by order of magnitude. Scores above BR of 85 are presented first and followed by a double asterisk. These scores are followed by BR scores in the 75–84 range with a single asterisk. BR scores in the 60–74 range are presented last. This pattern is followed for all three groupings: personality patterns, expressed concerns, and clinical syndromes.

Interpretation

The MACI manual (Millon, 1993) offers excellent guidelines on test interpretation, and the reader is strongly urged to review the manual. Using a four-step interpretive model, the clinician is advised to review important clinical information first, followed by modifying indexes, profile analysis, and profile integrations. After reviewing clinical information, response styles or modifying indexes are examined. Disclosure scores (i.e., Scale X) below 201 or above 589 indicate an invalid report.

FOUR STEP INTERPRETIVE MODEL

- *Step 1:* Review important clinical information.
- *Step 2:* Examine modifying indexes.
- *Step 3:* Look at profile analysis.
- *Step 4:* Examine profile integration.

After reviewing the modifying indexes, the test examiner reviews each section of the profile (i.e., Personality Patterns, Expressed Concerns, and Clinical Syndromes). Prior to examining profile configurations, it is recommended that clinicians analyze separate scale evaluations (Millon, 1993). Interpretation of the 12 personality patterns, according to Millon (1993), are as follows:

Personality Pattern Scales   Individuals who score high on the following scales possess the following characteristics:

- *Scale 1: Introversive*—is quiet, passive, and socially indifferent; has difficulty making friends

- *Scale 2A: Inhibited*—is shy, timid, and nervous in social situations; wants to be liked; is afraid of rejection and sensitive, yet often mistrusting and lonely
- *Scale 2B: Doleful*—has a gloomy mood; feels pessimistic, guilty, remorseful, and worthless
- *Scale 3: Submissive*—is soft-hearted, sentimental, kindly, and dependent; relies on others to lead
- *Scale 4: Dramatizing*—is talkative, charming, emotionally expressive, and frequently exhibitionist; likes excitement; is easily bored
- *Scale 5: Egotistic*—is self-centered and narcissistic, self-assured, and arrogant
- *Scale 6A: Unruly*—has a rebellious attitude and possible conflicts with parents, school authorities, and legal authorities; is antisocial
- *Scale 6B: Forceful*—is assertive, domineering, hostile, tough, fearless, and competitive
- *Scale 7: Conforming*—is respectful, rule oriented, conscientious, efficient, perfectionistic, controlled; lacks spontaneity; is serious and orderly
- *Scale 8A: Oppositional*—is passive-aggressive, sullen, and unhappy; can be disagreeable and moody, irritable, and hostile
- *Scale 8B: Self-Demeaning*—is self-defeating; demeans self; enjoys suffering; does not let others help
- *Scale 9: Boderline*—shows severe personality dysfunction, erratic interpersonal relationships, impulsive hostility, fear of abandonment, and self-destructive action

Expressed Concerns   Expressed concerns assess the teen's feelings about developmental issues as follows:

- *Scale A: Identity Diffusion*—is directionless, unclear about who he or she is, and unfocused about goals and values
- *Scale B: Self-Devaluation*—has problems with self-image and low self-esteem; doesn't like self
- *Scale C: Body Disapproval*—is unhappy with his or her maturation or morphology; expresses dissatisfaction with his or her physical attractiveness and social appeal
- *Scale D: Sexual Discomfort*—finds sexual thoughts and feelings confusing; is disagreeable and troubled by sexual impulses
- *Scale E: Peer Insecurity*—feels rejected by peers; wants social acceptance and is likely to withdraw when acceptance is not forthcoming

- *Scale F: Social Insensitivity*—is cool and indifferent to welfare of others; lacks empathy; shows little interest in warm or caring personal ties
- *Scale G: Family Discord*—sees families as a source of tension and conflict; has little support from parents; may be subjected to parental rejection, rebelling, or both
- *Scale H: Childhood Abuse*—feels shameful about verbal, physical, or sexual abuse from parents

Clinical Syndromes   Clinical syndromes are usually the initial focus of treatment and are more transient than personality characteristics, but they indicate clinical significance and need for intervention.

- *Scale AA: Eating Dysfunctions*—shows tendencies toward anorexia nervosa or bulimia
- *Scale BB: Substance Abuse Proneness*—shows a maladaptive pattern of drug or alcohol abuse that interferes with school, friendships, and family
- *Scale CC: Delinquent Predisposition*—is likely to violate rights of others; breaks rules and societal norms; may threaten others with weapons, lying, stealing, and other antisocial behavior
- *Scale DD: Impulsive Propensity*—has poor impulse control; is easily excited over small matters and easily provoked
- *Scale EE: Anxious Feelings*—is nervous, fretful, and apprehensive
- *Scale FF: Depressive Affect*—shows decreased activity relative to past; has feelings of guilt, fatigue, social withdrawal, loss of confidence, and feelings of inadequacy; is pessimistic about the future
- *Scale GG: Suicidal Tendency*—has suicidal thoughts and plans; has feelings of worthlessness and purposelessness, sense that others would be better off without them

Note: High scorers on this scale need professional attention (Millon, 1993).

Profile Coding   Both Axis I and Axis II diagnostic hypotheses can be generated from the MACI. Caution and clinical judgment are recommended in interpreting the report, however. As with all test data, the clinician should consider biographical, demographic, and behavioral self-report information as well as clinical judgment when making a diagnosis and treatment plan.

After examining individual scales for personality and clinical features, the therapist can begin profile analysis. The profile analysis should begin by distinguishing between the adolescent's personality style and clinical syndromes. For example, the therapist would separate Unruly (Antisocial) and Forceful (Sadistic) personality characteristics from Family Discord and Childhood Abuse, which are expressed concerns, and Depressive Affect and Suicidal Tendency, which are clinical syndromes. According to Millon (1993), these results represent three different dimensions: personality, expressed concerns, and clinical syndromes.

Interpretive reports are available from NCS. The NCS reports are computer generated and strongly opinionated. The interpretive reports are heavily inferential and overemphasize the role of personality in adolescent difficulties. Problems that may be situational (states) rather than traits are attributed to personality. For example, in the computer report for a teen who has divorced parents and a suicidal mother, the teen is labeled histrionic. The teen may have very real-world problems over which he or she has little control that are not personality characteristics. Also, the *DSM-IV-TR* cautions against diagnosing adolescents with Axis II disorders. Because they are young and not fully developed, adolescents are rarely diagnosed with personality disorders. Finally, the computerized reports focus on pathology and fail to acknowledge an adolescent's strengths. Extreme care must be taken if these reports are placed in an adolescent's school file or read by professionals untrained in testing. These reports are probably most useful to the therapist for generating diagnostic hypotheses. Keep in mind that the *Standards for Educational and Psychological Testing* (1999) requires that the test examiner demonstrate the validity of computer interpretations.

ETHNIC, GENDER, AND SOCIOECONOMIC DIFFERENCES

The norm group was predominantly Euro-American (79%). It was 7% African American, 6% Hispanic, 0% Asian, 3% Native American, 3% other, and 2% not reported (Millon, 1993). Socioeconomic data are not presented in the manual, and the impact of gender, ethnicity, and socioeconomic status are not discussed. As with all psychological tests, the tests should be interpreted within the cultural context of the adolescent's life.

PSYCHOMETRIC PROPERTIES

Standardization Sample and Norms

The MACI was normed on 579 adolescents and two-cross validation samples of 139 and 194 each. All of the subjects were patients in outpatient, residential, or other mental health centers. As stated earlier, this test was designed for use with clinical populations and should be used with clinical adolescents only. Nonclinical samples were 79% Euro-American and primarily aged 13–17. Eighteen-year-olds comprised only 3% of the sample and 19-year-olds only 1% (Millon, 1993). Although Millon states that the test was normed on 19-year-olds, the normative sample contains only three (Millon, 1993).

Reliability

Internal consistency reliability is good and ranges from .73 to .91 for various scales. Test-retest reliability ranges from .57 to .92 across scales based on a small sample ($N = 47$) and a test-retest interval of 3–7 days. No standard error of measurement is reported. More reliability data need to be collected on larger samples and at longer test-retest intervals (Millon, 1993).

Validity

Two tests of validity are reported in the MACI manual. One test of validity was measured by comparing clinicians' judgments with MACI test scores. Clinicians were presented with a list of personality patterns, expressed concerns, and clinical syndromes and asked to choose the one most similar to their patient's characteristics. These characteristics were then correlated with MACI test scores on two cross-validation samples B ($N = 139$) and C ($N = 194$). The resulting correlations were generally low. Only 5 out of 49 presented correlations exceeded .35, and most were between .10 and .20. Although such results are not unusual for this type of research, they do suggest that more validity research is necessary and that it should not be automatically assumed that the scales have construct validity. For example, identity diffusion correlates 0.00 with clinicians' judgments. The test examiner is advised to interpret these scales with caution (Millon, 1993).

As part of the validation process, Millon also correlated the scales with similar test instruments, such as BDI-II, the Beck Hopelessness Scale, the Beck Anxiety Inventory (BAI), the Eating Disorder Inventory–2 (EDI-2),

Rapid Reference 6.14
The Millon Adolescent Clinical Inventory (MACI)

- The MACI was designed for use with *clinical* populations only.
- The MACI aims to assess personality, self-reported concerns, and clinical syndromes.
- A sixth-grade reading level is required.
- The MACI requires a 30-min administration time.
- This test contains developmentally appropriate scales for teens, such as scales addressing eating disorders and conduct disorders.
- Standardization sample consisted of 579 adolescents, mostly aged 13–17 years and 79% Euro-American.
- Test-retest reliability ranges from .57 to .92 over 3–7 days ($N = 47$).
- Preliminary evidence of construct validity has been presented (e.g., Doleful correlates with the BDI, $r = .58$).
- Scales are *not* discrete dimensions. There is considerable item overlap.

Rapid Reference 6.15
Strengths and Weaknesses of the MACI

Strengths	Weaknesses
Brief, 30-min administration	Considerable item overlap
Theory based	Scales are not discrete dimensions
Scales parallel the *DSM*	Overemphasizes personality and underemphasizes situational variables
	New test, awaits further reliability and validity studies
May be useful for treatment evaluation	
Developmentally appropriate for teens (e.g., eating disorder items)	

Caution
- Interpretations should be approached as diagnostic hypotheses.
- Few minorities and older adolescents were included in the clinical sample.
- The MACI is not for use with nonclinical adolescents.

and the Problem Oriented Screening Instrument for Teenagers (Millon, 1993). Some evidence exists for convergent validity. Strong correlations in the predicted direction exist between the personality scale Doleful and the clinical syndrome scales Depressive Affect and Suicidal Tendency with the BDI (.58, .59, and .67). In addition, the clinical syndrome scale of Eating Dysfunction correlates .75 with Drive for Thinness and .88 with Body Dissatisfaction on the EDI-2. On the other hand, Anxious Feelings correlates .10 with the BAI and Peer Insecurity correlates −.02 with Social Insecurity on the EDI-2. Although many of the convergent validities are strong and in the predicted direction, the sample was very small ($N = 139$). Computing a large number of correlations on a small sample increases the error rate. Before clinicians can assume that the MACI scales have construct validity, these validities should be replicated on larger samples.

The most serious psychometric problem of the MACI is that there are too few test items (e.g., 160) to score so many scales (e.g., 30). As a result, there is considerable item overlap and the scales are intercorrelated. The scales should not be interpreted as if they are discrete dimensions.

SUMMARY

The MACI is a personality test based on Millon's theory, which is explained in his book *Toward a New Personality* (1990). The MACI parallels the *DSM-IV-TR* and is designed to identify personality disorders. It is interesting to note that the *DSM-IV-TR* cautions against diagnosing personality disorders in adolescents. Very rarely is an Axis II diagnosis given to an adolescent. Adolescents are still growing, and neither their neurology nor their personality is fixed. The MACI also contains scales (e.g., those addressing eating and conduct disorders) that are developmentally appropriate for adolescents. The MACI is brief and takes only about 30 min to administer. Although ease of administration is initially appealing, the brevity of the test contributes to a high intercorrelation among scales. Scales cannot be assumed to be discrete dimensions. A promising but relatively new test, the MACI awaits further reliability and validity research.

MINNESOTA MULTIPHASIC PERSONALITY INVENTORY–ADOLESCENT (MMPI-A)

PURPOSE, USE, AND BRIEF DESCRIPTION

The MMPI-A is the most widely used objective measure of adolescent adjustment. When the adolescent version was published by Butcher et al. (1992), it was designed to be very similar to the original MMPI so that approximately 50 years of research could continue to be applied to the interpretation of the test. Designed to be developmentally appropriate for adolescents, the MMPI-A contains item wording, norms, and scales specifically for an adolescent population. It contains scales and items focused on identity, family problems, school problems, low aspirations, and alienation. The new version aimed to be more current, more geographically representative, and more ethnically representative.

The MMPI-A consists of 478 true-false items grouped into validity, clinical, content, and supplementary scales. The validity scales are Cannot Say (*?*), Lie (*L*), F (Infrequency), *K* (Defensiveness), *VRIN* (Variable Response Inconsistency), and *TRIN* (True Response Inconsistency). The basic scales include Hypochondriasis (*Hs*), Depression (*D*), Hysteria (*Hy*), Psychopathic Deviate (*Pd*), Masculinity-Femininity (*Mf*), Paranoia (*Pa*), Psychasthenia (*Pt*), Schizophrenia (*Sc*), Hypomania (*Ma*), and Social Introversion (*Si*). The 15 content scales are similar to the adult content scales and measure anxiety, depression, conduct problems, and other psychological problems. They also contain items specific to adolescent development such as identity, alienation, aspirations, and family problems. The content scales are similar enough to the adult scales to allow similar interpretation but unique enough to focus on adolescent-specific concerns. Clinicians may find the content scales helpful in identifying perceived problem areas. Finally, the six supplementary scales assess substance abuse, immaturity, anxiety, and repression. Also included is the MacAndrew Alcoholism Scale–Revised (MAC-R).

ADMINISTRATION, SCORING, AND INTERPRETATION

Administration

The MMPI-A takes approximately 1 hour to administer and may be administered individually or in a group. If an adolescent is hyperactive, oppositional, or impulsive and cannot sit for an entire hour, the test may be administered with frequent breaks or over several time-limited intervals. The test must be administered under close supervision, and it is never acceptable for a teenager to take the test home to complete it. The validity scales (*L, F,* and *K*) and the basic scales can be scored on the first 350 items if the entire test cannot be completed. Content and supplementary scales are scored on the remaining test items. If necessary, the test may be stopped after the first 350 items. The test is appropriate for ages 14–18. A sixth-grade reading level is required. Adequate English language comprehension is necessary. To assess reading level, the clinician can ask the adolescent to read the first 5–10 items aloud. If still in doubt, a reading test, such as the Peabody Individual Achievement Test–Revised, can be given to assess reading level. If necessary, the test may be read to the teenager.

The MMPI-A is available in soft- and hard-cover booklets, audiocassettes, and computer forms from NCS. It is also available in many languages, including Spanish.

Scoring and Profiling

There are three ways to score the MMPI-A: by computer at NCS, by computer by the test examiner with NCS software, or by hand. Hand scoring is completed by a series of templates to obtain raw scale scores. Hand-scored tests should be separated by gender before being scored because the *Mf* scale has separate keys for boys and girls. Omitted and double-marked items (both T and F are endorsed) should be crossed out and treated as Cannot Say (*?*) scores. Raw scale scores are entered on a separate profile form by gender. MMPI-A authors do not recommend using the *K* correction because it was developed for adults and its generalizability to adolescents has not been demonstrated. On the profile sheet, left- and right-hand columns give the corresponding *T* scores values for raw scores. Dots are usually placed at the score points for each scale on the profile. A line is drawn to connect the dots on validity scales and again to connect basic scales, with a break between validity scales and basic scales.

Interpretation

After raw scores have been converted to *T* scores on the gender-appropriate profile sheet, *T*-score cutoffs are used to assist interpretation. In general, *T* scores greater than or equal to 65 indicate psychopathology on the basic scales. *T* scores between 60 and 64 *may* indicate pathology. The gray or shaded zone on the profile indicates marginal range elevations.

Rapid Reference 6.16
Minnesota Multiphasic Personality Inventory–Adolescent (MMPI-A)

- The MMPI-A is the most widely used objective measure of adolescent adjustment.
- It contains validity, basic, content, and supplementary scales.
- Adolescent version contains items and scales developmentally appropriate for adolescents, such as identity, alienation, school, and family problems.
- Administration takes approximately 1 hour.
- Use with ages 14–18.
- Sixth-grade reading level is required.
- The MMPI-A has been translated into many languages, including Spanish.
- The MMPI-A was standardized on both a community and clinical sample.
- The community sample consisted of 805 high school boys and 815 high school girls, aged 14–18 years, and from eight U.S. regions.
- The community sample was largely Euro-American (76%) with college-educated parents.
- The clinical sample consisted of 420 boys and 293 girls from inpatient and outpatient mental health or drug rehab units.
- Test-retest reliability varies by scale and ranges from .65 to .84.
- Test-retest reliability for Scale 4 (*Pd*) equals .80 with a standard error of 2.50.
- Critical item lists are *not* recommended with adolescents.
- Codetype analysis with adolescents is *not* recommended until further research is conducted.
- Validity research is still being conducted. Test authors assume research with adolescents on the original MMPI applies to the MMPI-A.

Interpretation begins by evaluating the validity scales to determine whether the profile is valid. Beginning with the *Cannot Say (?)* scale, a profile is considered invalid if 30 or more items are left unanswered. A *T* score greater than or equal to 65 on the *Lie (L)* scale indicates extreme denial of symptoms and the possibility of an all-false or fake-good response set. On the other hand, individuals with high *F (Infrequency)* scores are attempting to present themselves in a bad light—that is, they are trying to appear more troubled than they are. *F* scale scores between 80 and 89 warrant concern. Scores above 90 warrant serious concern. The *K (Defensiveness)* scale is interpreted as a denial of symptoms. *T* scores greater than or equal to 65 represent a facade of control and individuals who are very defensive denying psychological psychopathology. Again, the *K* correction is not used with adolescents.

VRIN (Variable Response Inconsistency) and *TRIN* (True Response) scales are still in the experimental stage. They were designed to help interpret *L* and *K. T* scores greater than or equal to 75 measure inconsistent or contradictory response styles. Butcher et al. (1992) emphasize that no validity indicator should automatically be relied on to invalidate a profile but that *L, F,* and *K* should be interpreted in the context of other clinical scales.

As previously mentioned, *T* scores greater than or equal to 65 indicate psychopathology and *T* scores between 60 and 64 may also indicate pathology on the basic scales. Extremely low scale scores may merit closer investigation. High scores on Scale 1, *Hypochondriasis (Hs)* indicate physical complaints or somatic symptoms. In teenage girls, high Scale 1 scores may suggest eating disorders. Scale 2, *Depression (D)* measures depression, suicidal somatic symptoms, anxiety, fear, worry, poor school performance, internalizing, guilt, low confidence, social withdrawal, shyness, timidity, and pessimism. Research with teens on Scale 2 suggests that they may be inclined to feelings of guilt, self-criticalness, and introspection, and they may be more inclined to suicidal ideation than are adults but are still open to discussing their feelings in therapy (R. P. Archer, 1997; Graham, 2000). High scores on Scale 3, *Hysteria (Hy)* indicate somatic problems, denial of symptoms, and a need for social acceptance. Although limited data with adolescents are available for Scale 3, Archer (1997) described teens scoring high on Scale 3 as dependent, nonassertive, and anxious. In sum, Scales 1–3 seem especially sensitive to somatic symptoms and depression. They have even been referred to as the "neurotic triad" (Greene, 1980).

Scale 4, *Psychopathic Deviate (Pd),* is one of the most researched scales with adolescents and frequently the most highly elevated scale on an adolescent profile (R. P. Archer, 1997). Teens with elevated Scale 4 scores often demonstrate acting-out behaviors, anger, delinquency, drug and alcohol abuse, school problems, conflict with authority, aggression, self-centeredness, impulsivity, hostility, and rebellion. Elevations on Scale 4 are also related to lying; cheating; stealing; temper outbursts; and school, family, and legal problems. Because so many descriptors apply to the adolescent scoring high on Scale 4, it can be difficult to sort out the appropriate ones. In this case, use of the Harris-Lingoes subscales may be helpful in separating out family discord, authority problems, and social or self-alienation. Because there may be a history of abuse, it is important to ask about this.

Scale 5, Masculinity-Femininity (*Mf*), was originally developed by Hathaway to measure homosexuality. Research conducted by Hathaway and Monachesi (1963) found boys with high Scale 5 scores tend to have more stereotypical feminine interests, higher grades, better school adjustment, and less acting out. Interpreting Scale 5 with girls is difficult. Research studies show mixed results (Butcher et al., 1992). Some studies indicate that high-scoring girls have more stereotypical masculine interests and less acting out (Hathaway & Monachesi, 1963). In contrast, MMPI-A normative research found these girls to be more aggressive with more conduct problems and poor anger control (Butcher et al., 1992).

Scales 6 through 9 tend to measure more serious psychopathology. Scale 6 *Paranoia (Pa)*, measures suspiciousness, feelings of persecution, rigidity, moral self-righteousness, aggressive acting out, and argumentative behavior. *Pa* is related to school problems (e.g., failing subjects and being suspended) for both boys and girls. In normal adolescents, *Pa* may be related to oversensitivity to comments and suspected attitudes of others. Scale 7, *Psychasthenia (Pt)*, appears to be a very good index of distress in adolescents (Graham, 2000). *Pt* indicates anxiety, tension, worry, fear, inability to concentrate, depression, poor self-concept, perfectionism, indecisiveness, shyness, self-criticalness, and restlessness. Symptoms on Scale 8, *Schizophrenia (Sc)*, include bizarre thought processes, confused and disorganized thinking, somatic symptoms, school performance problems, fearlessness, possible drug abuse and sexual abuse, internalizing, isolation, and behavior problems. Scale 8 is the most sensitive to psychoses in adolescents. Scale 9, *Hypomania (Ma)*, measures elevated mood, restlessness, flight of ideas, irritability, egocentricity, and cognitive and behavioral overactivity. Normal adolescents typically endorse more Scale 9 items than do adults, which could be related to enthusiasm and high energy common in teens. In some cases, this energy and restlessness could cause a tendency to stir up excitement and cause school problems.

Scale 0, Social Introversion (*Si*), is unique among the MMPI-A scales. Whereas Scales 1–9 measure neuroses, psychoses, and psychological adjustment, Scale 0 appears to measure a stable, temperamental trait. This scale is very stable across time and seems to measure shyness, introversion, difficulty making friends, depression, and in some extreme cases suicidal ideation. High scorers on Scale 0 are not likely to be delinquent or to use alcohol or drugs.

In addition to the validity and basic scales, the MMPI-A also contains 15 content scales and six supplementary scales. Scoring the content scales requires administration of all 478 items in the MMPI-A booklet and cannot be based on the first 350 items. Many of the adolescent content scales are similar to the adult content scales and include scales such as anxiety, depression, and bizarre mentation. Some are specific to adolescents, such as school problems, family problems, and low aspirations. The supplementary scales include the MacAndrew Alcoholism Scale–Revised (MAC-R), the Alcohol/Drug Problem Acknowledge (ACK) scale, the Alcohol/Drug Problem Proneness (PRO) scale, the Immaturity (IMM) scale, and Welsh's Anxiety (A) and Repression (R) scales. Content and supplementary scales should be used as additional sources of information to help the clinician interpret clinical scales but never in lieu of them. These content and supplementary scales can be especially useful when the clinician needs to clarify the meaning of basic scales. For more information and in-depth explanation of the validity, clinical, content, and supplemental research, the reader is directed to R. P. Archer (1997), Butcher et al. (1992), and Williams et al. (1992).

The test examiner is advised to look for converging lines of evidence. Descriptors that are replicated across scales and come from scales of highest evaluations are most likely to be true, especially if these descriptors are supported by clinical impressions, interviews, and other assessment tools. After profiling the basic, content, supplementary, and Harris-Lingoes subscales, if the clinician is still in doubt it is recommended that he or she review the actual items endorsed by the adolescent and discuss their meaning with the teenager. In general, the MMPI-A can be viewed as a 478-item structured interview.

ETHNIC AND GENDER DIFFERENCES

Considerable research has been conducted on MMPI gender and ethnic differences (Dahlstrom et al., 1986; Greene, 1987). Recent research is beginning to determine whether findings on the adult MMPI version apply to the adolescent version, or MMPI-A (Gumbiner, 1997, 1998). Gender differences are known to exist and for this reason boys and girls are profiled on separate forms (Butcher et al., 1992). It is absolutely essential that boys are profiled on male forms and girls are profiled on female forms. Not doing this risks invalidating the test results. Years of research on the adult version indicate that the test is generally valid for diverse ethnic groups. Some ethnic differences have been found but they are not sufficient enough to warrant new norms or to invalidate the test interpretation. However, the test examiner is advised to review chapter 4 and the MMPI-A manual before administering the test to a minority group member. Chapter 4 contains an in-depth discussion of the MMPI, MMPI-A, and diversity.

PSYCHOMETRIC PROPERTIES

Standardization Sample and Norms

Among the goals of the MMPI-A revision were ethnic and geographic representativeness. Two samples were collected: a normative sample and a clinical sample. The normative sample consisted of 805 boys and 815 girls sampled from schools in several geographic regions of the United States: California, Minnesota, New York, North Carolina, Ohio, Pennsylvania, Virginia, and Washington (Butcher et al., 1992). The ethnic composition of the sample was 76% Euro-American, 12% African American, and less than 3% Asian, Hispanic, Native American, or other minority. The test authors state that the test probably underrepresents the Hispanic population of the United States. Ages of the subjects ranged from 14 to 18. Educational and occupational level of the parents was predominantly college level or above. Approximately 65% of the fathers were either high-level professionals, professionals, or managers. The clinical sample consisted of 420 boys and 293 girls recruited from inpatient alcohol-and-drug treatment units, inpatient mental health facilities, day-treatment programs, and a special school program in the Minneapolis area.

Reliability

Internal consistency of the validity and basic scales is generally good. Most of the scales have high internal consistency (e.g., *Hs* is .78–.79 and *Sc* is .88–.89). Some have moderate internal consistency (e.g., *D* is .65–.66), and a few have low internal consistency (e.g., *Mf* is .40–.43; Butcher et al., 1992). Test-retest reliability is good and ranges from .65 to .84 depending on the clinical scale. For example, the test-retest reliability for *Pd,* which is commonly used with teens, is equal to .80 with a standard error of measurement of 2.50. The test-retest sample (45 boys and 109 girls) was small, and the time interval (1 week) was brief. Additional reliability studies are needed.

Rapid Reference 6.17
MMPI-A Scoring

- Be sure that raw scale scores are entered on the gender-appropriate profile form (e.g., boys on the boy profile and girls on the girl profile).
- Do not use the *K* correction with adolescents.
- Validity scales are connected with one line, and clinical scales are connected with a separate line. There is a break in the line between validity and clinical scores.
- Basic *T* scores ≥ 65 indicate psychopathology. *T* scores between 60 and 64 *may* indicate pathology.
- Scale 4 indicates acting-out behaviors and is frequently the most elevated scale on adolescent profiles. Harris-Lingoes subscales help better clarify the cause of the adolescent's responses on Scale 4 (e.g., family, school, etc.).

Note: From Butcher et al. (1992).

Validity

During the data collection phase for the MMPI-A, additional data were collected on the clinical and normative samples, including biographical information, life events information, the CBCL, and the Devereux Adolescent Behavior Rating Scale. Also included were parent ratings, treatment staff ratings, and hospital and school reports. One form of validity presented in the manual is a comparison of scale correlates. For example, the correlation of *Pd* with delinquency on the CBCL is compared between normative and clinical samples. Boys from the clinical sample tend to correlate .30 with delinquent behaviors on the CBCL; unfortunately, this is hard to interpret because no data are available for the normative sample. When describing the content scales, the authors make frequent reference to validity analyses and empirical evidence but offer no hard data. For scientific findings, the inquisitive reader is directed to research conducted by Ben-Porath, Williams, and Uchiyama (1989). In general, it is assumed that the MMPI-A performs similarly to the MMPI and that much of the validity research conducted on the parent test applies to the MMPI-A. However, because the MMPI was known to overpathologize for adolescents, this practice must be conducted cautiously.

Reliability and validity of critical items are limited in adolescent groups. For this reason, critical item lists are not recommended with teenagers.

Rapid Reference 6.18
Strengths and Weaknesses of the MMPI-A

Strengths	Weaknesses
Contains response style scales (faking bad, faking good, lying, and defensiveness).	Needs more research on new adolescent version, especially construct validity and test-retest reliability.
Has good internal consistency and reliability.	Very few minorities were in the standardization sample.
More than 50 years of research were conducted on the parent tool, the adult MMPI.	Teens in the standardization sample were primarily from well-educated, professional families.

Caution
Scales should be interpreted within the cultural and socioeconomic context of the adolescent.

Similarly, codetype analysis is not recommended with adolescents until further research is conducted (Butcher et al., 1992; Gumbiner & Flowers, 1997).

Several areas warrant more research on the MMPI-A. Because much of the research with adolescents was conducted on the adult version of the MMPI and applied to interpretation of the MMPI-A, nearly every research topic awaits replication on the new version. Among the research areas that need work are external validity correlates; studies of ethnic, educational, and socioeconomic differences; code type analysis; and critical item lists. Greene has urged the study of moderator variables, such as education and ethnicity for years (Greene, 1987). According to Anastasi and Urbina (1997), the MMPI-A is more of a "brand new instrument than a revision" whose ultimate usefulness will be determined by future research.

SUMMARY

The MMPI-A can be thought of as a 478-item structured interview. Published in 1992, the adolescent version is based on the MMPI but revised to be sensitive to adolescent issues such as identity, alienation, and school and family problems. In addition, the adolescent version aims to be geographically and ethnically representative and is normed on adolescents. The best uses of the MMPI-A are the assessment of psychosomatic symptoms, depression, conduct disorders, psychoses, and general psychopathology.

ROTTER INCOMPLETE SENTENCES BLANK (RISB)

PURPOSE, USE, AND BRIEF DESCRIPTION

Rotter, Lah, and Rafferty (1992) describe the Rotter Incomplete Sentences Blank (RISB) as a "semi-structured projective method" of assessing personality adjustment (p. 1). The test consists of forty sentence stems and objective scoring criteria. Sample stems are *I like—, The happiest time—*, and *My greatest worry is—*. The client completes the stem and the responses are assumed to reflect the individual's wishes, desires, fears, and attitudes. This sentence completion technique is designed to elicit self-statements that are assumed to measure adjustment or maladjustment. Adjustment is defined as "relative freedom from prolonged unhappy/dysphoric states (emotions) of the individual, the ability to cope with frustration, the ability to initiate and maintain constructive activity, and the ability to establish and maintain satisfying interpersonal relationships" (p. 4) (Rotter et al., 1992).

The first edition of the test manual was published in 1950. Based on an experimental form used in the U.S. Army, the two main objectives of the RISB were to provide a projective measure that was easy to administer and score and to provide helpful information for diagnosis. Published in 1992, the revision offers more current interpretation, updated normative data, and scoring criteria. In general, the 40 sentence stems are nearly identical to the original test to maintain continuity with previous editions and to allow the use of 50 years of research.

The RISB is used in college and university settings, industry, military settings, junior and senior high schools, research settings, hospitals, mental health clinics, and private clinical practices. It is used as a verbal projective measure prior to intake interviews, as a routine part of the intake interview, or as part of a complete assessment battery. The RISB was designed to save time for the clinician by providing valuable information to help design the first interview. The authors describe the RISB as an "index of overall adjustment for screening purposes" (Rotter et al., 1992).

ADMINISTRATION, SCORING, AND INTERPRETATION

Administration

There are three forms of the RISB: a high school form, a college form, and an adult form. It is recommended that the appropriate form be used. Administration of the RISB is easy. The examiner hands the respondent the response sheet and asks him or her to follow the directions on the sheet. Respondents complete the top portion with their name, age, sex, and so forth, and then complete the sentences. Directions on the test say, "Complete these sentences to express *your real feelings.* Try to do every one. Be sure to make a complete sentence." It may be necessary to tell the respondent there are no right or wrong answers or to reread the directions on the response sheet. Average administration time is approximately 20 to 25 minutes.

Scoring

The RISB manual provides objective scoring criteria and case study examples. A separate manual exists for males and females. An individual's 40 completed answers are evaluated according to empirically derived scoring examples to provide an overall index of adjustment called the Overall Adjustment Score.

The completed sentences are scored on a 7-point scale from 0 (*most positive*) to 6 (*most conflict*), with the total of the 40 items resulting in scores from 0 to 240. The sentences are scored by comparing them to examples in the test manual. The test manual offers helpful guidelines on scoring and for dealing with special problems such as omissions and incomplete sentences. Different criteria exist for males and females.

Interpretation

Original research conducted by Rotter, Rafferty, & Schachitz (1949) found 135 to be a useful cutoff score for discriminating maladjusted clients from adjusted ones. More recent research conducted by Lah (1989) found 145 to be a useful cutoff for the Overall Adjustment Score. The authors recommend caution and clinical acumen when interpreting these adjustment scores. In other words, there is no magic number that indicates adjustment or maladjustment, and other variables must be taken into consideration, such as the client's social circumstances, mental health, race, ethnicity, and the population comparison. Thus, it is recommended that the range of 130–152 be considered clinically meaningful.

In addition to the quantitative Overall Adjustment Score, a qualitative analysis may be useful to the clinician. Experienced clinicians will each have a unique manner of interpreting the RISB, but Rotter et al. (1992) recommend a theoretically grounded analysis. They recommend applying social learning theory, object relations, psychoanalytic, or systems theory. The authors emphasize that inferences and interpretations drawn from the RISB are hypotheses and should be carefully supported with data from records, interviews, other assessment tools, interviews with the family, direct observations, and clinical judgment.

PSYCHOMETRIC PROPERTIES

Interrater Reliability

Scoring of the RISB responses is very reliable. According to Rotter's (1949) original research the interrater reliability coefficients between scorers was .91 for a sample of 50 female subjects and .96 for 50 males. Additional research reported in the test manual and based on a review of 31 studies reported a range of a low of .72 to a high of .99 and a median of .93 for interrater reliability coefficients (Rotter et al., 1992).

Test-Retest Reliabilities

Test-retest reliabilities are sufficiently reliable to use the RISB to compare adjustment at the beginning of treatment to adjustment at the end of treatment. Test-retest coefficients for the RISB are in the medium to high range depending on the sample and time range. The test-retest reliabilities range from .54 (women) and .43 (men) for 6 months, .50 (women) and .52 (men) for the 1 year and .44 (women) and .38 (men) over 3 years (Rotter et al., 1992). A study conducted by Churchill and Crandall (1955) reported data that retested women at 13–24 months after the initial testing with a reliability coefficient of .70.

Validity

Extensive data have been collected assessing the validity of the RISB. Numerous studies using different types of experimental design and subject

Rapid Reference 6.19
Rotter Incomplete Sentences Blank (RISB)

- The RISB is an open-ended sentence completion measure of adjustment.
- Forty sentence stems aim to elicit the respondent's wishes, desires, fears, and attitudes.
- High school and college forms of the RISB have both been developed.
- Administration time is about 20–25 min.
- Separate scoring criteria exist for males and females.
- An overall adjustment score ranging from 130 to 152 is considered clinically meaningful.
- Theoretical interpretations may be grounded in social learning theory, object relations, psycho-analytic, or systems theory.
- Considerable validity studies have been conducted that demonstrate good construct and convergent validity.
- Test-retest reliabilities are .50 (women) and .52 (men) at 1 year.
- Considerable validity studies have been conducted that demonstrate good construct and convergent validity (Rotter et al., 1992)

populations are reported in the RISB manual. For example, subject populations include self-referrals for counseling, college dropouts, and marijuana users. Study designs include treatment outcome studies; measurement of anxiety, self-concept, and marital problems; and construct validity studies. Although most of the validity data on the RISB was collected on college students, various external criteria have been used to assess validity. Among them are students in counseling versus students not in counseling and instructors' ratings of maladjustment.

Original data collected by Rotter et al. (1949) indicated that a cutoff score of 135 on the RISB correctly identified 78% of the adjusted respondents and 59% of the maladjusted respondents. Numerous studies have correlated Overall Adjustment Scores with college students in counseling or not in counseling. Biserial correlations between the overall adjustment scores, and students seeking counseling were .42 for women and .37 for men (Rotter et al., 1992). When Lah (1989) compared a random sample of 120 college students to a random sample of clinic students at the university mental health center, he found correlations of .72 (women) and .67 (men) with Overall Adjustment on the RISB. Another form of known group analysis was to compare high and low anxiety students. Students

Rapid Reference 6.20
Strengths and Weaknesses of the RISB

Strengths

Nonthreatening way to begin battery.

Good screening tool.

Brief.

Flexible, adaptable to many clinical uses.

Easy to administer.

Good case study examples.

Fairly objective scoring criteria.

Good reliability.

Good validity.

Weaknesses

Most validity and reliability data were collected on college students.

Caution

There is no set cutoff score to discriminate maladjusted teens from well-adjusted ones. The teen's cultural and socioeconomic context should be taken into consideration when the clinician is interpreting the test.

---

were separated using the Taylor Manifest Anxiety Scale. It was found that the students with high anxiety scores had significantly greater RISB Overall Adjustment Scores. It can be concluded that the RISB is sensitive to anxiety.

Several construct validity studies have correlated the RISB with theoretically similar tests. In general, the correlations are acceptable. For example, the RISB correlates .51 with the BDI, .46 with the Taylor Manifest Anxiety Scale, and .32, .40, and .41 with the MMPI scales of Depression, Psychasthenia, and Social Introversion. It can be concluded that sufficient research has been conducted on the RISB to determine that it is a valid measure of adjustment.

Advantages to the sentence completion technique are that it is easy to administer, easy to score, quick, fun for the client, flexible, adaptable for clinical use, and amenable to group administration; it also requires no special training.

SUMMARY

The RISB is a sentence completion measurement of adjustment. It is easy to administer and scientifically valid. The manual is clearly written and offers helpful guidelines for scoring and interpretation. It can be used as a screening tool or as part of a complete battery and is sensitive to anxiety and depression. Because the RISB is brief and fun, it is a good way to begin a test battery.

THE STRONG INTEREST INVENTORY (SII)

PURPOSE, USE, AND BRIEF DESCRIPTION

The purpose of the Strong Interest Inventory (SII) is to help respondents make educational and vocational decisions. Harmon et al. (1994), emphasize that the Strong measures *interests* and not ability. One of the best uses of the SII is to help high school and college students plan career directions.

The SII is a venerable testing instrument. It has a long history of good empirical research and is one of the best testing instruments of any sort. Originally published by E. K. Strong in 1927 and updated in 1994 by Harmon et al., the SSI remains the most scientifically sound and widely used interest inventory. The SSI consists of 317 items that fall into five areas: General Occupational Themes, Basic Interest Scales, Occupational Scales, Personal Style Scales, and Administration Indexes. A brief description of each of these areas follows.

The *General Occupational Themes* (GOTs) are based on Holland's (1973) hexagonal model of career types. Based on 135 self-report items, the respondent's career interests are categorized into one or two themes. The six themes are Realistic, Investigative, Artistic, Social, Enterprising, and Conventional (R-I-A-S-E-C).

The *Basic Interest Scales* (BIS) are subdivisions of the General Occupational Themes but are more specific. There are 25 basic interest scales, such as agriculture, nature, athletics, art, and so on, that cluster into the GOTs. For example, science, mathematics, and medical science are all components of the Investigative Basic Interest Scale.

The *Occupational Scales* (OS) consist of 211 scales that compare the test taker to satisfied individuals of 109 occupations. A wide range of occupations is included from accountant to elementary school teacher and

forester. The best uses of the Occupational Scales are educational decisions, entry-level occupational choices, and career change.

The *Personal Style Scales* were added to the Strong in 1994 and measure
Work Style, Learning Environment, Leadership Style, and Risk Taking
and Adventure. The objective of these scales is to help people discover
their work preferences—for example, does the respondent prefer to work
independently or with people?

The *Administrative Indexes* are computer checks on the response style
of the test taker. Three statistics are calculated by computer: total responses; the percentage of *like, indifferent,* and *dislike* responses; and in-
frequent responses. These statistics provide the counselor with valuable
information about the validity of the profile.

For adolescents, the most useful scales are the GOT and BIS because
they help guide teens toward general career themes. At this stage in their
lives, most teens are more interested in career exploration than they are in
selecting a specific occupation. In contrast, the Occupational Scales are
more specific and more appropriate for employment choices.

ADMINISTRATION, SCORING, AND INTERPRETATION

Administration

The Strong Interest Inventory: Applications and Technical Guide (Harmon
et al., 1994) is clearly written and easy to use. This guide was written with
counselors in mind and is designed to help them interpret the test. The
manual contains many helpful guidelines, including checklists, for counseling test respondents. Because the inventory is long and well researched,
it is recommended that the examiner review the manual.

The SII takes between 40 and 60 min to complete, depending on the respondent's reading level and motivation. If necessary, the inventory can be
administered in more than one sitting. The inventory is useful with high
school students and is generally not administered prior to eighth grade.
By eighth grade, individuals begin to show stability in interests.

More than one version of the SII is available from the publisher. The
most widely used form (Form T317) is designed for professionals. Another form of the test is available that measures interests in vocations.

Translations

The 1985 SII was translated into Spanish using appropriate methodology. The authors present high correlations between the Spanish and English versions, which means that the Spanish version can be interpreted in the same manner as the English version. In addition, the authors describe a factor analytic study on the Spanish version, which provides data supporting Holland's hexagonal pattern (Harmon et al., 1994). There is also a French Canadian, a Hebrew, an Italian, and a British version of the 1985 SII. Research versions in other languages and translations of the 1994 SII are underway.

Scoring and Profile

The respondent completes a Form T317 for the 1994 SII. This form contains 317 items, most of which are answered at three levels: *like, indifferent,* or *dislike.* Instructions to respondents are to consider their interests only (not their abilities) when completing the inventory. Upon completion, the booklet is mailed to one of the publisher's scoring centers for computer scoring.

The 1994 profile was designed based on extensive feedback from users. Hundreds of counselors from high schools, vocational schools, colleges, government agencies, and businesses were consulted in its development. The profile aims to be user friendly by relying on plain, nontechnical language, interpretive keys, and explanations on the back of the profile. The profile consists of six pages. The first page provides a snapshot summary of the test taker's results. The summary ranks the respondent's general occupational themes, lists the five highest basic interests, and lists 10 occupations compatible with the respondent's interests. The remaining five pages go into more depth on the GOTs, BIS, OS, Personal Style Scales, and Administrative Indexes.

Interpretation

Counselors are advised to use the profile and test manual together when advising test takers. Although the profile is easy to interpret, the manual offers excellent guidelines for counseling and interpretation, including checklists. Computer scoring includes an in-depth interpretive report with suggested occupations.

ETHNIC AND GENDER DIFFERENCES

Gender differences exist on the SII at both the item and scale levels; these are empirical differences based on data from responses of thousands of respondents. For example, women tend to endorse more items related to decorating and clothing, whereas men endorse items related to mechanics, fighting, and sports. Because men and women respond differently to about one fourth to one third of the inventory items, separate norms exist for men and women. Information on the profile allows men and women to compare their scores with over 9,000 women and 9,000 men and with the opposite sex in various occupations. In general, same-gender comparisons will be the most predictive of career interests.

The SII manual discusses studies conducted with African Americans, Native Americans, and Hispanic Americans (Harmon et al., 1994). The authors claim that Holland's hexagonal career model, R-I-A-S-E-C, applies reasonably well to these groups and with disabilities. Ethnic comparisons on the 1994 SII are based on a sample of 2,445 individuals.

PSYCHOMETRIC PROPERTIES

The SII has been thoroughly researched over many years. Reliabilities and validities are based on large samples and calculated for each specific section of the test (e.g., GOTs, BIS, and the OS). Beginning with the original version of the inventory in 1927, E. K. Strong developed a strong tradition of empiricism. Reliability, validity, and follow-up studies are based on large samples (thousands) over decades.

Standardization Sample

The SII has been normed on hundreds of subjects for decades. The first predictive validity studies were conducted on the senior class of Stanford University students in 1927 by E. K. Strong himself. In 1955, he combined the test scores of these with several hundred of their peers ($N = 524$) and published his book, *Vocational Interests 18 Years After College*.

The most recent revision of the SII (1994) was administered to 55,000 individuals (Harmon et al., 1994). Exact figures on the sample size are difficult to extract from the manual because data are reported on various scales and separate studies. To examine gender differences, the GOTs were normed on over 18,000 men and women. Data are available on 2,445 minorities—approximately one third each African-American, Asian, and Latino, as well as a small proportion of Native Americans. Because reliability and validity studies are presented in the manual by scale, that same pattern will be followed below.

Reliability and Validity

The General Occupational Themes Internal consistency, as measured by Cronbach's alpha, is based on a sample of 18,951 women and men and is .90 or above for each of the occupational scales (Harmon et al., 1994). Test-retest reliabilities are based on smaller adult samples ($N = 191$) and range from .84 to .92 over a 3- to 6-month period. The reliabilities are slightly lower ($r = .84–.88$) for college students ($N = 84$), whose interests are still changing. In general, the GOTs are very stable over time.

Two forms of construct validity are offered in the manual. The SII correlates highly ($r = .77$) with another vocational inventory, the Vocational Preference Inventory, in the predicted direction (Harmon et al., 1994). The second form of construct validity is offered by ranking occupational groups on the 1994 SII. In general, the expected occupations fall into the appropriate dimensions (e.g., auto mechanic on Realistic and physicist on Investigative).

The Basic Interest Scales Cronbach's alpha on the BIS range from .74 to .94, indicating high internal consistency. Test-retest reliabilities over a 3- to 6-month period on the BIS range from .80 to .94 for adults. The stability of scores for adults over time is high. Test-retest reliabilities for high school and college students range from .50 to .90, depending on the retest time interval (Harmon et al., 1994).

The validity of the BIS is demonstrated by rank ordering the means of the 109 occupational groups in the 1994 SII on each scale. In general, the occupational rankings cluster in the predicted directions—for example, art teacher, medical illustrator, and artist rank high on Art BIS, whereas agribusiness manager, farmer, and plumber rank low on the Art BIS.

The Occupational Scales The most thoroughly researched component of the SII is the OS. The OS were originally designed by E. K. Strong in the 1920s and 1930s and have been extensively researched over the decades (Harmon et al., 1994). Test-retest reliabilities were computed over a 3- to 6-month period on four samples. The median correlations were .90,

Rapid Reference 6.21
The Strong Interest Inventory (SII)

- The SII is aimed at 8th- to 12th-graders.
- Administration time is 40–60 min.
- Profile and manual are clearly written and very useful for interpretation.
- Separate norms exist for males and females.
- The SII has been translated into many languages, including Spanish, French Canadian, Hebrew, and Italian.
- Psychometric data have been collected on thousands of subjects since the 1920s.
- Gender differences were normed on more than 18,000 men and women (Harmon et al., 1994).
- A combined total of 2,445 African Americans, Asians, Latinos, and Native Americans were in the standardization sample (Harmon et al., 1994).
- Test-retest reliabilities for the OS are very strong. Median correlations over a 3- to 6-month period are .90, .87, .85, and .84. Follow-up studies 12 years later indicate test-retest reliabilities as high as .72 for women and .73 for men.
- Research indicates that strong predictive validity is available for the SII. One half to two thirds of tested college students work in occupations predicted from their test scores.

.87, .85, and .84. In addition, follow-up studies as many as 12 years later indicate test-retest reliabilities of .72 for women and .73 for men (Swanson & Hansen, 1988).

Concurrent validity for the OS is measured in several ways: (a) as the scales discriminate from the General Reference Sample (GRS) (b) as the mean score of occupational samples (c) and as percent overlap. This percent overlap technique describes how well each scale discriminates from other scales. If the scale discriminates perfectly, there is zero overlap. If it does not discriminate, the overlap is 100%. The median overlap for both male and female scales was 36%. The OS vary widely in percent overlaps. Some scales are more tightly defined than others. Another measure of concurrent validity is the degree to which the OS discriminate from each other. The degree of discrimination is measured with a Q statistic, and in general the scales discriminate from each other quite well. For more information on this feature, the reader is directed to the test manual (Harmon et al., 1994).

Rapid Reference 6.22
Strengths and Weaknesses of the SII

Strengths

Very thorough assessment of career interests.

Contains 211 occupational scales.

Strong empirical base, well researched.

Good reliability.

Good validity.

Contains response style scales.

Manual is very helpful with interpretation and includes a checklist.

Weaknesses

Some scales perform unpredictably.

Caution
The SII measures interests *not* abilities.

In addition to concurrent validity, extensive research is also available on the predictive validity of the SII. These studies indicate a very high predictive validity for the SII. In general, one half to two thirds of all college students work in occupations that were predictable from their earlier test scores on the SII (Harmon et al., 1994).

The Personal Style Scales   Cronbach's alpha for the Personal Style Scales range from .78 to .91. Test-retest reliabilities are high and range from .81 to .92 over a 3-month interval. As with the other SII scales, construct and concurrent validities are based on rank ordering of occupations and college majors on the four Personal Style Scales. The rank orders provide strong support for the validity of the scale (Harmon et al., 1994).

SUMMARY

Based on over 60 years of research, The SII measures career *interests;* it is not a measure of ability. The SII contains 135 items categorized into six themes: Realistic, Investigative, Artistic, Social, Enterprising, and Conventional. It also contains 211 occupational scales. A very reliable, valid, and well-researched test, the best use of the SII with adolescents is for career exploration and educational planning.

THE WECHSLER INTELLIGENCE SCALE FOR CHILDREN–THIRD EDITION (WISC-III)

PURPOSE, USE, AND BRIEF DESCRIPTION

The Wechsler Intelligence Scale for Children–Third Edition (WISC-III), published in 1991, measures general intelligence, nonverbal intelligence, and verbal intelligence. It also contains subtests that can be used to assess cognitive strengths and weaknesses. The WISC-III grew out of previous Wechsler tests, including the original adult intelligence test, the Weschler-Bellevue Intelligence Scale from 1939, the first Wechsler Intelligence Scale for Children (WISC), and the more recent Wechsler Intelligence Scale for Children–Revised (WISC-R).

The WISC-III consists of 13 subtests grouped as Verbal or Performance Scales. The Verbal Scales include: Information, Similarities, Arithmetic, Vocabulary, Comprehension, and Digit Span. Digit Span is optional and can be substituted for other verbal tests. The Performance Scales include Picture Completion, Coding, Picture Arrangement, Block Design, Object Assembly, Symbol Search, and Mazes. Symbol Search and Mazes are supplementary tests. Kaufman and Lichtenberger (2000) recommend routinely substituting Symbol Search for Coding due to its stronger psychometric properties. They also recommend *not* using Mazes due to its psychometric weaknesses. The 13 subtests yield 3 IQ scores and four factor indexes. The IQ scores are Verbal IQ, Performance IQ, and Full Scale IQ. The factor indexes are Verbal Comprehension, Perceptual Organization, Freedom From Distractibility, and Processing Speed.

Verbal Subtests

The Information subtest measures a broad range of general knowledge, including common events, objects, places, and people. The Similarities subtest consists of pairs of contrasting words. The Arithmetic subtest contains arithmetic problems similar to the ones done in school. The Vocabulary subtest measures word meaning. The Comprehension subtest is made up of questions that focus on an understanding of interpersonal re-

Rapid Reference 6.23
The Wechsler Intelligence Scale for Children–
Third Edition (WISC-III)

- The WISC-III has 13 subscales grouped as Verbal or Performance scales. It measures general *g*, verbal comprehension, freedom from distraction, perceptual organization, and processing speed.
- Age limits are 6 years and 0 months to 16 years and 11 months.
- Subtest scores have means of 10 and standard deviations of 3.
- A careful reading of the manual is necessary prior to administration. Wording is important, and some tests are timed.
- FSIQ, VIQ, PIQ, and factor indexes have means of 100 and standard deviations of 10.
- The standard error of measurement and confidence intervals are reported by subscale in the WISC-III manual.
- Test-retest reliabilities are calculated for each full scale and subscale and are presented in the WISC-III manual.
- Test-retest reliability for VIQ = .94, PIQ = .87, and FSIQ = .94.
- The median test-retest reliability for the subscales is .74, and for the vocabulary subscale it is as high as .89.
- Studies of factor structure and convergent validity provide strong empirical evidence of construct validity (Wechsler, 1991).
- The WISC-III FSIQ correlates .74 with the Comprehension Test of Basic Skills.
- Factor analyses reveal four underlying structures. They are verbal comprehension, freedom from distractibility, perceptual organization, and processing speed.

lations, daily problems, and societal rules. Digit Span is a supplementary test that involves repeating a list of numbers forward and backward.

Performance Subtests

The Picture Completion subtest contains ordinary objects with missing elements; the respondent looks at a card and names the missing element. The Picture Arrangement subtest requires that the teen organize a series of pictures in a logical story sequence. The Block Design subtest consists of a series of red and white pictures of geometric design that the young

Rapid Reference 6.24
WISC-III Subscales

Verbal scales

- Information
- Similarities
- Arithmetic
- Vocabulary
- Comprehension
- Digit Span

Performance scales

- Picture Completion
- Coding
- Picture Arrangement
- Block Design
- Object Assembly
- Symbol Search
- Mazes

person copies with small red and white blocks. Object Assembly is a puzzle that the adolescent must put together to form common objects like a girl or a car. The Coding subtest involves copying symbols from a key to corresponding numbers. In the Maze subtest, the examinee solves paper-and-pencil mazes by drawing lines from the center of each maze to the outside without crossing any lines. In the Symbol Search subtest, the respondent finds a specific symbol in a series and marks a box.

Common uses of the WISC-III are global measurement of intelligence and the assessment of LDs, ADHD, giftedness, and mental retardation. Public Law 94-142, the Education for All Handicapped Children Act of 1975 and subsequent legislation (Individual Disabilities Education Act–IDEA of 1991 and IDEA Amendment in 1997) require an IEP for each disabled child. The WISC-III profile analysis has been very useful in this area. For an in-depth discussion of testing with diverse populations, see chapter 4.

ADMINISTRATION, SCORING, AND INTERPRETATION

Administration

Careful administration of the WISC-III is essential. The test examiner must closely follow directions in the test manual. Kaufman (1994), Kaufman and Lichtenberger (2000), and Sattler (2001) also offer very helpful guidelines. The validity of the test will be violated, scoring will be difficult, and norms and interpretation will be meaningless unless strict administration procedures are followed. The examiner's goal should be to follow test procedures and to be an objective, supportive examiner.

Before administering the test, the examiner should study the WISC-III test instructions and materials carefully. A stopwatch is necessary because some subtests are timed. Time limits must be observed. Questions should be read slowly and carefully. The chronological age of the child should be calculated accurately and the norms used appropriately. Responses need to be recorded verbatim, and ambiguous responses need to be probed. The WISC-III manual, Sattler (2001), and Kaufman and Lichtenberger (2000) offer excellent suggestions on probing. The record booklet should be completed properly and discontinuance procedures followed closely. Always follow the standard order of giving the subtests.

The WISC-III is designed to assess cognitive abilities of children and adolescents ages 6 years and 0 months to 16 years and 11 months. Some overlap of the WISC-III and the adult version, the WAIS-III, exists. Sixteen-year-olds can be tested on either version. It is recommended that a case-by-case decision be made based on the intellectual abilities of the teen. A gifted 16-year-old should be tested with the adult version. Adolescents 17 and over also should be tested with the WAIS-III.

Scoring

As noted previously, the WISC-III yields 13 subtest scores, three IQ scores, and four factor indexes. A score can be obtained for each subtest. In addition, FSIQ, VIQ, and PIQ can be obtained along with the factor indexes. After administering the test, the examiner will have raw scores. The raw scores are converted to standard scores. See the WISC-III manual for conversion tables (Wechsler, 1991). The subtest scores have means of 10 and standard deviations of 3. The FSIQ, VIQ, PIQ, and factor indexes have means of 100 and standard deviations of 15. Detailed instructions for scoring are available in the WISC-III manual and helpful guidelines are available in Kaufman and Lichtenberger (2000) and Sattler (2001).

Interpretation

A controversy exists regarding the interpretation of the WISC-III (Kaufman & Lichtenberger, 2000). This controversy is related to questions about the nature of intelligence itself. For a discussion of the intelligence controversy, readers are directed to chapter 2. Factor analyses of the WISC-III indicate a strong underlying factor of general intelligence also known as *g*. Some theorists believe that the only meaningful interpretation of the WISC-III is for *g*. On the other hand, profile analyses offer valuable information on a young person's strengths and weaknesses. The controversy is whether to obtain only a FSIQ score or to examine profile analysis. However, both FSIQ scores and profile analyses provide valuable clinical insight, especially when this information is combined with other clinical data such as behavioral observations, self-reports, parent reports, and teacher observations.

Profile Analysis for Learning Disabilities   An in-depth discussion of profile analysis for LDs can be found in chapter 4. All diagnoses of learning disabilities should be based on multiple methods and conducted by a team of professionals. According to Bannatyne (1974), WISC spatial scale scores are higher than conceptual scale scores, which are higher than sequential scales (special > conceptual > sequential) for LD students. Sattler (1992) ranks the WISC subtests from easiest to hardest for LD students as follows: Picture Completion, Picture Arrangement, Block Design, Object Assembly, Similarities, Comprehension, Vocabulary, Coding, Digit Span, Arithmetic, and Information. The ACID (Arithmetic, Coding, Information, and Digit Span) profile has been observed in LD students. However, after examining the research, Kaufman (1990) noted that the ACID profile does not add additional information over the Bannatyne. Most recent work cautions against using profile analysis for diagnostic purposes (Sattler, 2001). Sattler (2001) clearly states that there is no evidence that discrepancies indicate learning disabilities. He recommends using profiles only for hypotheses regarding cognitive efficiencies.

Rapid Reference 6.25
WISC-III Profile Analysis for LDs

- Profile analysis is controversial.
- All diagnoses of learning disabilities should be based on multiple methods and conducted by a team of professionals.
- Spatial > Conceptual > Sequential (Bannatyne, 1974).
- Easiest to hardest subtests are as follows: Picture Completion, Picture Arrangement, Block Design, Object Assembly, Similarities, Comprehension, Vocabulary, Coding, Digit Span, Arithmetic, and Information (Sattler, 1992).
- Most recent research provides no evidence that discrepancy scores indicate learning disabilities. Sattler recommends profile analysis strictly to formulate hypotheses about cognitive efficiency (Sattler, 2002).

PSYCHOMETRIC PROPERTIES

Standardization Sample and Norms

The WISC-III was standardized on a sample of 2,200 subjects representative of age, gender, ethnicity, geography, and parental educational level of the 1988 U.S. Census (Wechsler, 1991).

Standard Error of Measurement

The WISC-III manual provides considerable data on standard errors and confidence intervals (Wechsler, 1991). The manual also explains very clearly how to use this information when reporting test scores. The standard error of measurement is different for each scale and each age group. For this reason, the manual *must* be consulted. For example, the SEM for 10-year-olds on the PIQ scale is 4.50 (Wechsler, 1991). This SEM can be used to calculate a confidence interval around the PIQ score. In other words, it can be stated with 95% confidence that if the respondent's obtained test score equals 100, then the true score lies within ± 2 SEM of 100, which translates to a score between 91 and 109. On repeated testing, the respondent will very likely score between 91 and 109.

Reliability

Both internal consistency reliability (as measured by split-half reliability coefficients) and test-retest reliabilities for the WISC-III are very strong.

Split-half reliabilities for subtests across age groups average from .69 to .87, with a median equal to .78 (Kaufman & Lichtenberger, 2000). Split-half reliabilities for the IQ scores and factor indexes are as follows: VIQ = .95, PIQ = .91, FSIQ = .96, Verbal Comprehension Index = .94, Perceptual Organization Index = .90, Freedom From Distractibility Index = .87, and Processing Speed Index = .85 (Wechsler, 1991).

Even more important is that the test-retest reliabilities are very strong. The average Verbal Subtest test-retest reliabilities for all ages are as follows: Information = .85, Similarities = .81, Arithmetic = .74, Vocabulary = .89, Comprehension = .73, and Digit Span = .73. The Performance Subtest test-retest reliabilities are as follows: Picture Completion = .81, Coding = .77, Picture Arrangement = .64, Block Design = .77, Object Assembly = .66, Symbol Search = .74, and Mazes = .57 (Wechsler, 1991).

The test-retest reliabilities for IQ scores and factor indexes are as follows: VIQ = .94, PIQ = .87, FSIQ = .94, Verbal Comprehension = .93, Perceptual Organization = .87, Freedom From Distractibility = .82, and Processing Speed = .84 (Wechsler, 1991).

Validity

The WISC-III has very good validity. Many studies have been conducted supporting the validity of the WISC-III and are available in the manual (Wechsler, 1991). They include studies of the factor structure as well as correlations with other Wechsler scales, tests of ability, achievement tests, neuropsychological tests, and school grades. For example, the WISC-III FSIQ correlates with WRAT-R scores of Reading .53, Spelling .28, and Arithmetic .58. The correlation of the WISC-III FSIQ with group-administered achievement test scores, such as the Comprehensive Test of Basic Skills, is .74. Furthermore, the WISC-III FSIQ and grade point average correlate .47 (Wechsler, 1991).

Additional evidence for construct validity of the WISC-III comes from factor analytic studies. These studies support the underlying structure of four factors: Verbal Comprehension, Freedom From Distractibility, Perceptual Organization, and Processing Speed. In addition, the factor structure has been cross-validated on other populations, including large representative U.S. samples and children with mental retardation or LDs. For further information, the reader is directed to the WISC-III manual (Wechsler, 1991). Finally, factor rotations indicate substantial loadings on the first factor, which support the construct of general intelligence (*g*) underlying the FSIQ (Kaufman & Lichtenberger, 2000).

Rapid Reference 6.26
Strengths and Weaknesses of the WISC-III

Strengths	Weaknesses
Excellent reliability.	Test-retest reliability for some subtests (Object Assembly, Mazes, and Picture Arrangement) is weak.
Excellent validity.	Some Verbal subtests may be unfair to ethnic groups (Hispanics, African Americans, and Native Americans) and children referred for learning disabilities.
Excellent norms.	Short forms are not recommended, because they are less stable.
Excellent manual with clearly written administrative procedures and scoring criteria.	Norms are limited with older teens; the WAIS-III may be more appropriate with 16- to 17-year-olds.
Excellent instrument for testing of intelligence and cognitive strengths and weaknesses.	Some subtests are difficult to score.
Appropriate for preteens and teens through 16 years and 11 months.	

SUMMARY

The WISC-III measures general, nonverbal, and verbal intelligence. Subtests can be used to assess cognitive strengths and weaknesses. The WISC-III has excellent reliability and validity. Common uses of the test are global measurement of intelligence as well as assessment of LDs, ADHD, giftedness, and mental retardation.

THE WIDE RANGE ACHIEVEMENT TEST–3 (WRAT3)

PURPOSE, USE, AND BRIEF DESCRIPTION

The Wide Range Achievement Test–3 (WRAT3) was originally designed in the 1930s by Jastack as an addition to the Wechsler-Bellevue scales (Wilkinson, 1994). Whereas the Wechsler tests were designed to test intelligence, the WRAT was designed to test academic codes by focusing on reading, spelling, and arithmetic. The WRAT3 manual, written by Wilkinson, states that the purpose of the WRAT3 is to "measure the codes which are needed to learn the basic skills of reading, spelling, and arithmetic" (Wilkinson, 1994, p. 10). The WRAT was originally an addition to the Wechsler scales. Both Wechsler and Jastack believed that cognitive functioning was multifaceted and that the best form of cognitive assessment is multiple measurement. For this reason, Jastack designed the WRAT to add tests of word recognition, spelling, and mathematical computations to the assessment of intelligence already measured by the Wechsler-Bellevue scales.

The WRAT3 is made up of three subtests: reading, spelling, and arithmetic. The reading test is word decoding, which involves recognizing letters, naming letters, and pronouncing letters out of context. It does not assess comprehension. The spelling test asks examinees to write their names and record words to dictation, and the arithmetic test requires counting, reading number symbols, solving oral problems, and performing written computations. Because the reading subtest measures exclusively decoding and *not* comprehension, when combined with another test, such as the WISC-III, the WRAT3 can be very helpful at isolating types of reading problem. In other words, the examiner can determine whether a reading problem is due to language mechanics (e.g., decoding) or to comprehension. This information can be very helpful in planning an instructional program. In addition, the examiner can observe and record the types of errors an individual makes, which can also be helpful in designing an educational plan.

The best uses of the WRAT3 are to provide an estimation of grade level, to assess learning disabilities, to identify coding errors, and to help plan an educational program. For teens who have been truant, the WRAT3 can help provide an estimation of grade placement.

ADMINISTRATION, SCORING, AND INTERPRETATION

Administration

The WRAT3 manual is clearly written, well organized, and easy to follow. The entire test takes approximately 30 min to administer and can be administered to individuals from ages 5 to 75. As always, the test examiner is advised to carefully read the test manual. Clear and specific directions are given on the administration and scoring of the exam. The WRAT3 consists of two equivalent forms, a BLUE form and a TAN form. Either form may be used.

The examiner begins by carefully filling in the examinee's personal data, including birth date and current school grade. Any one of the three subtests can be administered first; there is no required order. For the reading test, the examinee begins by reading 15 letters from the alphabet, followed by pronouncing a list of 42 words of increasing difficulty, beginning with *in*, through *collapse*, and up to terpsichorean. The individual is given 10 to respond and the test is discontinued after he or she has missed 10 consecutive words.

The spelling test begins with name and letter writing, in which the examinee is asked to write his or her name. This section is followed by dictation. The examinee is asked to spell 40 words dictated by the examiner. The words are administered by increasing difficulty, beginning with *and* and ending with *vicissitude*. Similar to a school spelling test, the words are spoken by the examiner and then stated in a sentence.

There are a total of 55 items on the arithmetic test. The arithmetic test begins with very simple questions designed for children as young as 5, such as counting ducks. The questions become progressively more difficult; they include addition, subtraction, multiplication, division, and finally algebra. This content is very similar to math processes taught in school. Fifteen minutes are allowed for the entire math test.

Scoring

Scoring is straightforward. One point is given for each correct answer. The points are totaled for a raw score. Using the manual, the raw scores are converted to standard scores, percentile ranks, grade scores, and absolute scores by age of the examinee. For this reason, it is critical that the examiner has the exact birth date of the individual taking the test.

Interpretation

WRAT3 results can be reported in the form of six types of scores. They are raw scores, absolute scores, standard scores, grade scores, percentiles, and normal curve equivalents. The scores have different measurement properties (i.e., nominal-, ordinal-, interval-, or ratio-level data) and different uses. The manual gives a thorough explanation of the different scores. The raw score gives the exact count of items an individual achieved correctly. This score is converted to absolute, standard, grade, and percentile scores. The standard scores are deviation scores. Each age group has a mean scale score of 100 and a standard deviation of 15. There are 32 age-group norms for standard scores. These standard scores are useful for comparing scores between test takers and between test administrations for the same individual. Grade scores and percentiles are useful for communicating scores to parents and teachers. The absolute score is an interval-level score and most likely used for research.

PSYCHOMETRIC PROPERTIES

Standardization Sample and Norms

The current revision of the WRAT3, published in 1994, is based on nearly 60 years of test construction. Two equivalent forms were designed, the BLUE and TAN forms, using tested items from previous editions of the WRAT. The WRAT3 was standardized in 1992–1993 using a normative sample that was nationally stratified by age, geography, gender, ethnicity, and SES. The data closely represent the composition of the United States as indicated by the 1990 U.S. Census.

Based on a sample of 4,433 subjects, approximately 51% of the sample is male and 49% female. Twenty-three age groups were used, ranging from 5 years to 75 years. Subjects were sampled from the Eastern, Western, Northern, and Southern parts of the United States. The sample is approximately 72% Euro-American, 14% African American, 11% Hispanic American, and 4% other. Regarding occupational representativeness, 25% of the sample is managerial and professional; 31% technical, sales, and administrative support; 13% precision production, craft, and repair; 15% operator, fabricators, and laborers; and 16% service, farming, and fishing occupations. Chi-square analyses were conducted to make sure that these frequencies were representative of the national sample. In general, the test authors were thorough in ensuring the best possible gender, ethnic, socioeconomic, and geographical representativeness. Considerable in-depth data and statistics are available in the test manual.

During normative testing, both the BLUE and TAN versions of the WRAT3 were administered to the total norm sample of 4,433 subjects. The correlations of the reading, spelling, and arithmetic sections were .98, .98, and .98 respectively. These data mean that the two versions are essentially equivalent and can be used and interpreted interchangeably.

Standard Error of Measurement

The WRAT3 manual presents in-depth data on the *SEM* and confidence intervals. Standard errors are presented for each age group and each subtest. An excellent explanation of the meaning and use of standard errors is also provided. For BLUE and TAN scores of Reading and Spelling, error scores of 5 are recommended. For BLUE and TAN scores of Arithmetic, an error score of 6 is recommended. The error scores are used to develop confidence intervals for obtained test scores. For example, it can be said with 68% confidence that a true score is within one SEM of the obtained scores and with 95% confidence that the true score is within 2 SEM.

Reliability

Four types of reliability coefficients were computed: coefficient alpha, alternate form, person separation, and test-retest. All of the reliability coefficients are high. Median alphas, which measure internal consistency, range from .85 to .95. Alternate form correlations, which compare the two versions, correlate .98, .98, and .98 for each of the subtests: Reading, Spelling, and Arithmetic. Person Separation indexes, another form of internal consistency, range from .98 to .99. Finally, the test-retest data computed on a sample of 142 individuals ages 6–16 ranged from .91 to .98.

Validity

The WRAT3 was designed to measure the basic academic skills of word recognition (written decoding), spelling from dictation (written encoding), and arithmetic computation. Several forms of validity are reported in the test manual to assess how well the test measures these constructs. In general, the test is valid and the measurement and presentation of data are

Rapid Reference 6.27
Wide Range Achievement Test–3 (WRAT3)

- The WRAT3 is designed for ages 5–75.
- The test requires 30 min administration time.
- The WRAT3 measures academic codes of reading, spelling, and arithmetic.
- The WRAT3 gives an estimate of grade level.
- It is a nice complement to the WISC-III.
- It is helpful in assessing coding errors and forming educational plans.
- Psychometric data is based on a representative sample of 4433 subjects.
- Test-retest reliability ranges from .91 to .98.
- Standard errors are available in the manual by age group.
- Construct validity coefficients with the CTBS are .69 (reading), .84 (spelling), and .80 (arithmetic).

impressive. Content validity is assessed by the degree of difficulty of the test items. Each subtest contains easy items, moderate items, and difficult items. The items are arranged by ascending level of difficulty.

The test manual offers several measures of construct validity. The most appropriate here are agreement with other standardized measures of academic achievement. WRAT3 scores were correlated with appropriate subtests on the California Test of Basic Skills–4th Edition (CTBS-4), the California Achievement Test Form E (CAT), and the Stanford Achievement Test (SAT). Using a sample of 46 school-aged children, the WRAT3 COMBINED (both forms) tests and the CTBS were compared. Reading on the CTBS correlated .69 with Reading on the WRAT3 COMBINED. Spelling on the CTBS correlated .84 with the WRAT3, and Arithmetic Computations correlated .80 with the WRAT3 Arithmetic score. Using a group of 49 school-aged children, correlations of the WRAT3 with the CAT are .72, .77, and .41 for Reading, Spelling, and Arithmetic, respectively. Finally, the WRAT3 and SAT correlate .87, .76, and .81 for reading, spelling, and arithmetic based on a sample of 31 school-aged children; these are all strong correlations in the predicated direction. It can be concluded that the WRAT3 is a valid measure of academic achievement. The test construction procedures, the presentation of data, and the explanation are all very thorough.

Rapid Reference 6.28
Strengths and Weaknesses of the WRAT3

Strengths

Brief assessment of arithmetic, reading, and spelling.

Very useful for identifying reading problems.

Helpful in assessing grade level with a truant teen.

Good reliability and validity.

Generally representative sample.

Weaknesses

Not a measure of reading comprehension; measures decoding only.

Caution

The WRAT3 is a brief screening tool for academic problems. It should be used in conjunction with the WISC-III and teacher report for a thorough academic and intellectual assessment.

SUMMARY

The WRAT3 is a brief screening for academic problems. The three subtests measure reading, spelling, and arithmetic. The most recent revision, 1994, was based on decades of sound scientific research. The standardization sample was large, and the reliability and validity are very good. When combined with the WISC-III, the WRAT3 is an excellent assessment of grade level, LDs, and academic code cracking. It is very useful for planning an academic program for a teen who has missed school.

WOODCOCK-JOHNSON III TESTS OF ACHIEVEMENT (WJ III ACH)

PURPOSE, USE, AND BRIEF DESCRIPTION

The Woodcock-Johnson III Tests of Achievement (WJ III ACH) is an individually administered test of academic achievement. It consists of 22 tests related to school skills, such as reading and math. The WJ III ACH and the WJ III COG together form the WJ III, which was updated in 2001 by Woodcock, McGrew, and Mather (2001). The new norms are nationally representative and stratified to control for important variables such as geographic region, SES, ethnicity, and sex. Combined, the WJ III ACH and the WJ III COG provide a battery of individually administered tests assessing general intellectual ability, specific cognitive abilities, oral language abilities, and achievement. Test batteries can be administered in their entirety or selectively, depending on the needs of the assessment. More in-depth information on the history, standardization, reliability, and validity of both batteries can be found in this book in the section on the WJ III COG or in the many publications by Woodcock or Mather (Mather, Wendling, & Woodcock, 2001; Woodcock et al., 2001).

The WJ III ACH consists of 22 tests that measure reading, math, written language, oral language, and academic knowledge. It includes six tests of reading that measure decoding, speed, comprehension, phonology and orthography, vocabulary, and sound awareness. The WJ III ACH contains four math tests. The math tests measure computation, math fluency, problem solving, and quantitative reasoning/math knowledge. Six tests are devoted to written language. They assess spelling, writing fluency, written expression, editing, phonological and orthographic coding, punctuation/capitalization, and handwriting. There are five oral language tests, which measure listening/memory, understanding directions, word knowledge, oral comprehension, and story recall. The final category is academic knowledge, and it assesses acquired knowledge in the areas of science, social studies, and humanities.

The WJ III ACH tests can be administered as a complete battery or as selected tests depending on the purpose of the assessment. They can be used to measure general intelligence (*g*) or learning disabilities; their best use, however, probably is the assessment of academic strengths and weaknesses and educational planning.

Rapid Reference 6.29
Woodcock-Johnson III Tests of Achievement (WJ III ACH)

- The WJ III ACH is an individually administered test of achievement.
- It is designed for use with ages 2–95 years.
- The WJ III ACH takes approximately 60–75 min to administer.
- The WJ III ACH consists of 22 tests measuring reading, math, written language, oral language, and academic knowledge.
- The test battery may be administered in its entirety or selectivity, depending on the purpose of the assessment.

ADMINISTRATION, SCORING, AND INTERPRETATION

The WJ III tests are complex and require practice and training to administer and interpret. The test publisher, Riverside Publishing Company, provides excellent workshops and written training materials. The age range for administration is 2–95 years. The administration time for the Standard Battery is 60–75 min, and when the Standard Battery is combined with the Extended Battery, the test takes approximately 90 min. Individual administration of selected tests takes about 5–10 min per test. Scoring is done electronically with software purchased from the test publisher. More details on administration can be found in the WJ III COG section in this book and the examiner's manual accompanying the WJ III (Mather & Woodcock, 2001).

PSYCHOMETRIC PROPERTIES

Because the WJ III ACH and the WJ III COG were conormed on the same population, psychometric properties of the WJ III ACH are explained in the section on the WJ III COG.

WOODCOCK-JOHNSON III TESTS OF COGNITIVE ABILITIES (WJ III COG)

PURPOSE, USE, AND BRIEF DESCRIPTION

The Woodcock-Johnson III Tests of Cognitive Abilities (WJ III COG; Woodcock et al., 2001) measure cognitive abilities and cognitive functions. When the WJ III COG is combined with the WJ III ACH, the two batteries provide an overview of cognitive abilities, oral language, and achievement. Eight new tests assessing information processing were added to the 2001 version.

The original version of the Woodcock-Johnson was called the Woodcock-Johnson Psychoeducational Battery (1977) and consisted of three parts: a test of cognitive abilities, a test of achievement, and a test of interests. The test was atheoretical at first and based on experiments testing the ability to learn to read (Schrank et al., 2002). Woodcock began his career as an elementary school teacher, then was a school psychologist, and later became a director of special education, director of reading, and university professor. His early experience as a teacher explains the emphasis on reading and achievement in his tests. The WJ tests were devised by and for educators and have always been widely used in educational circles. Over the years, the battery became further refined. Theory was developed and factor analyses were conducted to test empirical validity (Schrank et al., 2002).

The 2001 version of the WJ III is based on factor analyses of previous versions and the Cattell-Horn-Carroll (CHC) theory. This theory is made up of three strata. The first stratum consists of narrow abilities, such as general information, spatial relations, sequencing, memory, and several other abilities. The second stratum is broader and made up of comprehension-knowledge, visual-spatial thinking, processing speed, and other broad abilities; and the third stratum is a general intellectual ability (GIA) factor. The narrow abilities are tested by subtests that combine into empirically valid factors.

The WJ III COG consists of 20 tests in two parts: a standard battery and an extended battery. The Standard Battery is made up of Tests 1–10, and the Extended Battery is made up of Tests 11–20. The 20 tests are verbal comprehension, visual-auditory learning, spatial relations, sound blending, concept formation, visual matching, numbers reversed, incomplete words, auditory working memory, visual-auditory learning-delayed, general information, retrieval fluency, picture recognition, auditory atten-

Rapid Reference 6.30
Woodcock-Johnson III Tests of Cognitive Abilities (WJ III COG)

- The WJ III COG is an individually administered test of cognitive abilities and cognitive function.
- It is suitable for use with ages 2 to 95 years.
- Separate norms exist for college students.
- The WJ III COG takes approximately 60–75 min to administer.
- The WJ III COG combined with the WJ ACH provide an overview of cognitive abilities, oral language, and achievement.
- The WJ III COG consists of 20 subtests in two parts: a standard battery and an extended battery.
- The test battery may be administered in its entirety or selectively, depending on the purpose of the assessment.

tion, analysis-synthesis, decision speed, memory for words, rapid picture naming, planning, and pair cancellation. Not all tests need to be given at every administration. Selective testing is advised, and tables to assist with the selection of tests for specific problems can be found in both the test manual and in *Essentials of WJ III Cognitive Abilities Assessment* (Schrank et al., 2002).

One of the unique characteristics of the WJ III is discrepancy scores. Although definitions of LDs are controversial, one traditional definition has been the ability-achievement discrepancy (Schrank et al., 2002). Several types of discrepancy scores are computed by the WJ III Compuscore computer software. They are intra-achievement, intracognitive, intra-individual, GIA/ACH, Oral Language/Achievement, and Predicted Achievement/Achievement discrepancy scores. These scores are based on WJ III norms and expressed in standard deviations and percentile ranks. Schrank et al. (2002) recommend caution in interpreting the discrepancy scores because the presence of a discrepancy does not automatically indicate the presence of an LD. Diagnosing an LD is complex and the educational field is in flux. According to some experts, current definitions of LDs are moving away from the ability-achievement model and toward domain-specific processes. Describing patterns of domain-specific strengths and weaknesses is an attribute of the WJ test batteries.

A major goal of the WJ III revision is to increase breadth and decrease reliance on the interpretation of narrow test abilities. Toward this end, narrow tests were organized into clusters. Test interpretation of clusters reduces the danger of overgeneralization from narrow specific abilities on one test to broad multifaceted abilities such as knowledge-comprehension.

ADMINISTRATION, SCORING, AND INTERPRETATION

Administration

The WJ III COG was normed on individuals from 2 to 90 years. Some of the tests are therefore appropriate for children as young as 2 years old. All of the tests can be administered to individuals from 5 to 95 years of age. Separate norms exist for college students. Some subtests take as little as 5 min to administer. The standard battery takes approximately 40 min, and the complete battery can take up to 2 hours.

Administration of the WJ III takes practice and experience. Reliability and validity depend on standardized administration. The Test Book comes in an easy-to-use easel format with very clear directions. Directions are provided on exact wording, eye contact, props, and probing. Correct answers for Spanish speakers are included. Some tests require a stopwatch or audiotape and headphones. It is important that the test examiner practice giving the tests prior to administration so that he or she is familiar with the procedures and can move smoothly through the battery. Certain tests have basal and ceiling criteria. These criteria are explained in the Test Book for each test. In addition to quantitative behavior obtained from the 20 tests, the Test Record provides a checklist to help the examiner record testing behavior. The observation checklist is very helpful and includes observations of spoken language, cooperation, attention-concentration, self-confidence, and attitude.

Scoring

Test item scores are calculated by the test examiner and entered on the test record. Clear and specific guidelines for scoring can be found in the WJ III testing materials and the *Essentials of WJ III Cognitive Abilities Assessment* (Schrank et al., 2002). These are then transferred to the WJ III Compuscore and Profiles Program (WJ III CPP; Schrank & Woodcock, 2001). The necessary computer software is included with the test kit. The computer program provides several scores, including General Intellectual Ability (GIA), standard scores with confidence bands, percentile ranks,

Rapid Reference 6.31
Administration and Scoring of the WJ III

- The WJ III ACH and WJ III COG can be administered to individuals from 5 to 95 years of age.
- The Standard Battery takes 40 min to 2 hours.
- Administration takes practice and experience.
- Some subtests have basal and ceiling criteria.
- The Test Book must be followed closely to ensure reliability and validity.
- Test item scores are calculated by the examiner and transferred to the WJ III CPP, which comes with the test kit.
- The WJ III CPP provides several test scores, including GIA, standard scores with confidence bands, percentile ranks, instructional ranges, discrepancy scores, a relative proficiency index, and a BIA score.

instructional ranges, discrepancy scores, a Relative Proficiency Index, and a Brief Intellectual Ability (BIA) score.

Interpretation

Like administration, interpretation of the WJ III is not simple. It takes training and experience. The test provides measures of general intelligence, specific cognitive abilities, discrepancy scores, and normative comparisons. These indexes are valuable and can be of use to parents and teachers as well as for diagnostic and remedial educational purposes. However, they require advanced training in psychometrics to interpret appropriately.

PSYCHOMETRIC PROPERTIES

An entire book is devoted to the psychometric properties of the WJ III. It is titled the *Woodcock-Johnson III Technical Manual* and provides in-depth explanations of test development, standardization sample, norms, reliability, and validity (McGrew & Woodcock, 2001). Decades of empirical research have been conducted on the WJ III. The Technical Manual is very clearly written, explains testing concepts, and provides valuable information on the factor structure of the tests. Students as well as experienced practitioners are advised to read the Technical Manual.

Standardization Sample

The WJ III was normed on a large nationally representative sample (Mc-Grew & Woodcock, 2001). Both the WJ III COG and the WJ III ACH were conormed on the same sample. The sample consisted of 8,818 individuals and was designed to approximate the 2000 U.S. Census. The sampling procedure was very thorough. Subjects were randomly selected from a stratified sample controlling for several community and subject variables such as geographic region, community size, sex, race, Hispanic origins, type of school, type of college or university, and educational-occupational status of adults. There were 1,143 preschool children, 4,783 K–12 students, 1,165 college and university students, and 1,843 adults.

Reliability

Internal consistency for the WJ III tests is high. A split-half reliability coefficient is used to measure internal consistency. The median internal consistency reliability coefficient across age groups for the GIA standard battery is .97 (median SEM = 2.60), and the internal consistency reliability coefficient for the GIA extended battery is .98 (median SEM = 2.12). Cluster score internal consistency reliability coefficients are in the high 80s or 90s, with SEMs ranging from 3.35 to 6.54. The subtest internal consistency reliabilities for the WJ III COG tests range from .76 to .97, and the reliabilities for the WJ III ACH tests range from .81 to .94. It can safely be concluded that the WJ III subtests are homogeneous and internally consistent.

The presentation of test-retest reliability scores for the WJ III in the Technical Manual is sketchy. For only 5 of the currently in-use 20 WJ III COG subtests are any data presented. Reliability statistics for the most widely tested age group (8–18 years) and the shortest testing interval (less than 1 year) is based on only 68 subjects, which is a combined cohort of children 8 through 18. The presented test-retest reliabilities are good (from .69 to .86), but clearly there is a need for more data on more subtests with larger samples and more subjects per age group.

More test-retest data are presented for ACH tests. Data are reported on 17 selected ACH tests and 12 ACH clusters, with sample sizes varying from 74 to 104 students depending on the test. The median test-retest reliability for adolescents aged 11–13 on the 17 ACH tests at 1-year intervals is .76 (range = .58–.89). The median test-retest reliability for adolescents aged 14–17 years is .76 (range = .60–.92). Test-retest reliability is also presented on 12 ACH clusters. The median test-retest reliability for the 11–13 age group is .88 (range = .80–.95). Moreover, finally the median test-retest reliability for the 14–17 age group is .89 (range = .79–.96).

Validity

The Technical Manual devotes an entire chapter to the topic of test validity. Four types of test validity are presented: test content, developmental patterns of scores, internal structure, and convergent validity. Considerable validity evidence has been presented on the WJ III tests from the WJ and WJ-R versions of the test as well (McGrew & Woodcock, 2001).

To ensure content validity, COG test items were selected to sample the major abilities of CHC theory. To ensure content validity of the ACH test items, items were selected to sample oral language and academic achievement. All of the items were reviewed by experts, such as teachers and psychologists. Finally, statistical techniques were employed to make sure the tests were homogeneous and did not tap unrelated error variance (McGrew & Woodcock, 2001).

Additional validity evidence is based on developmental patterns of clusters and tests. These data are summarized in growth pattern graphs. The data are cross-sectional, not longitudinal, and compare the performance of different cohorts of the ages of 5 years to 90 years. Even though the graphs are based on cross-sectional data, the developmental patterns over the life span are consistent with theory and previous research (McGrew & Woodcock, 2001). In general, most test scores increase and peak in early adulthood. Tests of speed, such as perceptual processing, increase more rapidly and decline faster. Only tests of verbal abilities such as knowledge, comprehension, and information continue to increase and plateau well into midlife and maturity. Because the developmental pattern is consistent with the research literature on cognitive abilities, brain development, and aging, these data are used as evidence of test validity (McGrew & Woodcock, 2001).

Further validity evidence is presented in the form of confirmatory factor analyses (CFA). Factor analyses and path models were created to test the CHC theory of broad factors, narrow abilities, and g. Factor loadings provide evidence for nine broad factors, as predicted by CHC theory and previous research. The strongest factor loadings are for comprehension-knowledge, quantitative, reading-writing, and long-term retrieval. All nine factors load on g. Three statistical tests of goodness of fit were conducted to empirically test the path models (McGrew & Woodcock, 2001).

Rapid Reference 6.32
Psychometric Properties of the WJ III ACH and the WJ III COG

- The WJ III is based on the CHC theory and extensive empirical research.
- The WJ III revision is based on a nationally representative normative sample of 8,818 individuals.
- The standardization sample approximates the 2000 U.S. Census. African Americans, Hispanic Americans, and Asian Americans are appropriately represented.
- Test-retest reliabilities are high, with a median test-retest reliability of .76 for adolescents aged 14–17 at 1-year retest interval.
- Considerable validity data is presented in the WJ III technical manual. Evidence of content and convergent validity as well as developmental patterns and factor analyses are presented.
- The WJ III cluster of comprehension-knowledge (Gc) correlation with the WISC-III VIQ equals .79.
- WJ III reading comprehension correlates .81 with the reading composite on the K-TEA.
- WJ III tests of math calculation skill correlates .67 with mathematics computation on the K-TEA.

Rapid Reference 6.33
Strengths and Weaknesses of the WJ III

Strengths

The WJ III is widely used in education.

Specific tests measure many academic ability and cognitive functions.

A nationally representative sample was used.

A strong theoretical and empirical foundation exists.

The computer profile offers many useful tests, including discrepancy scores.

Weaknesses

Version III needs more test-retest reliability research.

Final evidence of validity comes from convergent validity correlations with similar tests. Evidence for a strong verbal factor comes from the convergent validity of the WJ III cluster of Comprehension-Knowledge (Gc) with the WISC-III verbal IQ ($r = .79$). Fluid reasoning correlates .72 with General Conceptual Ability on the DAS Composites. WJ III Reading Comprehension correlates .81 with the Reading composite on the Kaufman Test of Educational Achievement (K-TEA) and the WJ III test of Academic skills correlates .70 with the Battery Composite on the KTEA. WJ III tests of Broad Math correlate .70 with the BCP on the K-TEA. Moreover, WJ III test of Math Calculation Skills correlates .67 with Mathematics Computation on the K-TEA. These convergent validities are all strong and in the predicted direction.

In sum, considerable work has been devoted to testing the empirical reliability and validity of the WJ III. Although there is still a need for more test-retest reliability, it can safely be concluded that the WJ III is a strong test both theoretically and empirically.

SUMMARY

The WJ III is an impressive test. It is designed specifically to assess cognitive abilities and achievement patterns. It has been widely used to diagnose learning disabilities. Its best uses, however, are for the assessment of individual academic strengths and weaknesses and for educational planning. The most recent version is based on a carefully selected, nationally representative sample.

The WJ III combines CHC theory with empirical tests of validity. It represents the best of theory, empirical research, and test construction. Still, it is a test and because it is so widely used it should be interpreted cautiously. Administering and scoring the test take training and practice. APA ethical guidelines recommend advanced training in statistics and measurement theory to interpret most psychological tests. No single test score should ever be interpreted in isolation, and all assessments should rely on multimethod techniques. Assessments of LDs should be made by teams of teachers, psychologists, and other professionals.

Appendix A

—————— ◆ ——————

Common Adolescent Tests and Their Best Uses

—— ◆ ——

Name of Test	Best Use
Achenbach System of Empirically Based Assessment (ASEBA)	Multimethod (parent, teacher, and teen) observational assessment of attention and conduct problems
Beck Depression Inventory–Second Edition (BDI-II)	Quick screening for depression and suicide
Conners' Rating Scales–Revised (CRS-R)	ADHD, oppositional behavior; rating scales by parent, teacher, and teen
Goodenough-Harris Drawing Test	Warm-up, rapport builder; clinical insight into family and self-perception
MacAndrew Alcoholism Scale–Revised (MAC-R)	Alcohol and substance abuse
Millon Adolescent Clinical Inventory (MACI)	*DSM-IV* diagnostic hypotheses; clinical adolescents, eating disorders, and family problems

Minnesota Multiphasic Personality Inventory–Adolescent (MMPI-A)	*DSM-IV* diagnostic hypotheses; conflict with authority, family problems; substance abuse, depression; response style scales
Rotter Incomplete Sentences Blank (RISB)	Warm-up, rapport builder; screening for personality adjustment
Strong Interest Inventory (SII)	Educational and vocational interests
Wescheler Intelligence Scale for Children–Third Edition (WISC-III)	General intelligence, verbal intelligence, nonverbal intelligence; learning disabilities; mental retardation
Wide Range Achievement Test–3 (WRAT3)	Brief screening for academic problems, grade level, LD, reading, spelling, and arithmetic
Woodcock-Johnson III (ACH)	In-depth assessment of academic codes, such as reading, math, written and oral language; good assessment of academic strengths and weaknesses for creating an educational plan
Woodcock-Johnson III (COG)	Cognitive abilities and cognitive functions; often used with the WJ III to assess learning disabilities

Appendix B

Diagnostic Issues and Suggested Tests

TEST NAME						
	ASEBA	BDI-II	CRS-R	Goodenough-Harris	MAC-R	MACI	MMPI-A
Problem							
Abuse		X				X	X
Academic Problem							
ADD/ADHD	X		X				
Alienation							X
Anxiety	X		X			X	X
Body Image				X		X	
Clinical Insight				X			X
Career Interests							
Cognitive Problems/ Inattention	X		X				
Conduct Disorder/ Delinquency	X		X			X	X
Depression	X	X				X	X
Eating Disorders						X	
Family Problems				X		X	X
Identity/ Self-Concept				X		X	X
Intelligence							
Learning Disabilities							
Oppositional/ Defiant	X		X			X	X
Peer Relations	X					X	X
Psychoses						X	X
Rapport		X		X			
Sexual Issues						X	X
School Problems	X						
Social Problems	X		X	X		X	X
Somatic Symptoms	X		X	X		X	
Substance Use Disorders					X	X	X
Suicide		X				X	
Test Taking Attitudes						X	X
Thought Disorder	X						X

TEST NAME					
	Rotter RISB	**Strong SII**	**WISC-III**	**WRAT3**	**WJ III**
Problem					
Abuse			X	X	X
Academic Problem					
ADD/ADHD					
Alienation					
Anxiety					
Body Image	X				
Clinical Insight	X				
Career Interests		X			
Cognitive Problems/ Inattention			X		X
Conduct Disorder/ Delinquency					
Depression	X				
Eating Disorders					
Family Problems					
Identity/ Self-Concept	X				
Intelligence			X		X
Learning Disabilities			X		X
Oppositional/ Defiant					
Peer Relations					
Psychoses					
Rapport	X				
Sexual Issues					
School Problems					
Social Problems	X				
Somatic Symptoms					
Substance Use Disorders					

Appendix C

Case Studies, Suggested Test Batteries, and Rationales

The following case studies are fictitious examples designed to illustrate how psychological tests might be used. The main purpose of the case studies is to demonstrate the features of specific tests in helping to clarify diagnostic issues. For example, administering a MACI might help clarify the absence or presence of an eating disorder. Themes common among adolescents (e.g., depression, poor grades, smoking pot, etc.) form the basis of the case studies. The case studies are also intended as practice in formulating diagnostic hypotheses for students. Diagnostic hypotheses are educated guesses about what a particular client's problem or issue might be. As hypotheses, they need to be tested and—if necessary—revised.

The sample test batteries were designed with several considerations in mind. First, the tests are listed in order of suggested administration, frequently beginning with a warm-up tool like a Rotter. Second, recognize that some teenagers are more receptive to testing than are others. A curious college student may be enthusiastic about taking many tests, whereas an incarcerated youth may be oppositional about taking any tests at all. The suggested batteries are only suggestions, and many other tests may be appropriate.

Remember that the case studies that follow are an academic exercise. The cases are completely fictitious, and the application of diagnoses, testing, and rationales are for the purposes of reasoning and applying psychological principles.

CASE STUDY: DEPRESSION

Presenting problem: possible depression, falling school grades, withdrawal, crying

REFERRAL SOURCE

Kristy (15) is referred by her school counselor because her grades have dropped dramatically, she cries a lot, she is spending a lot of time in her bedroom alone, and she is fighting viciously with her mother.

BACKGROUND HISTORY

Kristy is an attractive, healthy, and polite 15-year-old girl. Kristy has changed schools frequently since she was 8 years old. The longest she has ever been at one school is 3 years. She is friendly and gregarious but complains that the other kids "won't let her in" at her new high school.

Kristy's mother is divorced. The mother uses Kristy to send messages back and forth to the father. Kristy's father has remarried and has a "new family." She rarely sees her father. Kristy's mother was raised in wealthy circumstances and the divorce has caused her and her children considerable economic hardship. Kristy's mother did not finish college and has never been employed. Her mother spends her days watching TV and smoking cigarettes. She doesn't get dressed in the morning, go to the market, cook, or clean. Kristy doesn't want to bring friends home.

One night about 4 months ago, Kristy went into her mother's bedroom for help with a homework assignment. Kristy found her mother in bed, surrounded by empty pill bottles, and was unable to awaken her. Scared, Kristy called the paramedics. At the hospital, none of the medical personnel would explain to Kristy what happened. Kristy returned home to care for her younger sister while her mother was hospitalized.

Kristy scores high on standardized tests. Prior to her parents' separation and divorce, she was good student, but she is no longer interested in school. Her math teacher threatened to tell her father that she was "underachieving." She told the teacher that her father doesn't care about her. She feels that school is pointless and spends most of her time staring out of the window or doodling.

At home, Kristy spends most of her time in her bedroom. When she tries to study, her mother ridicules her and tells her that she is wasting her time thinking about college and will only end up pregnant before she graduates anyway. She listens to music, cries a lot, daydreams, sleeps a lot, and talks to friends on the phone.

DIAGNOSTIC HYPOTHESES

Assess for Major Depressive Disorder (296.2x, p. 327), Dysthymic Disorder (300.4, p. 349), Adjustment Disorder with Depressed Mood (309.0, p. 626), Bereavement (V62.82, p. 684), and Suicidal Ideation.

SUGGESTED TEST BATTERY AND RATIONALE

- RISB—Warm-up, rapport, clinical insight
- BDI-II—Quick screening for severity of depression and suicide
- MMPI-A—Depression, Scales 1, 2, 3; Harris and Lingoes (1955) scoring of Scale 4 (*Pd*) contains several items sensitive to family discord, authority problems, social alienation, and self-alienation; content scales: adolescent depression, adolescent family problems, adolescent school problems
- WISC-III—Assess intelligence
- WRAT3—Measure current academic level
- SII—Assess interests, plan educational and career goals

CASE STUDY: CHILD ABUSE

Presenting problem: physical abuse, neglect, possible sexual abuse, academic problems

REFERRAL SOURCE

Sarah is hospitalized for medical injuries secondary to abuse. You are a hospital psychologist and she is referred to you by the medical team.

BACKGROUND HISTORY

Sarah (13) was neglected and abused as a child. Her mother was unable to take care of her and frequently left her alone or in the care of her grandmother. The grandmother lived nearby and was a stable force in Sarah's life. Unfortunately, the grandmother passed away recently.

Sarah's mother has an inconsistent employment history and is unable to provide for the family. She has worked as a waitress and temp worker but can't keep a regular job. There was rarely food in the home. Sarah would borrow money from neighbors to buy peanut butter to feed her younger sister. Sarah's younger sister is deaf and blind. Sarah's mother frequently relied on Sarah to care for her little sister. She even kept Sarah home from school to take care of her. Sarah feels a tremendous responsibility for her younger sister. The school states that her attendance is poor and that she is about 2–3 years behind in school.

Recently, Sarah's mother has been bringing a boyfriend home. Late one night, Sarah heard the two fighting. She came in the room to try to protect her mother. The boyfriend grabbed Sarah, threw her against the wall, and beat her up. There was so much noise, the neighbors called the police.

The police had Sarah hospitalized and her sister placed in a temporary shelter. Sarah feels guilty and responsible for the police's coming and taking away her deaf and blind sister. She feels as if she failed to take care of her sister properly. Sarah misses her sister terribly and feels very guilty.

DIAGNOSTIC HYPOTHESES

Posttraumatic Stress Disorder (PTSD) (309.81, p. 427), Acute Stress Disorder (308.3, p. 431), Physical Abuse of a Child (V61.21, p. 682), Sexual Abuse of child (V61.21, p. 682), Neglect of a child (V61.21, p. 682), Academic Problems (V62.3, p. 685).

SUGGESTED TEST BATTERY AND RATIONALE

- Goodenough-Harris Drawing Test—Warm-up, trust, safety, rapport, clinical insight into family
- MACI—Assess abuse, Scale H: Childhood Abuse, especially Items 14, 72, 129, 137
- MMPI-A—*A-fam* (Adolescent Family Problems) correlates with sex-

ual abuse for girls and physical abuse for boys; *A-ang* (Adolescent-Anger); *A-lse* (Adolescent-Low-Self-Esteem)

- WISC-III—Assess intelligence and intellectual abilities; form an education plan
- WRAT3—Assess grade placement
- WJ III—Assess for learning disabilities and form an educational plan

CASE STUDY: BIPOLAR, SUBSTANCE ABUSE, ACADEMIC PROBLEMS, SUICIDAL IDEATION

Presenting problem: failing grades, substance abuse, possible bipolar disorder, risk for suicide

REFERRAL SOURCE

Kevin is referred to the college counseling center by the college provost due to his poor academic record and because of his drinking.

BACKGROUND HISTORY

Kevin (18) became very sad and morbid and told his friends that he no longer felt like living after his girlfriend broke up with him. He told his friends that first his mother left him, then his girlfriend left him. He has no reason to live. Kevin is a freshman in college. He was admitted to college with very high test scores, but his performance in class has been dismal. He is failing most of his classes and is on academic probation. He stays up very late at night with his friends drinking, taking drugs, watching movies, and listening to music. During the night, he draws. He draws pictures of women and clocks. The drawings are dark, bloody, and reminiscent of Freida Kahlo and Salvidore Dali. He sleeps most of the next day and has stopped going to class.

Kevin has been in love with his girlfriend, Katie, since ninth grade. They attended the same high school and college. In high school, she was very popular and he worshiped her. She was not interested in him because he was so weird and negative. Due to his persistence, they connected at the beginning of their freshman year in college. When they got together, he was elated. He stayed up all night writing poems and drawing her portrait. He rarely slept or ate and raced through his math assignments. He was very possessive of her and would not let her out of his sight. She felt as if she couldn't even visit friends or go to the library to study.

Due to a contraceptive failure, Katie got pregnant. She doesn't feel ready to get married and raise a family. She wants an abortion. Kevin's reaction to the pregnancy was to become obsessed with himself. He is worried about what his father will do to him when he finds out that he impregnated Katie. Kevin writes morbid poetry and accuses her of killing his baby. Kevin does not offer to help Katie with money. He also does not provide any emotional support. Moreover, he is preventing Katie from studying and seeing her friends. After many discussions, Katie feels as though she has no choice but to break up with Kevin.

DIAGNOSTIC HYPOTHESES

Bipolar II Disorder (296.89, p. 359), Alcohol Abuse (305.00, p. 196), Alcohol Dependence (303.90, p. 195), Substance Dependence (p. 176), Substance Abuse (p. 182).

ASSESSMENT PROCESS

- Start with suicide assessment (see Appendix B and Chapter 3).
- Refer Kevin for a medical exam and possible medication.
- Collect previous psychological evaluations.
- Contact Kevin's parents.

SUGGESTED TEST BATTERY AND RATIONALE

- Goodenough-Harris Drawing Test—Warm-up, rapport, clinical insight; Kevin is creative and likes drawing.
- BDI-II—Quick screening for depression and suicide
- MAC-R—Assess for alcohol and substance abuse
- MMPI-A—Depression (Scales 1, 2, 3) and Hypomania (Scale 9); Supplementary scales: ACK (Alcohol and Drug Problem Acknowledgement), PRO (Alcohol and Drug Problem Proneness)

- MACI—Rule out Axis II Personality Disorders: Doleful (Depression), Sensitive (Self-Defeating), Confident (Narcissistic), Unruly (Antisocial), Boderline tendencies, GG suicidal tendencies
- SII—Assess interests, form educational plan, and get teen on a career track

CASE STUDY: EATING DISORDER

Presenting problem: Losing weight, picking at food

REFERRAL SOURCE

Mother and aunt

BACKGROUND HISTORY

Ruthie (16) is a very high achiever and a leader at her high school. She is a cheerleader, on student government and maintains a 4.0 grade point average. She also has a part-time job on Saturdays working in a clothing store. The store sells the latest fashions, is filled with local teens, and broadcasts MTV on monitors throughout the store.

Ruthie's mother describes her as a "perfect" child. She has always been pleasant, eager to please, and helpful. Ruthie is the oldest child and helps a lot with her younger brothers and sisters. She cooks, cleans, feeds the babies, changes diapers, and sings and reads stories to her younger siblings. Recently, Ruthie's mother noticed that Ruthie's clothes were getting too big. Her mother asked her whether she was losing weight. Ruthie said that she was not. At the dinner table, Ruthie's mom noticed that Ruthie just picks at her food. Her mother fixes her favorite foods and tries to get Ruthie to eat, but Ruthie just runs off to her bedroom and says that she has to study. When her mother asked her whether anything was wrong, Ruthie said that she was just stressed out about getting into the right college, maintaining high grades, and taking her SATs. Ruthie insists that nothing is wrong.

Ruthie's mother saw a TV show on anorexia and got worried. She called her sister, a social worker, and asked her about it. The social worker suggested Ruthie and her mom seek professional help.

DIAGNOSTIC HYPOTHESES

Anorexia Nervosa (307.1, p. 544), Obsessive-Compulsive Disorder (300.3, p. 422), Self-Acceptance, Self-Esteem, and Self-Worth issues

SUGGESTED TEST BATTERY AND RATIONALE

- RISB—Warm-up, rapport builder, clinical insight into self-esteem, identity issues, fears, attitudes, likes, dislikes
- MACI—Scale C (Body Disapproval), Scale AA (Eating Dysfunctions)
- MMPI-A—Scale 2 (Depression) contains several descriptors for adolescent girls (e.g., eating problems, low self-esteem); *A-anx* (Adolescent-Anxiety), *A-obs* (Adolescent-Obsessiveness), *A-hea* (Adolescent-Health), *A-sod* (Adolescent-Social Discomfort); Items 30, 108, 408
- Goodenough-Harris Drawing Test—Nonthreatening way to wrap up battery, insight into body image

CASE STUDY: ATTENTION, CONDUCT, AND LEARNING PROBLEMS

Presenting problem: dyslexia, disrupts class, fights with peers

REFERRAL SOURCE

The school referred Jason (14) to private counseling for ADHD, fighting at school, poor grades, and parenting skills.

BACKGROUND HISTORY

Jason is 14 and in the seventh grade. He had a very difficult time learning to read and was held back in first grade. When he was little he was always hurting other children. His mother is very social. She took him to several play groups as a toddler, but the friendships never lasted long because he hit and bit the other children. The other mothers began to avoid Jason's mother. When Jason was 3, his mother gave birth to a little girl. Enamored with her daughter, Jason's mom left him with the nanny. Jason's mother spent her time playing tennis; going out to lunch with friends; and attending fashion shows, charity balls, and play groups with her daughter. Jason spent his time at home with the nanny.

When Jason started school, he began to have problems. Although he was athletic, none of the boys would play with him. They either got beat up or ended up in trouble with the teacher. Jason was very disruptive to the kindergarten and first-grade class. The teacher referred him to the school counselor, who met with the parents and suggested that he be tested, placed in a special school, and referred to a psychiatrist for Ritalin. Jason's first-grade teacher thought he was dyslexic and had ADHD.

Meanwhile, Jason's mother and father are getting divorced. She says that it is because they come from different social backgrounds. He is a plumber and wants her to live on his income. He wants to be the head of household. She has inherited considerable wealth. They live in a gated neighborhood in a house purchased by her father. Jason's father feels uncomfortable with most of the neighbors, and his mother complains about the plumbing truck parked in her front yard. She expects her husband to attend her charity balls. These differences were a source of constant conflict and have resulted in a divorce.

Jason's problems are now coming to a head at the end of seventh grade. He has made a poor adjustment to middle school. His grades are poor, the teachers don't like him, and he fights a lot. He has only one friend. This friend is new to the school and is also frequently in trouble.

DIAGNOSTIC HYPOTHESES

Attention-Deficit/Hyperactivity Disorder (ADHD) (314.00, p. 83), Conduct Disorder (312.8, p. 85), rule out Substance Abuse (p. 182), Reading Disorder (315.00, p. 50), Disorder of Written Expression (315.2, p. 53), Parent-Child Relational Problem (V61.20, 62.81, p. 681), Peer Relational Problem (V62.81, p. 681), Low self-esteem.

ASSESSMENT PROCESS

- Contact teachers and school regarding academic and social behavior.
- Collect previous reports from schools, doctors, and therapists, including medical history and medication.
- Get developmental history from parents.

- Refer for current medical exam.
- Perform an informal assessment for LD (Sattler, 2001).

SUGGESTED TEST BATTERY AND RATIONALE

- ASEBA—Teacher and parent observations of attention and conduct problems
- Goodenough-Harris Drawing Test—Warm-up, rapport, clinical insight into self-esteem and family relations
- CRS-R—Feedback and observations by teachers and parents on attention, concentration, impulsivity, and behavior
- MAC-R, MMPI-A—Rule out Substance Abuse, Scale 4 (*Pd*) pulls for conflict with family and authority; content scales: *A-ang* (Adolescent-Ang), *A-con* (Adolescent-Conduct Problems), *A-lse* (Adolescent-Low Self-Esteem), *A-fam* (Adolescent-Family Problems), *A-sch* (Adolescent-School)
- WISC-III—Assess intelligence, assess ability-achievement discrepancy for learning disability, identify weaknesses and learning style to prepare an educational plan, carefully review profile and subtests (ACID) (Arithmetic, Coding, Digit Span, and Information)
- WRAT3—Assess ability-achievement discrepancy for learning disability, gauge school level, assess reading decoding, check spelling
- WJ III—Assess for LDs, assess academic strengths and weaknesses, form an educational plan

CASE STUDY: CONDUCT DISORDER, ANTI-SOCIAL BEHAVIOR

Presenting problem: stealing, possible shooting, conflict with authority

REFERRAL SOURCE

Juvenile justice system, court-ordered evaluation.

BACKGROUND HISTORY

Gerald (17), an African American, has been in juvenile detention for 2 years. He was accused of stealing a car and shooting someone. He was identified from a photograph and insists he didn't do the shooting. He says he tried to steal the car but that he didn't shoot anybody. Gerald claims that "he's a thief but *not* a killer." According to Gerald, the police are out to get him. He is extremely angry. Putting him in jail has only given him more contacts and made him madder. Gerald says he knows how to play the game and follows the rules in jail. In fact, he has a very good record during the past 2 years and is very cooperative. While he was in juvenile hall, his grades have been all As and Bs.

Growing up, Gerald never had a chance. He had no mother and his dad was in and out of jail. Gerald's father is a thief and taught Gerald and Gerald's older brother his trade. During the periods when his father was in jail, Gerald lived with his grandmother or aunt. The aunt and grandmother are brokenhearted and say that Gerald would never shoot anybody. They are not aware of any guns in the house. Gerald's family is well liked, attends church regularly, and has lived in the same community for two generations. They have a lot of friends and are well respected. Previous reports from Gerald's teachers say that he was a very nice boy who got in with the wrong crowd. His grades were average and his school attendance inconsistent. The community in which Gerald lives has a history of conflict with the police. Members of the community feel that they cannot depend on the police to protect them and that the police are out to get them. They feel that they have to defend themselves from the police.

Gerald's first conflict with the police took place when he was 13. He was working in a grocery store after school to save money for a car. Once when his father was in jail, he stole some food for his family. Gerald was fingerprinted and lost his job. Two years later, his younger cousin was harassed by gang members. Feeling as though he had no one to whom to turn, Gerald approached a rival gang for protection. As part of the initiation, Gerald had to commit a felony. Gerald didn't want to hurt anybody, so he thought he would steal his old boss's car. He knew that his ex-boss could afford to replace the car. While Gerald and the other gang members were stealing the car, the boss came out of the store. One of the gang members shot at the boss. Gerald was shocked.

This case is referred by the juvenile justice system. An evaluation is needed to determine Gerald's placement. He is approaching 18, and the judge needs to make a decision. No one is sure what happened. The psychologist is asked to evaluate Gerald for lying and criminal conduct and to give a future prognosis.

ASSESSMENT PROCESS

Consider the social, cultural, and economic context of the behavior.

DIAGNOSTIC HYPOTHESES

Conduct Disorder (312.8, p. 90), Child or Adolescent Antisocial Behavior (V71.02, p. 684)

SUGGESTED TEST BATTERY AND RATIONALE

- RISB—Warm-up; rapport builder; insight into likes, dislikes, fears, goals, regrets, interpersonal relations, feelings, attitudes
- MMPI-A—Scale 4, Psychopathic Deviate (*Pd*) assesses delinquent behavior; Harris-Lingoes pull for conflict with authority; Content scales: *A-ang* (Adolescent-Anger), *A-con* (Adolescent-Conduct Problems) is associated with legal problems, stealing, and lying, *A-fam* (Adolescent-Family Problems) indicates a history of family problems, delinquent, hostile behavior
- CRS-R—Ratings by others, teachers, family, Probation Officer, and self on oppositional behavior, social problems, anger, and fighting; norms for African Americans

CASE STUDY: OPPOSITIONAL-DEFIANT

Presenting problem: Angry, substance abuse, running away, depression, suicidal behavior

REFERRAL SOURCE

Lauren's parents brought her to your private practice for evaluation and treatment.

BACKGROUND HISTORY

Lauren (16) was brought to therapy by her parents because she ran away with her boyfriend. Her parents were unable to find her for 2 weeks. Her boyfriend, Michael, is 18 and has been arrested twice.

Lauren was always a sweet and dependable girl. She made good grades in elementary school. Her mother noticed that Lauren began to get moody about the time her periods started. Last year when she was 15, she was diagnosed with cervical cancer that was caused by a medication Lauren's mother took during her pregnancy with Lauren. The cancer was successfully treated and is not life threatening. However, the doctors told Lauren not to wait too long to have children because she may have trouble giving birth. Since the diagnosis, Lauren has completely changed. She is full of rage toward her mother. Lauren is rarely at home and spends all of her time with her boyfriend.

Lauren's boyfriend, Michael, has a history of polysubstance abuse and has been in juvenile hall twice. Once when Lauren was with him, she overdosed and had to be taken to the hospital. Michael's mother likes Lauren and thinks she is a good influence on her son. She lets them spend the night together at her house. Michael briefly broke up with Lauren. When they broke up, she cut her wrists. A week later, they got back together. Lauren's mother tried to talk to her about Michael. Lauren became furious, stormed out of the house, and wasn't seen for 2 weeks. She recently came home and her parents brought her to therapy.

DIAGNOSTIC HYPOTHESES

Oppositional Defiant Disorder (313.81), Major Depressive Disorder (296.2x), Substance-Related Disorder, Suicidal Ideation.

SUGGESTED TEST BATTERY AND RATIONALE

- RISB—Warm-up, rapport builder, clinical insight into self-esteem and relationships
- CRS-R—Teacher and parent rating of oppositional behavior
- BDI-II—Quick screening for severity of depression and suicide
- MMPI-A—Scale 4 (*Pd*) measures conflict with authority; Harris-

Lingoes on Scale 4 break down source of anger (parents, school, etc.); Scale 2 (*D*) Depression; Content scales: Adolescent-Depression, Adolescent-Alienation, Adolescent-Anger, Adolescent-Conduct Problems, Adolescent-Low Self-Esteem, Adolescent-Family Problems
* MAC-R—Assess alcohol and substance abuse
* SII—Assess interests, plan career goals
* WRAT3—Assess current academic level

CASE STUDY: PSYCHOSES

Presenting problem: schizophrenia, thought disorder, delusional disorder, bipolar disorder, substance abuse, conduct disorder

REFERRAL SOURCE

You are court appointed to determine whether Alex (19) is sane. The jury is trying to decide whether he should go to prison or a mental hospital.

BACKGROUND HISTORY

Since early childhood, Alex was observed to have behavior problems. While he was in preschool, Alex organized a gang of three other 4-year-old boys to push a smaller boy face down in the sand and steal his shovel. He also used a balloon string to strangle a little girl. When the preschool director asked him what he thought would happen to the little girl, he answered coldly, "She will die." When the director called Alex's parents and requested a conference, Alex's father was too busy working and Alex's mother was busy with her daughter. Neither parent showed up. When Alex started elementary school, he was so rough and disruptive, the teacher urged his parents to send him to a doctor. At 5, he was diagnosed with ADHD by a pediatrician and given Ritalin. Over the years, Alex was shuffled between many doctors. He has been diagnosed with ADHD, paranoia, bipolar disorder, and schizophrenia, and he has been on many types of medications. Alex's mother reports that raising him has been hell and that she can't cope with him. His father thinks he will grow out of it and be normal.

At age 13, Alex was taken to a major medical center. When doctors interviewed him, he told them that he was smarter and better than everyone else, including them. The doctors told Alex's parents that he was delusional; he was prescribed antipsychotic medications and sent to a special boarding school. Alex's father remembers a similar situation with his brother when his brother was about the same age. When Alex turned 16, his father bought him an expensive and powerful automobile. Alex went off his medications and crashed the car. He says that voices told him to do it. Fortunately, no one was hurt. His father quickly replaced the automobile, and Alex crashed it a second time.

When Alex was 18, Alex's father sent him to a large public university. Alex did not want to go. He thought the other kids would be out to get him. He wanted to stay at home and attend the community college. His father insisted that he go and believed that with time Alex would grow out of his problems. Alex failed his first semester. While he lived in the dormitories he went off his medications and experimented with marijuana, LSD, and Ecstasy. One night he got drunk, took out a college girl, ran through a red light, and twisted his car around a pole. The girl was killed; Alex was not. He is now on trial to determine his sanity and sentence.

ASSESSMENT PROCESS

- Collect as many medical records and previous psychological evaluations as possible, including history of medications.
- Conduct a developmental history from parents and doctors.
- Collect academic and behavioral records from elementary and high schools.
- Talk to university administrators.
- Consult with a major medical center and consider an MRI (magnetic resonance imaging).

DIAGNOSTIC HYPOTHESES

Schizophrenia (295.30), Delusional Disorder (297.1), Bipolar Disorder (296.xx)

SUGGESTED TEST BATTERY AND RATIONALE

- MACI—Scale 5 (Egoistic), Scale 6A (Unruly), Scale 6B (Forceful), Scale 9 (Boderline); all measure antisocial and boderline tendencies
- MMPI-A—Scale 4 (*Pd*) assesses conflict with others; use Harris-Lingoes to identify sources of conflict; Scale 6 (*Pa*) Paranoia, Scale 8 (*Sc*) Schizophrenia, Scale 9 (*Ma*) Hypomania all assess psychoses; Content scale: Adolescent-Bizarre Mentation assesses auditory, visual, and olfactory hallucinations and paranoid ideation; Harris-Lingoes for Scale 6 measure persecutory ideas, poignancy, and naïveté.
- MAC-R—Substance abuse

CASE STUDY: GANG CONFLICT

Presenting problem: conduct disorder

REFERRAL SOURCE

Rueben's attorney has advised his parents to refer him for a psychological evaluation and therapy.

BACKGROUND INFORMATION

Rueben (16), a Mexican-American, murdered a rival gang member. Rueben grew up in the barrio. His father is a manager of a landscaping crew and his mother works at the elementary school. Both parents grew up in the same barrio. They have a large extended family, have many friends, and are well respected in their community. On Sunday, the whole family attends Catholic church together. Both the mother and father were in gangs when they were younger.

Rueben was never much of a student in school. He did not participate in sports either, but he was very social. He always had several friends and was well liked. One boy in particular, Jesus, was his best friend for as long as he can remember. They spent all their time together when they were little. They were together at school, after school, on weekends, and during the summer. Friends and neighbors describe them as good kids. Jesus's older brother is a very influential gang member. When Jesus was about the right age, his brother brought him into the gang. They also inducted Rueben. Rueben's parents didn't like this situation, but they felt that they were unable to do anything. Recently, a rival gang member stabbed and killed Jesus to threaten his older brother, the gang leader. Rueben, who is intensely loyal to Jesus, wanted revenge. He got a gun and murdered the boy who killed Jesus.

DIAGNOSTIC HYPOTHESES

Conduct disorder (312.82)

ASSESSMENT PROCESS

Be sure to assess for reading level and English fluency.

SUGGESTED TEST BATTERY AND RATIONALE

- CRS-R—Parents' and teachers' rating of conduct
- MMPI-A—Scale 4 (*Pd*) assesses conflict with authority; content scale: *A-ang* (Adolescent-Anger)

CASE STUDY: PEER PROBLEMS

Presenting problem: bullies at school

REFERRAL SOURCE

Rebecca's parents brought her into your private practice because the girls at school are bullying her.

BACKGROUND INFORMATION

Rebecca (12) just started middle school. She has ambitious Jewish parents and lives in an affluent community. Rebecca was identified as intellectually gifted early in elementary school. She always excelled in school. Because she is gifted, her parents pamper her. She is allowed to buy anything she wants at the mall. She regularly spends several hundred dollars in a day. For Rebecca's 13th birthday, her parents are planning an elaborate Bat Mitzvah celebration; and when she turns 16, her parents have already promised her the car of her choice. She plans to go to Europe after high school, attend a prestigious private university, and inherit a comfortable trust fund.

Recently, Rebecca decided she didn't like the color of her room, although it had just been professionally decorated the previous year. She demanded that her parents repaint it. When her parents said no, she threw a temper tantrum. Her parents, both attorneys, were stressed out and tired from work so they gave in to her demands.

Rebecca is in therapy now because she says that the other girls at school pick on her. She says a group of girls are bullying her and calling her names. She badly wants to be popular, but the other girls don't like her. They say mean things and leave her out of activities. She is often in tears. Rebecca says that the other girls don't like her because she is prettier and smarter. According to her, the other girls are anti-Semitic. Rebecca has had problems getting along with other girls since she began elementary school. She also fights a lot with her brothers and parents.

DIAGNOSTIC HYPOTHESES

Adjustment disorder with disturbance of conduct (309.3)

SUGGESTED TEST BATTERY AND RATIONALE

- RISB—Warm-up, insight into her self-image
- ASEBA—Parents and teachers score to assess social problems
- MACI—Expressed concerns scales measure peer relations, social relations, family discord, and identity issues

CASE STUDY: SEXUAL IDENTITY, SOCIAL ISOLATION

Presenting problem: sexual identity problems, loneliness, isolation

REFERRAL SOURCE

Your friend, a high school counselor, has recommended to David's father and stepmother that they bring David to see you.

BACKGROUND INFORMATION

David (15) feels alone and says that no one understands him. He says he has known he was different since he was about 5 or 6. He doesn't know why he feels different. When asked if he has a girlfriend, he says he is not interested in girls. When the other guys in the locker room talk about girls, he just pretends to go along. He has no interest in girls. At school, he stays by himself. He eats lunch alone. When he was younger, he ate lunch with the girls. He enjoyed playing games like jump rope and galloping ponies with the girls. His teachers are worried about him because he has no friends and he wears a trench coat to school.

David lives with his father. His father is bisexual and currently remarried but is seldom at home. The father travels a lot for his work. The stepmother is left with the responsibility of raising David and his sister along with her other children. David's biological mother was diagnosed with depression and was unable to take adequate care of David and his sister. The house was always dirty and rarely had enough food for the children. The mother stayed in the house all of the time and liked the children to keep her company. She often kept them home from school to be with her. The children are about 2–3 years behind in school. David has high scores on standardized tests but expresses no interest in going to college or pursuing any career goals.

Three years ago, David's father left his wife, took the children, and moved out of state. He met his current wife in a bar, and after knowing each other only briefly, they were married. She became pregnant and they had a new baby together. Both parents drink a lot. The stepmother had children of her own and was having difficulty making ends meet before she met David's dad. Between them they have 5 children. David and his sister are extra work for her. She cleans and cooks and they mouth off to her.

They don't help with the housework but she doesn't complain. Her previous husband beat her. She says David's dad is a good man. He brings home a paycheck and he doesn't beat her.

DIFFERENTIAL DIAGNOSIS

Identity Problem (313.82), Academic Problem (v62.3)

SUGGESTED TEST BATTERY AND RATIONALE

- Goodenough-Harris Drawing Test—Warm-up, rapport builder, insight into self-image
- CBCL—Feedback from teachers and parents on social skills
- MACI—Identity issues, sexuality
- WISC-III—Examine discrepancy between ability and achievement, obtain an IQ score and pattern of strengths
- WRAT3—Measure grade level
- WJ III—Assess academic strengths, weaknesses, and LDs
- SII—Assess interests, form a career plan

CASE STUDY: SMOKING POT, POOR GRADES

Presenting problem: learning disabilities, academic performance, substance abuse

REFERRAL SOURCE

You work in a residential treatment center for adolescents and you are conducting a routine intake interview.

BACKGROUND HISTORY

Ryan (16) is in an adolescent residential treatment center for substance abuse. He was pulled over by the police for driving under the influence. His mother went through his room and found marijuana. She also found in-structions for making a bomb that he downloaded from the Internet.

While he was growing up, Ryan was the class clown. His teachers fre-quently complained about his being too silly and disrupting the class. Be-cause he was so funny and entertaining, he was always well liked by his peers; however, academic work was hard for him. He struggled with read-ing and math. Because he was a hard worker, had tutors, and received a lot of help from the teachers, he was able to achieve Bs and Cs on his report card. However, he always found it hard to sit still and concentrate. The teacher asked the parents to take him to a doctor for ADHD. When Ryan was in third grade, the doctor started him on Ritalin. It seemed to help him focus and be more manageable in the classroom.

Ryan is wildly popular with his peers. He is athletic, funny, and musical. He plays guitar with his friends in a band. His favorite music is reggae mu-sic, and when he's not playing music, he is at the beach surfing. His room is filled with posters of Bob Marley and surfers. He also attends a lot of concerts. Although he has always been well liked by the other kids, they describe him as "hyper." When he was younger and bored, he occasionally threw balls at cars and neighbors' houses. He frequently rang doorbells and ran away.

His parents brought him to the residential treatment center. They are both working and have good insurance. They are very devoted to their son and family and want you to help get him sober. They are concerned about his school placement and about the type of the friends he has. He has a lot of school truancies and won't be able to graduate high school with his peers. They ask you for your help with his substance abuse problem and school placement.

ASSESSMENT GOALS

- Assess substance abuse.
- Assess learning disabilities and educational placement.

ASSESSMENT PROCESS

- Obtain all previous medical and educational records, including diag-noses and prescribed medications.

- Talk with teachers.
- Obtain a developmental history from parents.

DIAGNOSTIC HYPOTHESES

Reading disorder (315.00), mathematics disorder (315.1), disorder of written expression (315.1), disorder of written expression (315.2), substance-related disorders

SUGGESTED TEST BATTERY AND RATIONALE

- Goodenough-Harris Drawing Test—Warm-up, rapport builder
- ASEBA—Parental and teacher observation of ADHD
- MMPI-A—Assess substance abuse with Alcohol and Drug Acknowledgement (ACK) and Alcohol and Drug Problem Proneness (PRO) scales
- MAC-R—Assess alcohol abuse
- WISC-III—Diagnose intellectual strengths and weaknesses
- WRAT3—Assess grade level
- WJ III—Assess academic strengths, weaknesses, and LDs

CASE STUDY: ANXIETY

Presenting problem: stress, anxiety, excessive worrying, possible panic attacks, obessessive-compulsive traits

REFERRAL SOURCE

Michelle brought herself into the university counseling center.

BACKGROUND INFORMATION

Michelle (17) has come to see you at the university counseling center. She arrives 10 minutes early for her appointment and is waiting when you come out to meet her. Even though it is finals week, she is immaculately groomed. Her hair, makeup, and clothes are all perfect.

After you greet Michelle and ask her how she is doing, she tells you that she feels as though she is losing her mind and going to die. Yesterday, her heart began to race so fast, she thought she was going to have a heart attack. She had trouble breathing. She drinks a lot of coffee, has headaches, feels dizzy, and grinds her teeth. She can't sleep at night or concentrate on her studies. As she talks to you, she speaks very rapidly, wringing her hands and moving around a lot.

Yesterday, Michelle went the health center, where she was diagnosed with anxiety and referred to your office. Michelle is very worried because she can't study. She looks at the pages, but the words don't sink in. She copies her notes over and over, but it doesn't help. She doesn't know what is wrong with her. According to Michelle, she has never been like this before. Always the best student in the class, Michelle was valedictorian of her high school. In high school, she got all As, high SAT scores, and was student body president. Now she is at a major university and feels as though she can't compete. She is afraid she is going to flunk out, and she is terrified of her father. When she thinks of what her father will do to her, she begins to cry.

DIAGNOSTIC HYPOTHESES

Generalized Anxiety Disorder (300.02), Anxiety Disorder NOS (300.00), Adjustment Disorder with Anxiety (309.24).

SUGGESTED TEST BATTERY AND RATIONALE

- RISB—Rapport; clinical insight into self-image and worries; used extensively with college students
- Goodenough-Harris Drawing Test—Self-concept, family issues
- MACI—Scale 7: Conforming, Scale G: Family Discord
- MMPI-A—Scale 7 (*Pt*) measures anxiety, tension, worry, poor concentration, perfectionism; content scales: *A-anx* (Adolescent-Anxiety), *A-fam* (Adolescent-Family Problems)

Appendix D

—— ◆ ——

APA Ethical Principles of Psychologists and Code of Conduct (2002)

Standard 9—Assessment

—— ◆ ——

9. ASSESSMENT

9.01 BASES FOR ASSESSMENTS

(a) Psychologists base the opinions contained in their recommendations, reports, and diagnostic or evaluative statements, including forensic testimony, on information and techniques sufficient to substantiate their findings. (See also Standard 2.04, Bases for Scientific and Professional Judgments.)

(b) Except as noted in 9.01 c, psychologists provide opinions of the psychological characteristics of individuals only after they have conducted an examination of the individuals adequate to support their statements or conclusions. When, despite reasonable efforts, such an examination is not practical, psychologists document the efforts they made and the result of those efforts, clarify the probable impact of their limited information on the reliability and validity of their opinions, and appropriately limit the nature and extent of their conclusions or recommendations. (See also Standards 2.01, Boundaries of Competence, and 9.06, Interpreting Assessment Results.)

(c) When psychologists conduct a record review or provide consultation or supervision and an individual examination is not warranted or necessary for the opinion, psychologists explain this and the sources of information on which they based their conclusions and recommendations.

9.02 USE OF ASSESSMENTS

(a) Psychologists administer, adapt, score, interpret, or use assessment techniques, interviews, tests, or instruments in a manner and for purposes that are appropriate in light of the research on or evidence of the usefulness and proper application of the techniques.

(b) Psychologists use assessment instruments whose validity and reliability have been established for use with members of the population tested. When such validity or reliability has not been established, psychologists describe the strengths and limitations of test results and interpretation.

(c) Psychologists use assessment methods that are appropriate to an individual's language preference and competence, unless the use of an alternative language is relevant to the assessment issues.

9.03 INFORMED CONSENT IN ASSESSMENTS

(a) Psychologists obtain informed consent for assessments, evaluations, or diagnostic services, as described in Standard 3.10, Informed Consent, except when (1) testing is mandated by law or governmental regulations; (2) informed consent is implied because testing is conducted as a routine educational, institutional, or organizational activity (e.g., when participants voluntarily agree to assessment when applying for a job); or (3) one purpose of the testing is to evaluate decisional capacity. Informed consent includes an explanation of the nature and purpose of the assessment, fees, involvement of third parties, and limits of confidentiality and sufficient opportunity for the client/patient to ask questions and receive answers.

(b) Psychologists inform persons with questionable capacity to consent or for whom testing is mandated by law or governmental regulations about the nature and purpose of the proposed assessment services, using language that is reasonably understandable to the person being assessed.

(c) Psychologists using the services of an interpreter obtain informed consent from the client/patient to use that interpreter, ensure that confidentiality of test results and test security are maintained, and include in their recommendations, reports, and diagnostic or evaluative statements, including forensic testimony, discussion of any limitations on the data obtained. (See also Standards 2.05, Delegation of Work to Others; 4.01, Maintaining Confidentiality; 9.01, Bases for Assessments; 9.06, Interpreting Assessment Results; and 9.07, Assessment by Unqualified Persons.)

9.04 RELEASE OF TEST DATA

(a) The term *test data* refers to raw and scaled scores, client/patient responses to test questions or stimuli, and psychologists' notes and recordings concerning client/patient statements and behavior during an examination. Those portions of test materials that include client/patient responses are included in the definition of *test data*. Pursuant to a client/patient release, psychologists provide test data to the client/patient or other persons identified in the release. Psychologists may refrain from releasing test data to protect a client/patient or others from substantial harm or misuse or misrepresentation of the data or the test, recognizing that in many instances release of confidential information under these circumstances is regulated by law. (See also Standard 9.11, Maintaining Test Security.)

(b) In the absence of a client/patient release, psychologists provide test data only as required by law or court order.

9.05 TEST CONSTRUCTION

Psychologists who develop tests and other assessment techniques use appropriate psychometric procedures and current scientific or professional knowledge for test design, standardization, validation, reduction or elimination of bias, and recommendations for use.

9.06 INTERPRETING ASSESSMENT RESULTS

When interpreting assessment results, including automated interpretations, psychologists take into account the purpose of the assessment as well as the various test factors, test-taking abilities, and other characteristics of the person being assessed, such as situational, personal, linguistic, and cultural differences, that might affect psychologists' judgments or reduce the accuracy of their interpretations. They indicate any significant limitations of their interpretations. (See also Standards 2.01 b and c, Boundaries of Competence, and 3.01, Unfair Discrimination.)

9.07 ASSESSMENT BY UNQUALIFIED PERSONS

Psychologists do not promote the use of psychological assessment techniques by unqualified persons, except when such use is conducted for training purposes with appropriate supervision. (See also Standard 2.05, Delegation of Work to Others.)

9.08 OBSOLETE TESTS AND OUTDATED TEST RESULTS

(a) Psychologists do not base their assessment or intervention decisions or recommendations on data or test results that are outdated for the current purpose.

(b) Psychologists do not base such decisions or recommendations on tests and measures that are obsolete and not useful for the current purpose.

9.09 TEST SCORING AND INTERPRETATION SERVICES

(a) Psychologists who offer assessment or scoring services to other professionals accurately describe the purpose, norms, validity, reliability, and applications of the procedures and any special qualifications applicable to their use.

(b) Psychologists select scoring and interpretation services (including automated services) on the basis of evidence of the validity of the program and procedures as well as on other appropriate considerations. (See also Standard 2.01 b and c, Boundaries of Competence.)

(c) Psychologists retain responsibility for the appropriate application, interpretation, and use of assessment instruments, whether they score and interpret such tests themselves or use automated or other services.

9.10 EXPLAINING ASSESSMENT RESULTS

Regardless of whether the scoring and interpretation are done by psychologists, by employees or assistants, or by automated or other outside services, psychologists take reasonable steps to ensure that explanations of results are given to the individual or designated representative unless the nature of the relationship precludes provision of an explanation of results (such as in some organizational consulting, preemployment or security screenings, and forensic evaluations), and this fact has been clearly explained to the person being assessed in advance.

9.11 MAINTAINING TEST SECURITY

The term *test materials* refers to manuals, instruments, protocols, and test questions or stimuli and does not include *test data* as defined in Standard 9.04, Release of Test Data. Psychologists make reasonable efforts to maintain the integrity and security of test materials and other assessment techniques consistent with law, contractual obligations, and in a manner that permits adherence to this Ethics Code.

Appendix E

◆

Test Ordering Information

◆

Test	Publisher
Achenbach System of Empirically Based Assessment (ASEBA)	ASEBA 1 South Prospect St. Burlington, VT 05401-3456 Fax: 802-656-2602 E-mail: ASEBA@uvm.edu http://www.ASEBA.org
Beck Depression Inventory (BDI)	The Psychological Corporation 19500 Bulverde Rd. San Antonio, TX 78259 1-800-872-1726 http://www.psychcorp.com
Conners' Rating Scales–Revised (CRS-R)	NCS Assessments P.O. Box 1416 Minneapolis, MN 55440 1-800-627-7271 Fax: 1-800-632-9011
Goodenough-Harris Drawing Test	The Psychological Corporation (see BDI information)

Millon Adolescent Clinical Inventory (MACI)	NCS Assessments (see CRS-R information)
Minnesota Multiphasic Personality Inventory– Adolescent (MMPI-A)	NCS Assessments (see CRS-R information)
Rotter Incomplete Sentences Blank (RISB)	The Psychological Corporation (see BDI information)
Strong Interest Inventory (SII)	Consulting Psychologists Press, Inc. P.O. Box 10096 3803 E. Bayshore Rd. Palo Alto, CA 94303-0979 1-800-624-1765 650-969-8901 Fax: 650-969-8608 http://www.cpp-db.com
Wechsler Intelligence Scale for Children–Third Edition (WISC-III)	The Psychological Corporation (see BDI information)
Wide Range Achievement Test–3 (WRAT3)	Wide Range, Inc. P.O. Box 3410 15 Ashley Place, Suite 1A Wilmington, DE 19804 1-800-221-9728 http://www.widerange.com
Woodcock-Johnson III (WJ III)	The Riverside Publishing Co. 425 Spring Lake Dr. Itasca, IL 60143 http://www.riverpub.com

References

Achenbach, T. M. (1966). The classification of children's psychiatric symptoms: A factor-analytic study. *Psychological Monographs, 80* (Serial No. 615).

Achenbach, T. M. (1978). The Child Behavior Profile: I. Boys aged 6–11. *Journal of Consulting and Clinical Psychology, 46,* 478–488.

Achenbach, T. M. (1991). *Manual for the Child Behavior Checklist/4-18, YSR, and TRF profiles.* Burlington: University of Vermont Department of Psychiatry.

Achenbach, T. M. (1993). Implications of multi-axial empirically based assessment for behavior therapy with children. *Behavior Therapy, 24,* 91–116.

Achenbach, T. M., & Edelbrock, C. S. (1981). Behavioral problems and competencies reported by parents of normal and disturbed children aged four through sixteen. *Monographs of the Society for Research in Child Development, 46* (1, Serial No. 188).

Achenbach, T. M., Howell, C. T., Quay, H. C., & Conners, C. K. (1991). National survey of problems and competencies among four- to sixteen-year-olds. *Monographs of the Society for Research in Child Development, 56* (3, Serial No. 225).

Achenbach, T. M., & Rescorla, L. A. (2001). *Manual for the ASEBA school-age forms & profiles.* Burlington: University of Vermont Research Center for Children, Youth, and Families.

Albert, N., & Beck, A. T. (1975). Incidence of depression in early adolescence: Preliminary study. *Journal of Youth and Adolescence, 4,* 301–307.

American Psychiatric Association. (1997). DSM-IV *sourcebook* (Vol. 3). Washington, DC: Author.

American Psychiatric Association. (2000). *Diagnostic and statistical manual of mental disorders* (4th ed., text revision). Washington, DC: Author.

American Psychological Association. (1992). Ethical principles of psychologists and code of conduct. *American Psychologist, 47,* 1597–1611.

American Psychological Association. (1993). *Violence and youth: Psychology's response. Vol. I: Summary report of the American Psychological Association Commission on Violence and Youth* (pp. 440, 441, 468). Washington, DC: Public Interest Directorate, American Psychological Association.

American Psychological Association. (2002). *Ethical principles of psychologists and code of conduct.* Retrieved from http://www.apa.org, Feb. 14, 2003.

Anastasi, A., & Urbina, S. (1997). *Psychological testing* (7th ed.). Upper Saddle River, NJ: Prentice Hall.

Archer, J. (1991). The influence of testoserone on human aggression. *British Journal of Psychology, 82,* 1–28.

Archer, R. P. (1997). *MMPI-A Assessing adolescent psychopathology.* Mahwah, NJ: Erlbaum.

Archer, R. P., Maruish, M., Imhof, E. A., & Piotrowski, C. (1991). Psychological test usage with adolescent clients: 1990 survey findings. *Professional Psychology: Research and Practice, 22,* 247–252.

Aristotle. (1941). *Rhetorica* (W. R. Roberts, Trans.). In McKoen (Ed.), *The basic works of Aristotle.* New York: Random House.

Babbie, E. (1997). *The practice of social research.* Belmont, CA: Wadsworth.

Bandura, A. (1997). *Self-efficacy: The exercise of control.* New York: W. H. Freeman & Co.

Bannatyne, A. (1974). Diagnosis: A note on recategorization of the WISC scaled scores. *Journal of Learning Disabilities, 7,* 272–274.

Barnes, G. M., Farrell, M. P., & Banerjee, S. (1995). Family influences on alcohol abuse and other problem behaviors among Black and White adolescents in a general population sample. *Journal of Research on Adolescence, 4,* 183–202.

Basham, R. B. (1992). Clinical utility of the MMPI research scales in the assessment of adolescent acting out behaviors. *Psychological Assessment, 4,* 483–492.

Baumrind, D. (1967). Child-care practices anteceding three patterns of preschool behavior. *Genetic Psychology Monographs, 75,* 43–88.

Beck, A. T., Steer, R. A., & Brown, G. K. (1996). *BDI-II manual.* San Antonio, TX: The Psychological Corporation.

Beebe, D. K. (1991). Emergency management of the adult female rape victim. *American Family Physician, 43,* 2041–2046.

Bem, S. L. (1974). The measurement of psychological androgyny. *Journal of Consulting and Clinical Psychology, 42,* 155–162.

Berger, K. (2000). *The developing person through childhood and adolescence.* New York: Worth.

Berger, K., & Thompson, R. A. (1991). *The developing person through childhood and adolescence.* New York: Worth.

Berman, A. L., & Jobes, D. A. (1999). *Adolescent suicide assessment and intervention.* Washington, DC: American Psychological Association.

Berube, R. L., & Achenbach, T. M. (2001). *Bibliography of published studies using ASEBA instruments: 2001 edition.* Burlington: University of Vermont.

Blos, P. (1989). The inner world of the adolescent. In A. H. Esman (Ed.), *International annuals of adolescent psychiatry* (Vol. 1). Chicago: University of Chicago Press.

Bronfenbrenner, U. (1986). Ecology of the family as a context for human development: Research perspective. *Developmental Psychology, 22,* 723–742.

Bronfenbrenner, U. (1995). The bioecological model from a life course perspective. In P. Moen, G. H. Elder, & K. Luscher (Eds.), *Examining lives in context.* Washington, DC: American Psychological Association.

Butcher, J. N. (1987). *Computerized psychological assessment.* New York: Basic Books.

Butcher, J. N., Graham, J. R., Dahlstrom, W. G., & Bowman, E. (1990). The MMPI-2 with college students. *Journal of Personality, 54,* 1–15.

Butcher, J. N., Williams, C. L., Graham, J. R., Archer, R. P., Tellegen, A., Ben-Porath, Y., et al. (1992). *MMPI-A Manual for administration, scoring, and interpretation.* Minneapolis: University of Minnesota Press.

Campbell, J. C., & Soeken, K. L. (1999). Forced sex and intimate partner violence: Effects on women's risk and women's health. *Violence Against Women, 5*(9), 1017–1035.

Campos, L. P. (1989). Adverse impact, unfairness, and bias in the psychological screening of Hispanic peace officers. *Hispanic Journal of Behavioral Sciences, 11,* 122–135.

Churchill, R., & Crandall, V. J. (1955). The reliability and validity of the Rotter Incomplete Sentences Test. *Journal of Consulting Psychology, 19,* 345–350.

Cloninger, C. R. (1991, January). *Personality traits and alcoholic predisposition.* Paper presented at the conference of the National Institute on Drug Abuse, University of California, Los Angeles.

Cohen, J. (1988). *Statistical power for the behavioral sciences* (2nd ed.). Hillsdale, NJ: Erlbaum.

Conger, J. J. (1977). *Adolescence and youth: Psychological development in a changing world* (2nd ed.). New York: Harper and Row.

Conners, C. K. (1997). *Conners' Rating Scale–Revised.* New York: Multi-Health Systems.

Costello, C., & Stone, A. J. (1994). *The American woman 1994–95.* New York: W. W. Norton & Company.

Cunningham, J. L. (1998). Learning disabilities. In J. Sandoval, C. L. Frisby, K. F. Geisinger, J. D. Scheuneman, & J. R. Grenier (Eds.), *Test interpretation and diversity* (pp. 317–347). Washington, DC: American Psychological Association.

Dahlstrom, W. G., Lachar, D., & Dahlstrom, L. E. (1986). *MMPI patterns of American minorities.* Minneapolis: University of Minnesota Press.

Daniels, P., & Plomin, R. (1985). Origins of individual differences in infant shyness. *Developmental Psychology, 21,* 118–121.

Darves-Bornoz, J. M., Lepine, J. P., Choquet, M., Berger, C., Degiovani, A., & Gaillard, P. (1998). Predictive factors of chronic posttraumatic stress disorder in rape victims. *European Psychiatry, 13,* 281–287.

Donaldson, M. A., & Gardner, R. (1985). Diagnosis and treatment of traumatic stress in women after childhood incest. In C. R. Figley (Ed), *Trauma and its wake* (pp. 356–377). Bruner/Mazel.

Dunn, Loyd M., & Dunn, Leota M. (1981). *Peabody Picture Vocabulary Test–Revised: Manual for Forms L and M.* Circle Pines, MN: American Guidance Service.

Eagly, A. H. (1995). The science and politics of comparing women and men. *American Psychologist, 50,* 145–158.

Education of All Handicapped Children Act of 1977, 20 U.S.C. §1401 *et seq.*

Elkind, D. (1961). Quantity conceptions in junior and senior high school students. *Child Development, 32,* 551–560.

Elkind, D. (1976). *Child development and education: A Piagetian perspective.* New York: Oxford University Press.

Elkind, D. (1985). Reply to D. Lapsley and M. Murphy's *Developmental Review* paper. *Developmental Review, 5,* 218–226.

Erikson, E. (1963). *Childhood and society.* New York: W. W. Norton & Company.

Erikson, E. (1968). *Identity: Youth and crisis.* New York: W. W. Norton & Company.

Erme, R. F. (1979). Sex differences in childhood psychopathology: A review. *Psychological Bulletin, 86,* 574–595.

Fasick, F. A. (1994). On the "invention" of adolescence. *Journal of Early Adolescence, 14,* 6–23.

Federal Bureau of Investigation. (1991). *Uniform crime reports.* Washington, DC: U.S. Department of Justice.

Finklehor, D., Hotaling, G., & Lewis, I. A. (1984). Sexual abuse in a national survey of adult men and women: Prevalence, characteristics, and risk factors. *Child Abuse & Neglect, 14,* 530–541.

Freud, A. (1958). *The ego and mechanisms of defense.* New York: International Universities Press.

Friedman, H. S., Tucker, J. S., Schwartz, J. E., Tomlinson-Keasey, C., Martin, L. R. Wingard, D. L., et al. (1995). Psychosocial and behavioral predictors of longevity: The aging and death of the "Termites." *American Psychologist, 50,* 69–78.

Friedman, J. M. H., Asnis, G. M., Boeck, M., & DiFiore, J. (1987). Prevalence of suicidal behaviors in a high school sample. *American Journal of Psychiatry, 144,* 1203–1206.

Frisby, C. L. (2001). Culture and cultural differences. In J. Sandoval, C. L. Frisby, K. F. Geisinger, J. D. Sheunemean, & J. R. Grenier (Eds.), *Test interpretation and diversity* (pp. 51–73). Washington, DC: American Psychological Association.

Gantner, A., Graham, J., & Archer, R. P. (1992). Usefulness of the MAC scale in differentiating adolescents in normal, psychiatric, and substance abuse settings. *Psychological Assessment, 4*, 133–137.

Gardner, H. (1983). *Frames of mind: The theory of multiple intelligences.* New York: Basic Books.

Geisinger, K. F. (2001). Psychometric issues in test interpretation. In C. L. Sandoval, C. L. Frisby, K. F. Geisinger, J. D. Sheunemean, & J. R. Grenier (Eds.), *Test interpretation and diversity* (pp. 17–30). Washington, DC: American Psychological Association.

Gilligan, C. (1982). *In a different voice.* Cambridge, MA: Harvard University Press.

Gilligan, C. (1992, May). *Joining the resistance: Girls' development in adolescence.* Paper presented at the symposium on development and vulnerability in close relationships, Montreal, Quebec.

Goldsmith, H. H., & Gottesman, I. I. (1981). Origins of variation in behavioral style: A longitudinal study of temperament in young twins. *Child Development, 53*, 91–103.

Goodenough, F. L. (1926). *Measurement of intelligence.* New York: Harcourt, Brace, & World.

Gordon, T. (1975). *PET: Parent effectiveness training.* New York: New American Library.

Graham, J. R. (2000). *MMPI-2: Assessing personality and psychopathology.* New York: Oxford University Press.

Greene, R. L. (1980). *MMPI: An interpretive manual.* New York: Grune & Stratton.

Greene, R. L. (1987). Ethnicity and MMPI performance: A review. *Journal of Consulting and Clinical Psychology, 55*, 497–512.

Gumbiner, J. (1996). *Daniel: A readiness success story* [Brochure]. Orange, CA: Author.

Gumbiner, J. (1997). Comparison of scores on the MMPI-A and MMPI-2 for young adults. *Psychological Reports, 81*, 787–794.

Gumbiner, J. (1998). MMPI-A profiles of Hispanic adolescents. *Psychological Reports, 82*, 659–672.

Gumbiner, J., & Flowers, J. V. (1997). Sex differences on the MMPI-1 and MMPI-2. *Psychological Reports, 81*, 479–482.

Gynther, M. D. (1972). White norms and Black MMPIs: A prescription for discrimination? *Psychological Bulletin, 78*, 386–402.

Gynther, M. D. (1989). MMPI patterns of Blacks and Whites: A review. *Journal of Clinical Psychology, 45*, 878–883.

Hall, G. S. (1904). *Adolescence* (Vols. 1–2). Englewood Cliffs, NJ: Prentice Hall.

Harmon, L. W., Hansen, J. C., Borgen, F. H., & Hammer, A. L. (1994). *Strong Interest Inventory: Applications and technical guide.* Palo Alto, CA: Consulting Psychologists Press.

Harnqvist, K. (1968). Relative changes in intelligence from 13 to 18. *Scandinavian Journal of Psychology, 9*, 50–82.

Harris, D. B. (1963). *Children's drawings as measures of intellectual maturity: A revision and extension of the Goodenough Draw-a-Man Test.* New York: Harcourt Brace Jovanovich.

Hathaway, S. R., & Monachesi, E. D. (1963). *Adolescent personality and behavior: MMPI patterns of normal, delinquent, dropout, and other outcomes.* Minneapolis: University of Minnesota Press.

Heck, A. (1988). *The burden of Hitler's legacy.* Frederick, CO: Renaissance House.

Hiskey, M. S. (1966). *The Hiskey-Nebraska Test of Learning Aptitude.* Lincoln, NE: Union College Press.

Holland, J. L. (1973). *Making vocational choices: A theory of careers.* Englewood Cliffs, NJ: Prentice Hall.

Honzik, M. P., Macfarlane, J. W., & Allen, L. (1948). The stability of mental test performance between two and eighteen years. *Journal of Experimental Education, 17*, 309–324.

Husen, T. (1951). The influence of schooling upon IQ. *Theoria, 17*, 61–88.

Jensen, A. R. (1980). *Bias in mental testing.* New York: Free Press.

Johnston, L. D., O'Malley, P. M., & Bachman, J. G. (1995). *National survey results on drug use from the Monitoring the Future Study: Vol. 1. Secondary school students.* Ann Arbor, MI: Institute of Social Research.

Jung, C. G. (1965). *Memories, dreams, reflections.* New York: Vintage Books.

Kagan, J., Reznick, J. S., & Snidman, N. (1987). The physiology and psychology of behavioral inhibition in children. *Child Development, 58,* 1459–1473.

Kaplan, S., & Pelcovitz, D. (1997). Incest. In American Psychiatric Association (Ed.), DSM-IV *Sourcebook* (Vol. 3, pp. 805–857). Washington, DC: American Psychiatric Association.

Kandel, D. B., & Davies, M. (1986). Adult sequelae of adolescent depressive symptoms. *Archives of General Psychiatry, 43,* 255–262.

Karle, H. R., & Velasquez, R. J. (1996). *The comparability of the English and Spanish versions of the MMPI-2.* Manuscript submitted for publication.

Kashani, J. H., Beck, N., Hoeper, E. W., Fallahi, C., Corcoran, C. M., McAllister, J. A., et al. (1987). Psychiatric disorders in a community sample of adolescents. *American Journal of Psychiatry, 144,* 584–589.

Kashani, J. H., Reid, J., & Rosenberg, T. (1989). Levels of hopelessness in children and adolescents: A developmental perspective. *Journal of Consulting and Clinical Psychology, 57,* 496–499.

Kaufman, A. S. (1990). *Assessing adolescent and adult intelligence.* Boston: Allyn & Bacon.

Kaufman, A. S. (1994). *Intelligent testing with the WISC-III.* New York: Wiley.

Kaufman, A. S., & Lichtenberger, E. O. (1999). *Essentials of WAIS-III assessment.* New York: Wiley.

Kaufman, A. S., & Lichtenberger, E. O. (2000). *Essentials of WISC-III and WPPSI-R Assessment.* New York: Wiley.

Keefe, J., Sue, S., Enomoto, K., Durvasula, R., & Chao, R. (1994). Asian American and White college students' performance on the MMPI-2. In J. N. Butcher (Ed.), *Handbook of international MMPI-2 research* (pp. 204–235). New York: Oxford University Press.

Kempe, R., & Kempe, C. H. (1984). *The common secret.* New York: W. H. Freeman.

Kerlinger, F. N., & Lee, H. B. (2000). *Foundations of behavioral research.* New York: International Thomson.

Kerlinger, F. N., & Pedhazur, E. J. (1973). *Multiple regression in behavioral research.* New York: Holt, Rinehart, and Winston.

Kohlberg, L. (1958). *The development of modes of moral thinking and choice in the years 10 to 16.* Unpublished doctoral dissertation, University of Chicago.

Kohlberg, L. (1976). Moral stages and moralization: The cognitive-developmental approach. In T. Lickona (Ed.), *Moral development and behavior.* New York: Holt, Rinehart, and Winston.

Koppitz, E. M. (1968). *Psychological evaluation of children's human figure drawings.* New York: Grune & Stratton.

Koppitz, E. M. (1984). *Psychological evaluation of human figure drawings by middle school pupils.* Orlando: FL: Grune & Stratton.

Koss, M. P. (1993). Rape: Scope, impact, interventions, and public policy responses. *American Psychologist, 48,* 1062–1069.

Koss, M. P. (2002). *Arizona rape prevention and education project.* Retrieved from http://www.u.arizona.edu/~sexasslt/arpedep/, November 24, 2002.

Koss, M. P., & Heslet, L. (1992). Somatic consequences of violence against women. *Archives of Family Medicine, 151,* 342–357.

Kovacs, M. (1990). Comorbid anxiety disorders in childhood-onset depressions. In J. D. Maser & C. R. Cloninger (Eds.), *Comorbidity of mood and anxiety disorders* (pp. 272–281). Washington, DC: American Psychiatric Press.

Lah, M. I. (1989). New validity, normative, and scoring data for the Rotter Incomplete Sentences Blank. *Journal of Personality Assessment, 53,* 607–620.

Laosa, L. M., Swartz, J. D., & DiazGuerrero, R. (1974). Perceptualcognitive and personality development of Mexican and Anglo-American children as measured by human figure drawings. *Developmental Psychology, 10,* 131–139.

Larson, R., & Lampman-Petraitis, C. (1989). Daily emotional states as reported by children and adolescents. *Child Development, 60,* 1250–1260.

Lewin, K. (1936). *A dynamic theory of personality.* New York: McGraw-Hill.

Lindberg, F. H., & Distad, L. J. (1985). Post-traumatic stress disorders in women who experienced childhood incest. *Child Abuse & Neglect, 9,* 329–334.

Lord, M. (2001, April 1). Drinking: Here's looking at you, kids. *U.S. News & World Report,* p. 63.

Maccoby, E. E. (1966). *The development of sex differences.* Stanford, CA: Stanford University Press.

Maccoby, E. E. (1987, November). Interview with Elizabeth Hall: All in the family. *Psychology Today,* pp. 54–60.

Maccoby, E. E., & Jacklin, C. N. (1974). *The psychology of sex differences.* Palo Alto, CA: Stanford University Press.

Machover, K. (1949). *Personality projection in the drawing of the human figure.* Springfield, IL: Charles C. Thomas.

Marshall, J. (1989). Re-visioning career concepts: A feminist invitation. In M. B. Arthur, D. T. Hall, & B. S. Lawrence (Eds.), *Handbook of career theory* (pp. 275–291). Cambridge, England: Cambridge University Press.

Mather, N., & Woodcock, R. W. (2001). *Examiner's manual: Woodcock-Johnson III Tests of Cognitive Abilities.* Itasca, IL: Riverside.

Mather, N., Wendling, B. J., & Woodcock, R. W. (2001). *Essentials of WJ III Tests of Achievement Assessment.* New York: Wiley.

McCarthy, M. (1989). *Greater depression in women and a greater concern for thinness: Is there a relationship?* Unpublished manuscript.

McCrae, R. R., & Costa, P. T. (1987). Validation of the five factor model of personality across instruments and observers. *Journal of Personality and Social Psychology, 52,* 81–90.

McGrew, K. S., & Woodcock, R. W. (2001). *Technical manual: Woodcock-Johnson III.* Itasca, IL: Riverside.

McDonald, R. L., & Gynther, M. D. (1963). MMPI norms associated with sex, race, and class in two adolescent samples. *Journal of Consulting Psychology, 27,* 112–116.

Mehryar, A. H., Tashakkori, A., Yousefi, F., &

Khajavi, F. (1987). The application of the Goodenough-Harris Draw-A-Man Test to a group of Iranian children in the city of Shiraz. *British Journal of Educational Psychology, 57,* 401–406.

Mercer, J. R. (1979). *Technical manual: System of Multicultural Pluralistic Assessment (SOMPA).* New York: Psychological Corporation.

Meyer, G. J., Finn, S. E., Eyde, L. D., Kay, G. G., Moreland, K. L., Dies, R. R., et al. (2001). Psychological testing and psychological assessment: A review of evidence and issues. *American Psychologist, 56,* 128–165.

Millon, T. (1990). *Toward a new personology: An evolutionary model.* New York: Wiley.

Millon, T. (1993). *MACI manual.* Minneapolis, MN: National Computer Systems.

Monahan, J. T., & Steadman, H. J. (1994). *Violence and mental disorder: Developments in risk management.* Chicago: University of Chicago Press.

Myers, D. (1999). *Social psychology.* Boston: McGraw-Hill College.

National Institute on Drug Abuse. (2001). *High school and youth trends, 2000: Monitoring the future study.* Retrieved from http://www.nida.nih.gov/Infofax/HSYouthtrends.html, November 24, 2002.

National Institute of Mental Health. (1990). *National plan for research on child and adolescent mental disorders* (DHS Publication No. ADM 90–1683). Washington, DC: U.S. Government Printing Office.

National Institute of Mental Health. (2001). *The numbers count.* Retrieved from http://www.nimh.nih.gov/publicat/numbers.cfm, November 24, 2002.

Nolen-Hoeksema, S. (1990). *Sex differences in depression.* Stanford, CA: Stanford University Press.

Norris, F. H. (1992). Epidemiology of trauma: Frequency and impact of different potentially traumatic events on different demographic groups. *Journal of Consulting and Clinical Psychology, 60,* 409–418.

Olin, S. S. (2002). *Report of the surgeon general's*

conference on children's mental health: A national action agenda. Retrieved from http://www.surgeongneral.gov/topics/cmh/childreport.htm

Padilla, A. M., & Medina, A. (1996). Cross-cultural sensitivity in assessment: Using tests in culturally appropriate ways. In L. A. Suzuki, P. J. Meller, & J. G. Ponterotto (Eds.), *Handbook of multicultural assessment: Clinical, psychological, and educational applications* (pp. 3–28). San Francisco: Jossey-Bass.

Petersen, A. C., Compas, B. E., Brooks-Gunn, J., Stemmler, M., Ey, S., & Grant, K. E. (1993). Depression in adolescence. *American Psychologist, 48,* 155–168.

Piaget, J. (1952). *The origins of intelligence.* New York: International Universities Press.

Plake, B. S., & Impara, J. C. (Eds.). (2001). *The fourteenth mental measurements yearbook.* Lincoln, NE: Buros Institute of Mental Measurements.

Plato. (1955). *The Republic* (D. Lee, Trans.). New York: Viking.

Pratt, S. I., & Moreland, L. (1998). Individuals with other characteristics. In J. Sandoval, C. L. Frisby, K. F. Geisinger, J. D. Scheuneman, & J. R. Grenier (Eds.), *Test interpretation and diversity* (pp. 349–371). Washington, DC: American Psychological Association.

Roberts, R. E., Attkission, C. C., & Rosenblatt, A. (1998). Prevalence of psychopathology among children and adolescents. *American Journal of Psychiatry, 155*(6), 715–725.

Rotter, J. B., Lah, M. I., & Rafferty, J. E. (1992). *Rotter Incomplete Sentences Blank.* San Antonio, TX: Harcourt Brace & Co.

Rotter, J. B., Rafferty, J. E., & Schachtitz, E. (1949). Validation of the Rotter Incomplete Sentences Blank for college screening. *Journal of Consulting Psychology, 13,* 348–356.

Rosenthal, R., & Jacobson, L. (1992). *Pygmalion in the classroom.* New York: Irvington.

Rothbaum, B. O., Foa, E. B., Riggs, D. S., Murdock, T., & Walsh, W. (1992). A prospective examination of post-traumatic stress disorder in rape victims. *Journal of Traumatic Stress, 5,* 455–475.

Rutter, M., Graham, P., Chadwick, O. F. D., & Yule, W. (1976). Adolescent turmoil: Fact or fiction? *Journal of Child Psychology and Psychiatry, 17,* 35–56.

Sandoval, J., Frisby, C. L., Geisinger, K. F., Scheunemean, J. D., & Grenier, J. R. (Eds.). (1998). *Test interpretation and diversity achieving equity in assessment.* Washington, DC: American Psychological Association.

Santrock, J. W. (2000). *Adolescence.* New York: McGraw-Hill.

Sattler, J. M. (1992). *Assessment of children.* San Diego, CA: Author.

Sattler, J. M. (2001). *Assessment of children: Cognitive applications.* San Diego, CA: Author.

Sattler, J. M. (2002). *Assessment of children: Behavioral and clinical applications.* San Diego, CA: Author.

Saunders, B. E., Villeponteauz, L. A., & Lipovsky, J. A. (1992). Child sexual assault as a risk factor for mental disorders among women: A community survey. *Journal of Interpersonal Violence, 7,* 189–204.

Schildkrout, M. S., Shenker, I. R., & Sonnenblick, M. (1972). *Human figure drawings in adolescence.* New York: Brunner/Mazel.

Schrank, F. A., Flanagan, D. P., Woodcock, R. W., & Mascolo, J. T. (2002). *Essentials of WJ III Cognitive Abilities Assessment.* New York: Wiley.

Schrank, F. A., & Woodcock, R. W. (2001). WJ III Compuscore and Profiles Program [Computer software]. Itasca, IL: Riverside.

Searles, P., & Berger, R. J. (1987). The current status of rape reform legislation: An examination of state statutes. *Women's Rights Law Reporter, 10,* 25–43.

Seligman, M. E. P. (1992). *Helplessness: On depression, development, and death.* New York: W. H. Freeman & Co.

Shiffrin, R. M., & Atkinson, R. C. (1969). Storage and retrieval processes in long term memory. *Psychological Review, 76,* 179–193.

Spearman, C. E. (1927). *The abilities of man.* New York: Macmillan.

Standards for educational and psychological test-

ing. (1999). Washington, DC: American Psychological Association.

Stern, W. (1914). *The psychological methods of testing intelligence.* Baltimore: Warwick & York.

Sternberg, R. J. (1986). *Intelligence applied: Understanding and increasing your intellectual skills.* San Diego, CA: Harcourt Brace Jovanovich.

Strong, E. K., Jr. (1955). *Vocational interests 18 years after college.* Minneapolis: University of Minnesota Press.

Sue, D. W., & Sue, D. (1990). *Counseling the culturally different.* New York: Wiley.

Sue, S., & Sue, D. W. (1974). MMPI comparisons between Asian-American and non-Asian students utilizing a student health psychiatric clinic. *Journal of Counseling Psychology, 21,* 423–427.

Suomi, S. J., & Harlow, H. F. (1976). Monkeys without play. In J. S. Bruner, A. Jolly, & K. Sylva (Eds.), *Play.* New York: Basic Books.

Suzuki, L. A., Ponterotto, J. G., & Meller, P. J. (Eds.). (2001). *Handbook of multicultural assessment: Clinical, psychological, and educational applications* (2nd ed.). San Francisco: Jossey-Bass.

Taylor, S. E. (1998). *Health psychology.* Boston: MacGraw-Hill Higher Education.

Terman, L. M. (1925). *Genetic studies of genius: Vol. I. Mental and physical traits of a thousand gifted children.* Stanford, CA: Stanford University Press.

Thomas, A., Chess, S., & Birch, H. G. (1963). *Behavioral individuality in early childhood.* New York: New York University Press.

Tomlinson-Keasey, C. (1972). Formal operations in females from 11 to 54 years of age. *Developmental Psychology, 6,* 364.

Triandis, H. C., & Brislin, R. W. (1984). Cross-cultural psychology. *American Psychologist, 39,* 1006–1016.

Turner, S. M., DeMers, S. T., Fox, H. R., & Reed, G. M. (2001). APA guidelines for test user qualifications. *American Psychologist, 56,* 1099–1113.

U.S. Bureau of the Census. (1990). *Languages spoken at home and ability to speak English for United States, regions, and states.* (DHHS Publication No. CPH-L-133). Washington, DC: Government Printing Office.

U.S. Bureau of the Census. (November 1, 2002). *Profiles of general demographic characteristics 2000.* Retrieved from http://www.census/gov

Vernberg, E. M. (1990). Psychological adjustment and experience with peers during early adolescence: Reciprocal, incidental, or unidirectional relationships? *Journal of Abnormal Child Psychology, 18,* 187–198.

Wechsler, D. (1991). *WISC-III manual.* San Antonio, TX: The Psychological Corporation.

Wilkinson, G. S. (1994). *The Wide Range Achievement Test administration manual.* Wilmington, DE: Wide Range.

Willingham, W. W., Ragosta, M., Bennett, R. E., Braun, H., Rock, D. A., & Powers, D. E. (1988). *Testing handicapped people.* Boston: Allyn & Bacon.

Williams, C. L., Butcher, J. M., Ben-Porath, Y. S., & Graham, J. R. (1992). *MMPI-A content scales assessing psychopathology in adolescents.* Minneapolis: University of Minnesota Press.

Woodcock, R. W., McGrew, K. S., & Mather, N. (2001). *Woodcock-Johnson III Tests of Cognitive Abilities.* Itasca, IL: Riverside.

Wyatt, G., & Peters, S. (1986). Issues in the definition of child sexual abuse in prevalence research. *Child Abuse and Neglect, 10,* 231–240.

Zola, I. K. (1966). Culture and symptoms: An analysis of patient's presenting complaints. *American Sociological Review, 31,* 615–630.

◆ Author Index

◆ *Subject Index*